IN DEFENSE OF FREEDOM

Why Free Market and Capitalism Work

ÁLVARO MARTÍN SÁNCHEZ

I WOULD LIKE TO DEDICATE THIS BOOK TO...

"All my family who since the beginning have been supporting me and criticizing constructively many of my articles for a future improvement, and who were the only ones reading my blog when I started two years ago..."

"To Daniel Lacalle for writing his magnificent books, articles, and reports from where I have learned mostly all I know about economics nowadays."

"To Podemos and its totalitarian leader, because without them and their desire of turning the Spanish economic model into one similar to Venezuela, I would have never been so interested in economic freedom and consequently I wouldn't have written this book!"

"Finally, to all the free market supporters in Spain, and especially to those ones who believe that we don't have any option of having a voice: remember that if we continue fighting for the free market, it is just a matter of time and common sense to persuade people about our ideas..."

INDEX

PROLOGUE

If there is a cause that deserves to be defended with all our passion and strength it is the cause of freedom. Because our liberties are under threat. It is a subtle, quiet, constant attack and it is often delivered with a smile. The message is repeated every day in the media, in universities, in lectures and articles. Capitalism does not work and individual initiative is the root of all evil. The solution to all the problems of modern society is not more freedom of choice and a merit based, prosperous society. The solution is interventionism and government control.

This message is delivered with a smile and the idea that if one does not agree, it is because of selfishness and perverse incentives. How can anyone be against equality, helping the poor and solving society's problems in a sustainable and egalitarian way? No one is. The problem is that interventionists have appropriated themselves with the ownership of real generosity and true goodwill, when the reality is completely different.

It is only through freedom and a capitalist, market economy that we can provide a better future for the majority. The problem is that defenders of freedom have always believed that reality would sink in and society would recognize the benefits of an open society that rewards hard work and success, because it creates more growth, prosperity and reduction in poverty. And freedom defenders were wrong. Every little mistake of capitalism has been magnified to reject the entire system. Every tiny imbalance has been used as an excuse to defend interventionism. We are told that we should give up more of our individual rights and our liberty for a greater good, which is not society, but government. The bait is to promise eternal subsidies and entitlements from redistribution policies. A promise of heaven if we give up our freedom and allow politicians to manage every aspect of our life.

There is a problem. It does not work, has never worked and never will. It is our duty as economists, entrepreneurs, workers, intellectuals or simple citizens to constantly debunk the false myths of the interventionist agenda. And we must do it every day, every hour without rest, because the movement against individual freedom does not stop. It is relentless, it is powerful, it is empowered because interventionists believe they have the moral high ground, even if it is false as proven by hundreds of years of history. But interventionists do not care. They will always blame the outside enemy, the markets, another country, anything, of their failure. Any excuse will be used to defend the argument that "this time it is different" and you, the average citizen, should trust that the failed policies of the past will work this time. When it fails again there will always be some invented conspiracy theory to justify the disaster and, more importantly, for the same interventionists to present themselves as the solution to the problems they have created.

We must fight every day. In schools, at home, in university, at work. We must fight to say loud and clear that we are the defenders of the system that truly works in achieving the objective of improving the lives of all people. Capitalism is not a bad word. It is a beautiful word. And freedom of choice, the opportunity to do what any person decides to do with responsibility and freedom are values we must fight for, tooth and nail.

When I met Alvaro Martin I was amazed at how such a young talent could have the talent, commitment and the clarity of ideas that he displays in this excellent book. It is rare to find someone that, as such a young age, has such a profound understanding of important economic matters, and his precise argumentation in the much-needed task of debunking the interventionist agenda.

This book provides readers of all ages with the tools to destroy the lies of socialism and the hidden agenda of interventionism. It is an essential read for the younger generation that suffers the pressure of the enormous propaganda machine that sells itself as generous, social and egalitarian and hides the evil face of totalitarianism.

Alvaro Martin, with his articles and this book, has created a body of work that is impressive for any expert, let alone for someone who is still in college. But he must persevere. The future is going to be very difficult. It is not "cool" or "sexy" to defend freedom. And he, like many others, will be criticized as anti-social. So, my dear Alvaro, the battle has just begun. Do not forget it.

These are momentous times. Never since the years before the Second World War has individual freedom been more in danger. The voice of a new generation that embraces liberty and free proves us that there is hope and that the war on freedom will be lost.

There is nothing social about interventionism. It is simply theft for the benefit of a manipulating elite.

Capitalism and a free market society is the answer to society's demands of a better future for every citizen and their families.

The quest for prosperity does not need to be achieved at the expense of liberty, because it is liberty what guarantees prosperity.

We are not wrong. Fight for freedom.

Daniel Lacalle.

27 April, 2017.

PhD Economist and Fund Manager. Author of bestsellers "Life In The Financial Markets" and "The Energy World Is Flat" as well as "Escape From the Central Bank Trap". Frequent collaborator with CNBC, Hedgeye, Wall Street Journal, El Español, A3 Media and 13TV. Holds the CIIA (Certified International Investment Analyst) and masters in Economic Investigation and IESE.

INTRODUCTION

Just three years ago, I started to receive Economy lessons at school, and the truth is that the first class that I had did not give me an extremely good impression about the mother of all sciences. After entering the class I found several groups of very mixed people, which I would never have imagined in any topic related to Economy, since there were present from the people who was popping over there and having a relaxed chat, to the very hard-working and prepared students, passing through the typical ones that had chosen the subject for being which they considered to be "the easiest one"... However, I can assure you that not a too agreeable surprise was waiting for them.

I decided to sit down in the first row after entering the classroom since I had proposed myself to pay extreme attention in these classes, since Economy was a subject in particular in which I had some special desires to stand out. In the first class, without a single Economy word being spoken, or without at least being able to analyze a graph, we started to study the weekly development of the Ibex 35... Therefore I thought the teacher assigned to my class by the school did not have an actually clear idea about introducing students into this matter, which for us was completely new. I have to admit that I was wrong, and from here --being sure that Anthony Mitchell is reading these lines--, I have to admit that I was completely mistaken, because what I thought that I would not like turned out to be having my first contact with the financial economy, which is the main reason for me, with only 15 years, to be writing this book and presenting my free-market ideology; in a humble way, of course, but with a strong desire to announce to the world many of my opinions: how it would be necessary to manage the economy, the things that from my perspective are right, and also commenting about those ones we should change.

Automatically, at the end of my first Economy course at school, and of course without a lot of knowledge about what I was doing, I decided to jump right into writing an economic blog (www.elrincondelparquet.com), with the beginning of writing completely my material, with my mistakes and wise moves... but especially with my own words and thoughts, which you will be able to appreciate in the final chapter of this book: *"What would I do if... I were the minister of economy"*. At first, the blog did not start too well, since it was not receiving too many visits and I was not either even capable of raising interesting topics to write about, and there was a small period in which I thought about leaving it, thinking that perhaps it was too much work, or simply I was committing a mistake on having dedicated so much time to something that might not even be turning out to be fruitful.

Finally, since you can observe I have continued here and haven't stopped writing not just once per weekend, alternating articles about the stock-exchange market with articles about economic policy, doing proposals and giving my opinion about a very wide status of topics, which I consider really important, and putting all my effort into each of these valued articles, since they are my best way of expression and direct contact with almost 4000 readers who nowadays visit my web every month.

Throughout all these years I have been able to observe how many of my friends have changed opinions in many topics, being clearly outstanding the economic model, looking for the most efficient one, always having freedom as a primordial and essential aspect, being there people like myself who put the greatest ink and role on its defense, and other people who, if simply took a second to think what they defend, would quickly change their opinion, bearing also in mind to those who have a solid, endorsed and worthy opinion about a different or even opposite thought from mine. With all of them, I have had infinity of debates, many of them organized by the teacher, and others like the ones organized on a Friday evening concerning refreshments and a few chips, being interesting both equally, and enriching in thought and development.

But, there is a question that I always answer with the same dignity, and with an upstanding moral, being sure of what I say, but especially, about how I say it, taking not even a second to open my mouth when they ask me: "And you: why are you in defense of freedom?"

1-THE MIRACLE OF GLOBALIZATION

Globalization has affected my family and myself several times during my 15 years of life. Being a student at an international school has made me think repeatedly about the benefits that opening our frontiers and offering our country for a free allocation of global resources should have. I remember that some months ago, I took the decision of buying a necklace for a friend of mine that was coming to Spain for some days for a visit from Ireland. I have to admit that I was a bit delayed with the shopping and I had to use Amazon as my last resource to grant a good image. God bless Amazon. When I looked into the prices, it was curious that the same neckless, of exactly the same material and with the same identification number was being produced in two different factories at two completely different prices. I won't tell the price because I still want to keep contact with my friend. I should advise that the production was of high quality, so it didn't come from any Asian country or low added-value manufacturing region. The first option was being produced in Mexico with a quite elevated price, while the second one was produced in Italy, and for my surprise, the original price --without even a discount-- was less than half in comparison with the Mexican necklace. It was my lucky day. This is a pretty clear example of globalization in our daily life because the Italian necklace wasn't being produced at lower labor costs or with cheaper materials, but it suffered on its final price much lower governmental impositions as tariffs, taxes or quotas, as on the other side, the Mexican one did. Having the same product produced in two different countries and with various ranges of distribution is one of the smallest examples of globalization nowadays, which has been the greatest victory of market freedom over interventionism in the last 200 years, right behind the Industrial Revolution.

Globalization has supposed the internationalization of trade in a freer and less restrictive environment, which has resulted in the mean term in a larger economic growth for most of the countries in the world, overall emerging and undeveloped economies being the ones who have benefited the most from it. Nowadays, and in contrast from 40 years ago, big firms are planning, designing and investing thinking about a future with open barriers, lower tariffs and many more trading and selling possibilities due to technological improvements. Political boundaries have always been an obstacle in our professional development and business settling. But everything hasn't been done yet, and even though market freedom has harmonized national sovereignty and provided a much wider range of resources for countries and mean citizens, we still should advance towards a world with harmonized norms, standards, tariffs and practices in relation to regions, looking for a transition towards a Europe of nations and not nations of Europe.

Globalization has meant the greatest increase in international commerce in a very long time, and a clear example of it has been the global exports growth, which has risen from 14% on 1970 up to 24% nowadays[1], having a clear effect on global trade over GDP which has

---

[1] https://www.wto.org/english/res_e/statis_e/its2015_e/its2015_e.pdf

increased by more than 241%[2] thanks to these liberalization policies. The country which has demonstrated the greatest international cooperation after the EU and in collaboration with it has been the US, which since the 60s has incremented its FDI ratio by more than 300%[3], taking a really important share in the global FDI level, which in 1997 reached the $400 billion, and over 37% of that capital was inflowed into emerging economies to reduce the development gap, overall not due to State imposition but for better business opportunities, investment diversification and low governmental restrictions. Globalization is usually attached to two essential factors of the XX century: first of all, the decline of Soviet Communism after the Second World War, which started with the Berlin Wall's fall and the disappearance of the Soviet government, freeing 400 people from the hands of an oppressive Communist government, representing one of the most historically commanded-economic systems. In the second place, the Third World countries and emerging economies have discovered how to profit from the de-industrialization process of the developed countries due to technological development, and have offered lower labor and working capital costs, attracting tons of manufacturers and chemical industries to these nations. Coming out from the debt crisis of the 80s has been one of the main successes for developing economies, which nowadays are able to welcome larger levels of FDI due to growing financial security and investors' trust, just like occurred in Chile after the decade of the 70s or in China, or much more recently with Argentina, following the election of Mauricio Macri and finally India, which has delocalized much of the textile manufacturing production in China.

---

[2] http://data.worldbank.org/indicator/NE.TRD.GNFS.ZS?locations=1W

[3] http://ofii.org/sites/default/files/Foreign%20Direct%20Investment%20in%20the%20United%20States%202016%20Report.pdf

After observing the failure of Communism, several countries have been able to deregulate their industries and free up their production towards international markets. A clear example of this factor has been the Four Tigers of Asia (Singapore, Taiwan, Hong Kong and Korea) which although in the 1950s were taken into account as undeveloped nations, nowadays have reached the living standards of the vast majority of industrialized economies, having GDP per capita levels[4] similar to those in the richest European and American nations[5].

The success of liberal economic policies has been furthermore noticed over the devastating effects of protectionism and crude socialism, promoting bilateral trade agreements and reducing armed conflicts. Since the 80s decades, more than 80% of the LDCs have reduced their trade barriers and impositions, and more than 139 governments have accepted to join the WTO[6]. More than 90% of the countries have changed their trade policies in the last 50 years towards much more liberalized and internationally integrated economic systems.

Numbers in reference to Globalization have clearly shown to be outstanding, but for our patriotic and protectionists friends, we should show which effects it has got on particular economies and the benefits it has offered to the mean citizen rather than just global growth and development. Even though some friends of mine look at me really strange, I still think that globalization has been a key factor for the establishment of democracy in many countries around the world during the XX and XXI centuries, being the end of numerous dictatorships starting by the Spanish

---

[4] http://www.tradingeconomics.com/singapore/gdp-per-capita
[5] http://data.worldbank.org/indicator/NY.GDP.PCAP.PP.CD?locations=DE
[6] https://www.wto.org/english/thewto_e/whatis_e/tif_e/org6_e.htm

one, which I'm referring minimally in the book preventing to be seen as a reporter of LaSexta. It has been clear that the greatest winners of Globalization have been consumers in LDCs and those in countries which during the last centuries developed isolationists policies, as they have been able to enjoy a wider range of goods and services with a higher quality of production offering a better VFM (Value For Money), and consequently decreasing prices of those goods due to cheaper production and distribution processes. In most of the cases, the process of liberalization --and in the case of Europe the single currency-- has prevented extreme devaluations and an increase of the value of savings, eliminating as a factor the Financial Crisis of 2008. Even though many anti-globalization parties have insisted on its negative effects on poor people, once again they have been proven to be lying, as the mean global GDP per capita has raised from $445 in 1960, up to... $10,057 in 2016[7]! This factor could be exposed mainly due to a delocalization of production in developed countries which has shifted into LDCs, being smart to deregulate their labor schemes and trade policies and allowing FDI into the countries, generating consequently lower unemployment levels and a greater mean income level.

Protectionism has only implied along history the exploitation of consumers which are offered poor services and low quality of goods, with hyper-inflated prices in contrast to the real market value, due to a unreal level of competitiveness into the national market, shown by the poor level of cars driven by citizens in the Soviet part of Berlin; they were buying Ladas instead of West Berlin, where you could easily see Mercedes and Fords circulating down the street. With Globalization LDCs have gained

[7] http://data.worldbank.org/indicator/NY.GDP.PCAP.CD?locations=1W

access to immense markets where they can export and import freely, giving their citizens the profitability of developed economies through their goods and services, and those developed nations access to cheaper labor, in contrast to their original nations, and cheaper raw materials and commodities, due to a larger distribution and diversification of resources in the global market. My father, who is a financial investor and has worked internationally, and who is also one of my best references into the economic world, always used to tell me: "Don't put all your eggs in the same basket, because if your basket falls, you'll lose everything you have." This phrase came up to my mind while writing this book and after connecting all the data in relation to the market share of emerging economies.

World Gross Domestic Product (GDP) by Region Expressed in Purchasing Power Parity, Reference Case, 1990-2030

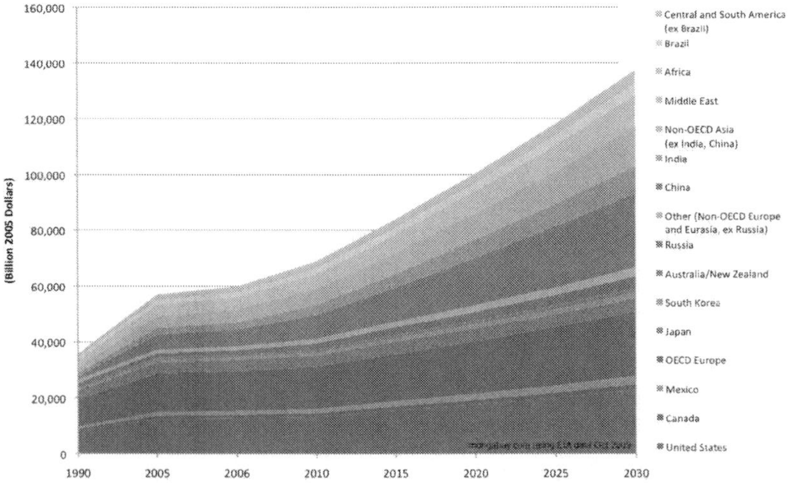

Market freedom has always provided capital with a greater future of growth and has boosted international investment all around the world. Usually, it was thought that saving money was the best possible option for the mean worker, and anciently some people didn't trust banks, as occurred in LDCs where the savings level was excessive in relation to their capital levels. Global markets were able to fill all their possible investment areas through the process of globalization, having a clear example in 1998, where more than $166 billion[8] outflowed from developed economies around the globe to emerging economies, which later invested this money into allegedly secure and long-term growth assets as American bonds, even though they would lately be proved otherwise.

Free market impulse and international trade have also been a key factor in infrastructure development around the world, as foreign capital has financed recently modern types of infrastructure, and overall in a private and decentralized way, for example profitable airports or electricity generation plants, just like the cooperation between the Europeans: it's remarkable the case of French and British to build up the English Channel, with a cost of $12 billion[9]. Multinational companies have also been a key factor in enabling services between different countries, and once again for the economic interest, so, why should we fight against them and impose restrictions, when they just bring social and economic development? China and India have made use of this factor to promote a protected and efficient service of railways, with help of the development of manufacturing and exporting industries by having access to cheaper materials faster. LDCs were conscious that their only possibility of success was opening up their economies for international trade, with the unique objective of gaining larger access to manufacturing markets in advanced nations. Liberalizing and privatizing is always positive, but doing it globally

[8] http://unctad.org/en/Docs/wir1998_en.pdf
[9] http://www.telegraph.co.uk/travel/destinations/europe/france/articles/The-Channel-Tunnel-20-fascinating-facts/

and with international cooperation was the best possible decision emerging economies could take, doing a favor not just to their international consumers, but to themselves, through larger employment, greater income levels, and further social and economic restructuring.

Globalization has brought hope to the poorest countries by promoting economic growth, shifting into a poverty reduction. The IMF has affirmed in several occasions that sustained economic and social development in LDCs has always been attached to a reduction of poverty and inequality lowering the development gap[10]. Poverty has clearly fallen in 77 out of 88 undeveloped economies in the world since the start of globalization in the 60s. The greatest poverty reductions have occurred in countries which have liberalized their economic system completely by offering fiscal and labor incentives to those countries in the developed world which opted to invest into them. If we consider the poverty definition of people living under $1 a day, we could say, according to statistics that poverty has been reduced between 1993 and nowadays by more than 100% in contrast to the 1.2 billion people living under the threshold of poverty in the 90s. Globalization has helped to improve medical services, extending life expectancy in undeveloped nations and offering better life projects for people with difficulties.

Many people opposing globalization along with protectionist organizations have blamed market freedom for the poverty nowadays established in the world, but the reality is that market freedom and overall international trade have just been used to reduce it alongside. It has been clear that those regions where nowadays we can find a greater

[10] https://getrevising.co.uk/resources/how_trade_reduces_the_development_gap

concentration of poverty and greater levels of unemployment have been the ones as Latin America (Venezuela mostly), with a poverty rate of 32.1% of the population living under $1 a day since 2006[11], or sub-Saharan Africa, have the most centered in centralization policies and protectionist measures trying to isolate themselves from international markets and developed world investors.

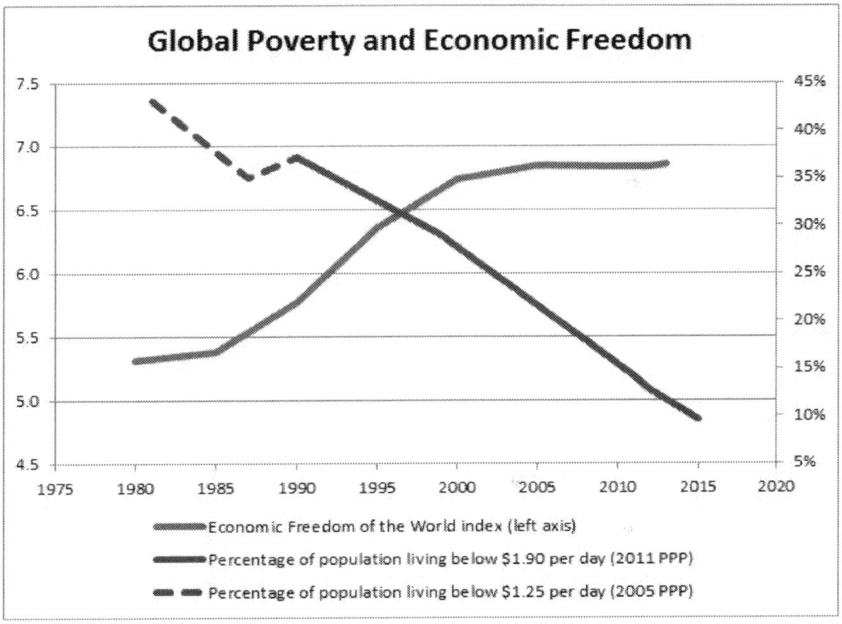

Globalization and market freedom have been proved to be the best weapons in war against poverty and in search of economic growth. Globalization has not only helped with economic growth in developed countries, but much wider it has helped to promote employment and

[11] http://www.indexmundi.com/venezuela/population_below_poverty_line.html

social development in emerging economies, breaking up the usual leftist argument against multinationals and market freedom. To me, Globalization has been the clearest example of market freedom and the development of libertarian ideas in the last century. Throughout this book, we will try to draw a detailed analysis of the different points and sectors where implementing market freedom policies is essential for growth and individual liberty, starting with a clear example of the route all nations should follow towards freedom, and which has demonstrated why capitalism works. The miracle of Globalization. In Defense of Freedom.

2-IT IS POSSIBLE TO LIBERALIZE THE ECONOMY AND MAINTAIN BASIC PUBLIC SERVICES AT THE TIME

A city is a human settling with a high population density: people do not live dispersed, but grouped. But these community establishments do not arise, apart from exceptions, because the State has created them in a planned way moving necessarily the whole population towards them, but because groups of individuals have settled in unoccupied territories, have appropriated of them, have built them and have fixed in them their residence. But what characterizes the city is not only the continuity of many housings but the necessary presence of common spaces which every resident can make use of[12].

Out of necessity, then, in cities, typical problems of coexistence arise: in these agglomerations, it is inevitable that the actions of a few people end up affecting others and that it's necessary to agree on how to support the cost of the spaces and the common services. It is a question of

[12] http://www.centralparknyc.org/assets/pdfs/surveyreport_april2011.pdf

two problems that the economists usually call of "externalities" and of "government properties." For example, a public work that produces a lot of gas will generate a negative externality; also, the system of illumination on the streets must be financed by all the residents, since if the individual temptations of outstaying were generalized, and to "scrounge" (by the face), the streets would remain without illuminating (what some economists would name 'a government property', although severely we should call it 'a communal good')[13].

The existence of externalities and government properties makes necessary some kind of social coordination: it is necessary to "regulate" which conducts are permissible and which are not, and it is necessary to "impose" who pays how much for these goods and common services. This implies that, traditionally, the State has adopted the competence of regulating the externalities and providing the government with properties. In the municipal ambience, many of these competitions have been cornered by the town hall, fundamentally in two ambiences: town-planning design and management of the common services (safety, provision of drinking water, sewerage, networks of public transport, garbage and other residues collection, public system of illumination or protection of the environment). As a clear example, we can position easily Spain which spends 43.8% of its GDP on public services and communal goods[14]. It is not that these are the only competences that have relapsed into the hands of the town halls, but perhaps they constitute the hard nucleus of the same ones: it is not complicated to imagine how a stadium

---

[13] https://www.cambridge.org/core/journals/european-journal-of-sociology-archives-europeennes-de-sociologie/article/div-classtitlecan-communal-goods-be-human-rightsdiv/F86BEDED04DB582E427E4754A889D465
[14] http://www.datosmacro.com/estado/gasto

or a private sports center might be constructed, but it takes a fancy complicated time to conceive how the streets and the sewerage might be regulated or how a harmonic growth of the cities would be achieved without the intervention of the State.

A very good solution would be the implied individuals to start negotiating and coming to an agreement on how the costs of the externalities or the government properties were distributed. For example, if a person wants to listen to music to its maximum volume at midnight, he might negotiate with his neighbors or pay an indemnification to them in exchange for the fact that he was allowed to listen to music in the night, or that he was giving up listening to it in exchange for the fact that the rest of neighbors were indemnifying him; in return, if the agreement was unviable, all the implied parts might resort to a court of arbitration that was expressing a verdict proposing an equitable solution (most likely, rejecting the right to listen to music in the night hours). Nevertheless, this type of solution is not too practical to settle thousands, tens of thousands or hundreds of thousands of problematic cases that could appear within the limits of a city.

Hence the second possible private solution has many other success tints: the co-ownership of the common spaces, including the co-ownership on the norms that regulate the coexistence in a city. The private ownership does not exist only in its individual form, but also in its communal form: if a human group creates a settlement, it seems reasonable that each of them is an individual owner of his housing and, in turn, a co-owner of the spaces or common goods (streets, system of illumination, sewerage...). One of these common goods is the government of the city: the organ entrusted to establish norms deprived of coexistence as well as determining which common services must be offered and how we must pay for them (quota per owner, quota per resident, quota per square meter of individual property, quota per property value, etc.).

Deeply, then, in absence of the State there would emerge cities (in a wide sense of the word: including urban developments or neighbors' communities of very different size and arrangement from the current centralized cities) governed by governmental bodies deprived with certain resemblance to the current town halls but with a crucial difference: these cities would be a fruit of the free and voluntary agreement between the parts and not of the unilateral imposition of some of them on the set. In the same way that the military invasion of a country does not legitimate the occupation government, the constitution of State town halls against the will of the owners of the real State should not be seen like legitimate either. In this sense, the perspective that is usually adopted is erroneous: a voluntary city is not a political community where all the citizens plan the destination of the whole municipality jointly; a voluntary city is an owners' community or, rather, a political community of owners' communities, as citizens are normally and into the status better managers of their own and private resources than the State[15].

Since the different private cities would be autonomous among themselves, each of them might establish different regulations that would allow every individual to change the municipality with one more juridical frame according to his values and preferences: the competition between cities would minimize the costs of the services and would maximize their

[15] http://www.deccanherald.com/content/591572/citizens-demand-better-management-resources.html

quality. Also, the cities might constitute consortiums, unions or private provinces directed to production of those goods of collective nature which size was coming out of the ones handled by only one municipality (for example, a regional highway or a consortium to regulate public transports which connect both cities.)

In sum, in the absence of the State there would keep on being cities — municipal governmental bodies and community services — but constituted in a flexible and voluntary way for all the parts.

EXPENDITURE IN PUBLIC SERVICES IN SPAIN:

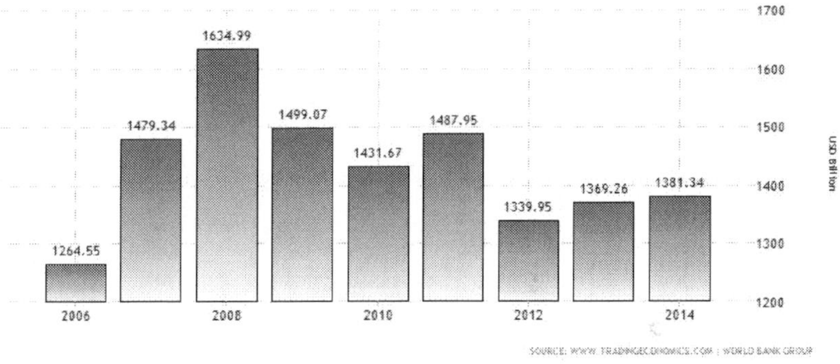

At present, it is obvious that the State has blocked in almost every part of the world the emergence of private cities and, in its place, it has imposed town halls that are mere followers of the State administration. But it does not remove it so there could be reversed this undesirable process of creating more efficient and competitive cities. For it, three routes can be used.

The first route, the most authentically private, is the creation from zero of new cities. A real State promoter (in a wide sense, this is, including the cooperative promotion of the future owners) in charge of construction of thousands of housings can, simultaneously, take responsibility of the town-planning and the construction and maintenance of the common spaces (highways, sewerage, system for illumination, parks, squares, etc.) : it will have only to accord, along with the property of every building, a co-ownership quota on the common areas of the city, including between them its governmental bodies (dedicated, between other business, to agree unanimously on the articles of association that will establish the rights and the obligations of every co-owner on the areas and common services). Another more ambitious option would be that the promoter who was constructing the houses would devote himself to rent them and to be the one running with the maintenance costs and the regulation of the common areas.

In the first case we would have a communal private ownership, in the second one an individual private ownership: in both cases, the problems of externalities and government properties associated with the provision of municipal services would remain entirely settled.

In the United States there are 62 million people[16] — one-fifth of the population — who live in communities deprived of owners. When a person acquires a building placed in these communities it is, in turn, acquiring a co-ownership quota on the spaces (streets, sewerages, system of illumination, swimming pools...) and on the governmental bodies that determine so much the articles of association by which they are ruled --all the co-owners, as well as the services that they must be lent (cleanliness, safety...). The regulations approved by the organ deprived of government can be in some cases very lax, but in others, they can become quite

[16] http://www.unfpa.org/urbanization

detailed (architectural norms or lifestyles), depending on what the perception of the residents is of the importance of the different externalities.

The problem of charter cities is, as we have already seen, that Occident is less and less an example of democracy and, furthermore, the citizens of many countries of the Third World associate them with a kind of neocolonialism which they distrust intensely. Hence many defenders of charter cities have ended up by joining another even more interesting proposal: the free cities. The free cities are free and autonomous cities not only with regards to the national legislation but to the western one: every city composes its own legislative code without having to be sent to a preexisting institution. In this sense, free cities are more flexible than charter cities when it comes to adapting themselves to the legislative environment of the country that lodges them (without having to import specific western institutions that cannot fit in the society of certain cultures) and allow them to encourage an experimentation of decentralized and competitive normative frames.

The first country of the world that has amended its Constitution and has enabled the establishment of free cities legislatively — under the name of "shaped cities" — has been Honduras since the middle of 2013. Spain should continue its way, allowing legally to be private promoters (in the shape of capitalist partnerships or cooperatives) to those who should establish autonomous and independent frames from the national and municipal legislation. To sum up, communities deprived of owners break the monopoly of State town halls on the provision of municipal services: it is a private government fruit not of the compelling imposition, but of the free agreement between the parts.

The liberal State should recognize as autonomous cities all those municipalities of new private creation, giving place to a very healthy institutional, juridical and administrative competition not only between the different cities but between the cities and the proper central government. Now then, despite of everything we could promote the creation of new autonomous cities managed by private promoters or in union diet (group all), as the Spanish population does not seem to be going to grow very much in the present future, it will be difficult that new cities are erected inside our country. Said otherwise: cities of the future Spanish residence are already created in its practical totality, and their management relapses into already constituted town halls. We have been able to observe during these last years than 88% of the best and safest cities to live in the world are overall privately managed[17].

It is here where it would be necessary to exploit the second route to achieve a management deprived of the municipal services: the right of a communal division as the route to come closer to cities that are communities deprived of owners. At the present, a city is an incomplete co-ownership: its constitution has not had too much to see with a free and voluntary agreement between owners, and its management develops with absolute scorn towards these. This implies that, ultimately, its government has been taken by political oligarchies that do and undo at their pleasure without worrying the most minimal thing for the needs of the co-owners

---

[17]http://www.independent.co.uk/news/17-best-cities-to-live-world-voted-by-expats-a7421701.html

(the same happens with the central government of the nation, to the highest scale and with worse results).

One of the advantages of the private cities is that it would be the co-owners who would determine the municipal infrastructures: every community might choose to be more austere on its expenses and common services; to reduce the community taxes or to include more services that should be financed between all the co-owners. A similar phenomenon already takes place in the neighbors' communities of the real State or in the private urban developments: those ones with elevators, gardeners, central heating, swimming pools or tennis courts are more expensive than those who only include the maintenance of the common spaces. In turn, every person might choose which community to belong to (where to acquire its building), according to these parameters.

In spite of the previous thing, a brief estimation can indeed be carried out at the costs of the private municipalities. In 2012, the Spanish town halls were handling a budget of 47.000 million euros[18]; nevertheless, a good part of these rubrics, of course, would not be supported in the private cities — it is not probable that the organ deprived of community government would be taking control of the education, health, agriculture, industry, energy, R+D, commerce, pensions, culture or promotion of the employment, unless the private city was adopting the same way; legitimate form of a commune — and other functions would be re-formulated almost completely — tourism, sport or general services—. If we tighten closer, to take into account the expenses that the organs deprived of government that would be maintained — security of the

[18] https://www.boe.es/diario_boe/txt.php?id=BOE-A-2012-15651

public from crime, housing and town planning, community well-being, infrastructures and certain general services — the entire expense, even today, scarcely would overcome 20.000 million euros[19]. Despite everything, and bearing in mind that the inefficiencies in the management have gone so far as to be estimated in close to 20 percent, probably the entire expense these private communities would handle would range between the 15.000 and 20.000 million.

MUNICIPAL EXPENSE IN THE CITY OF MADRID:

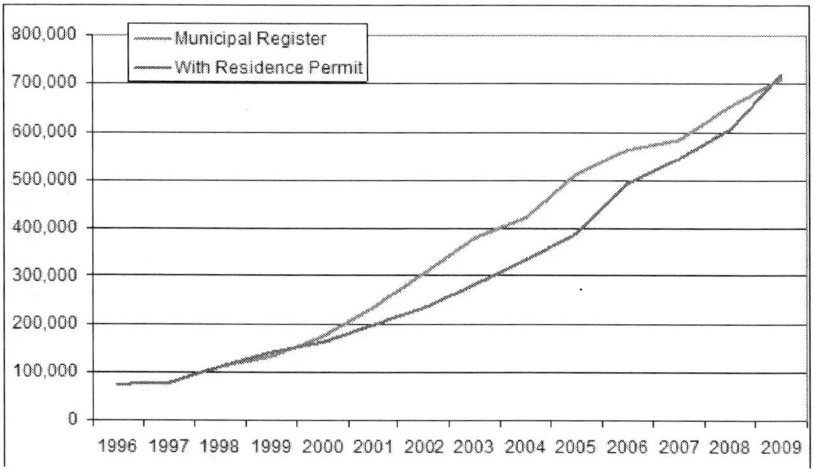

For most of the people, the protection of the environment has turned into an almost exclusive competence of the public sector. The conventional intuition says that the State is the only entity capable of protecting our environment from the "predators to which inexorably it would be submitted by capitalism"; and the fact is that, apparently, the

19 http://contenidos.ceoe.es/resources/image/inversion_infraestructuras_publicas_espana_propuesta_mejora_marco_legal_2013.pdf

natural forces of the market drive to the depletion of the resources and to the ecological deterioration.

The Spanish State spent in 2013 almost 9.500 million euros in the protection of the environment[20]. 70 percent of this expense was attached by the local authorities on account fundamentally of the management of urban garbage and of the residual waters; which is to say, of some of the local services that we have already included in the previous situation. The rest of payments in the rubric of the environment (reduction of the contamination or protection of the biodiversity) scarcely were overcoming 2.500 million euros. More than through the expense, consequently, the Spanish State takes control and "protects" the environment through all kinds of regulations on the people and the companies (legislations on natural spaces, on hunting and fishing, on cattle routes, on conservation of fauna and wild flora, on mounts, on residues and contamination, on quality of the air, on protection of groundwater, on coasts or on environmental impact, etc.). Previously we have tried to show that the minimal State should give the widest space to the autonomy of the will of the parts, minimizing the existence of norms of imperative type. Nevertheless, in the case of the environment, it does not stop turning out to be clear how this autonomy of the will would drive to a scrupulous respect for the environment. After all, two or more people can agree not to destroy the environment, but with that, there appears a third one that refuses to add up to this private consensus... it would seem that at first, it might damage it with absolute impunity. How to prevent it? Minimizing

20 http://www.madrid.es/UnidadesDescentralizadas/Presupuestos/PresupuestosAnuales/Presupuesto2013/Proyecto%20Presupuesto%202013/FicherosProyecto2013/presupuesto2013-medioambiente.pdf

the grade of regulative interventionism of the State; which ones of those who aren't worried about the environment end up with it?

But protecting the environment in the absence of the big State, Interventionist State, worries me. Not only because I derived a certain esthetic pleasure of meditating or of submerging in nature, but because a reasonable care of the environment (reduction of the contamination, protection of the biodiversity, management of not renewable natural resources...) is essential to guarantee its present and future well-being. Consequently, it is interesting for the human being to take care of the environment since not doing so generates discomfort and costs; its interest, also, is increasing over all what is its wealth. In this sense, if the State were essential to take care of the environment, certainly it would not be for the fact of imposing by the force on the human being a few motivations that are extremely tight: if most of the people despreocuppied of the way, the elected politicians in a few democratic elections will be, also, ruling with scarce environmental sensibilities; and if most of the people had a deep interest towards protecting the environment, this will be protected even without the State.

Obviously, when we say that human being is interested in protecting the environment could want to give to understand that it consists in preserving it in its primary status. Leaving aside the radical environmentalism that tries to erase any trace of the human being on the Earth, it is slightly blameworthy that the human beings would want to modify the environment to adapt it to our needs: the houses where we live have been constructed on a soil earlier empty and from a material (the concrete) that is obtained by the development of a quarry; the meal on which we feed proceeds of domesticating and the cattle breeds in captivity of showing industrially in the ground cultivation that would be foreign; as the highways arise of asphalted area so that they circulate only a few vehicles impelled by a fuel extracted from the subsoil; or the role in which I'm writing comes from the pulp of vegetable cellulose. Therefore, it is obvious that we are going to keep on transforming the environment, and it is positive that this way continues to be. Perhaps the reasonable environmental worry can come from the fact that we do not transform it in an irreversible way or with a tremendous degradation of the rest of the ecosystem (what some of them have named “sustainable development"). More, again, the human being is inclined naturally to not degrade his environment extraordinarily and to not remain devoid of natural resources. From 25 years to now, just in Europe, nearly 8,000,000 million proposals have been launched from the private sector for the maintenance of the ecology and the protection of the environment[21].

Being a generalized worry between the human species — especially, in the wealthiest societies who have covered their basic needs — if the environment is not safeguarded it will only be able to because the human being is placed in an institutional context in which it is encouraged to treat it to his environment. In this sense, the typical institutional context in which the natural incentives of the individual are distorted in a direction opposite to the one of the care of the environment is that in fact, the private ownership of the environment is not quite definite. For example, if the contamination that a person expresses was harming this person exclusively, it is obvious that it would have strong incentives in reducing it, but if, on the other hand, it could move this deterioration entirely to

[21] https://www.oecd.org/daf/inv/investment-policy/WP-2001_1.pdf

others, he will feel the temptation of contaminating without limits. Also, if the consumption of natural resources a person does only reduces the portion available for himself but not the available for the rest, he will have strong motives for an overload of the environment.

The first solution to this inconvenient rising for assigning and the environment defines rights of individual private ownership, especially so the costs of the deterioration remain also privatized. This way, if an individual contaminates the foreign private ownership, it will be necessary to understand that he is attacking this foreign private ownership, therefore his owner will be able to demand from him that he should stop contaminating or he should compensate him for the damage received (and meanwhile if the cost of the contamination is positive and increasing, the polluter will have incentives to reduce his pollution). For example, in California, there has been a custom to assign the use of the water discharges as the beginning first in steals, first in the right, so that first who used the water, maintains a priority right on its use. If another person who settled later in an adjacent area wants to use more water of the surplus, he will have to buy the "use rights" to the first one. In this sense, if an individual can only use the foreign resources in case he pays its price, he will have much more zeal at the time of economizing on them and rationing its use (the more scarce these resources are): paradigmatically, the prices system on the raw material promotes a continuous tendency to investigate new technological forms that allow not only to economize on these resources but to find new deposits or nearby substitutes which increase its availability.

Another very important route through which the individual private ownership protects the environment are the environmental foundations. The most important example is constituted by the National Trust of the United Kingdom[22]: an organization entirely private, founded in 1895 with the intention of preserving the natural and cultural legacy of the country. To give credibility to this mission, National Trust declared from a beginning that his properties would be inalienable in the future (that is to say, they might never be sold to a third one, at least to mortgage), dedicating them permanently to the free enjoyment of the whole of British citizens. This way, throughout their 120 years of history, National Trust has been receiving enormous donations deprived both from money — that grounds and historical monuments destine to acquire precisely — and of heredities — properties that their owners donated to National Trust so that it protects them and uses them for the sake of the community—. At the present days, National Trust is the organization with more members and volunteers of the whole United Kingdom (in particular, four million members and 70.000 volunteers who dedicate more than four million hours annually to preserve and restore the environmental and cultural properties of National Trust), it is also the biggest owner of land of the country (it owns 1.150 kilometers of coast and more than 250.000acres of ground)[23], it relies on a few funds superior to 1.300 million[24] euros and receives annually more than two million visitors.

Consequently, the private ownership of particular individuals and associations derived from the environment allows settling many of the

[22] https://www.nationaltrust.org.uk/our-cause
[23] https://www.fginsight.com/news/we-are-pro-good-farming-claim-national-trust-rural-chiefs-3441
[24] https://www.nationaltrust.org.uk/features/grants-and-funding

environmental problems, but not all of them. Those environments with multiple users and whose use is indivisible and generates numerous externalities on third people will be hardly governable in diet of individual private ownership: for example, a river is difficult to break down into numerous individual private properties, given that the use that is carried out in its high course affects inevitably the users located in the average and low courses. In general, ecosystems cannot be administered by means of the sum of individual private properties: they are such complex and interdependent systems that the externalities are usually of a complexity bigger than the one that can be annotated and be quantified in a very specific way; or said otherwise, the causality relations, far from being unequivocal, are quite ambiguous (does not remain clear who is responsible for which negative consequences) and, therefore, it is very complicated to establish the terms of a negotiation and of a cost share-out.

In such cases, the solution that historically has tended to be developed has been the communal private ownership on the ecosystems (farming grounds, fishing grounds, aquifers, forests). The communal private ownership maintains, in the one hand, several of the advantages of the individual private ownership (the protection of the environment coincides with the interest of the owners) and, in the other hand, it avoids some of his defects (externalities are significantly reduced): and the fact is that the power of performance of the proprietors inside the ecosystem is not unlimited, but remains submitted to the communal, well-known institutions are in charge of the set of norms and managing organisms that have developed across the negotiation between the owners, due to their knowledge, their experience and their adaptation to the changes in the environment. The intention of these communal institutions is distributing the fruits of the ecosystem between the proprietors but avoiding to degrade the ecosystem that provides such fruits.

NATIONAL TRUST IN THE UNITED KINGDOM:

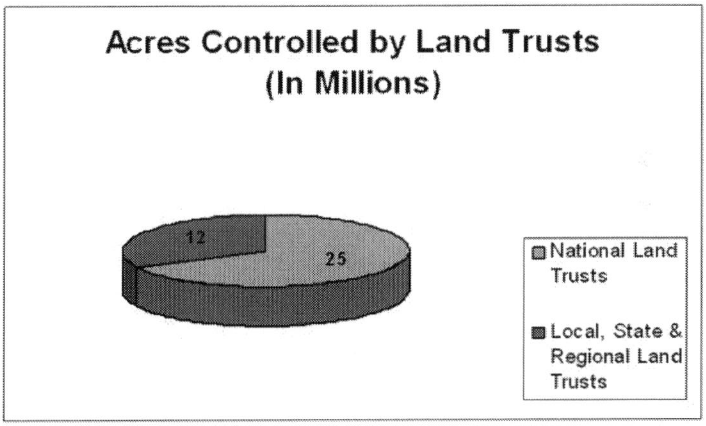

The feature shared by all the communal institutions that have protected successfully the environment for centuries has been the normative flexibility of the communal organs, to specify clearly when, where, how and who can make use of the communal resources, as well as to establish how many systems of supervision where all the proprietors inform rotator schemes in a gradual way. The normative flexibility implies that the State must not intervene in the assertion of all these rules.

In other words, both the norms and the systems of alertness of these institutions must emerge from the proper land-owners, that is to say, they do not have to be granted for or delegated to external agents (especially the State). The advantage of this creation and internal supervision of the norms is double: for what it refers to the creation, the proprietors usually have a lot of more and better practical information than the State to raise and to establish very concrete norms that contribute to an effective safe-conduct for the environment; when it comes to supervision, if the proprietors are implied during rotation in inspecting the grade of fulfillment of the others, they can verify with their own eyes that the respect to the norms is very high, that the institution is not cracked and that, therefore, they can keep on expiring themselves with the norms without feeling defrauded by the others.

The communal private ownership, consequently, has been an excellent traditional tool to solve the environmental problems inside a community. And it has achieved it for being " private ownership," this is because its co-owners were enjoying an exclusive use on certain ecosystems and had afforded to exclude of the domine both the State and the proprietors who wanted to make a use opposite to the one determined by the communal institutions. With this its over-exploitation has been avoided, its responsible management has been encouraged and, especially, it has returned to the pathway the administration of these ecosystems inside the civil society and the market, achieving a wide and dynamic coordination with the rest of human needs: for example, some Japanese villages had chosen to sell or to rent their communal grounds to hotels or ski resorts before the enormous demand that these services were possessing and, therefore, the high price that their buyers were ready to pay them; others, on the other hand, have preferred to preserve them. The important thing is that, finally, the grounds ended up being assigned to those social uses that were turning out to be more valuable, as for example in the UK nearly 40% of the population supported National

Trust and more than 25% made some kind of financial donation through 2012[25], implying that the private sector can also defend environmental interests and that it's not only a matter of interventionists.

Overall, we, citizens, will need to ask for State's size reduction. The problem is not many people not wanting this, but they being scared of it. They deeply think that services and grants wouldn't reach them if it wasn't for a big, conglomerated State. But no. It's not true. Santa Claus doesn't exist, and it's time to start realizing it. By eliminating the vast majority of unnecessary public expenditure and grants; as for example in environmental protection, the State will be able to offer lower taxes on income and expenditure, allowing the population to privately make an assignation of their capital freely into the services and goods they find necessary for them, being able to increase their saving levels when they consider so. The first step for a prosperous and free society is uncovering the myth of hyper-inflated public services and grants. To, later on, reduce the government's size.

[25] https://www.nationaltrust.org.uk/features/grants-and-funding

3-WHAT WILL HAPPEN TO INFRASTRUCTURES IN A PURE-MARKET ECONOMY?

The big infrastructures tune in for ground, sea, and air in the different cities of a country, which to the foreigner look like activities that "naturally" must be a competence of the public sector. Certainly, it is difficult for us to imagine how the private sector might be in charge of constructing highways, lines of railroad, ports or airports without everything degenerating into an oligopolistic chaos. It has been found that globally in 2014 nearly 3.7 trillion of dollars were destined for further development of public infrastructure projects[26].

And, nevertheless, during the XIX century the main communication routes were constructed and managed by private entrepreneurs: in 1830, it is believed that 25 percent of 105.000 kilometers of highways that existed in Great Britain were highways deprived of toll, being also the main and more crowded routes; taking into account both in the United Kingdom and in Spain, the immense most of the railroad lines during the XIXth century were erected and administered by private enterprises; and, in turn, the system of English channels of navigation was also constructed essentially by private entrepreneurs. The companies entrusted to build up

[26] https://www.arcadis.com/media/3/7/E/%7B37E96DF6-82D5-45A6-87D8-5427637E736D%7DAG1015_GIII%202016_ONLINE%20FINAL_SINGLE%20PAGES.pdf

and to manage these works were financed expressing actions to the big public and, later, were harvesting their income from the tariffs (or tools) that were charged to the users for that one used infrastructure, increasing its efficiency and reinvesting their benefits into improving the actual services to increase their effective demand.

It is true that the system was distant from being entirely free: highways, routes of railroad and channels needed of a previous parliamentary authorization to initiate the works; in case of the highways, also, this authorization was remaining limited to 21 years, and needed later of their renewal; frequently, the prices of the services were direct or by implication regulated (for example, the company that constructed the first line of railroad of the history, between Manchester and Liverpool, was forbidden to pay to its shareholders a dividend of more than 10 percent)[27]; and, especially, the concessionary companies which had almost always the faculty of expropriating to the landowners the grounds they needed for the works. But, nevertheless, the reference to the nineteenth-century private transport keeps being useful to understand how the sector of the big infrastructures might work without the need to be provided by the State.

The infrastructures might be constructed perfectly and without interventionist help of the State applying the same logic used on the rest of goods — logic shifted by the historical experience — it is necessary to think that the private sector of transports would develop in the absence of the State in a similar way to that of any other: firstly , a strong initial investment would be necessary, directed to acquire the productive factors

[27] http://onlinelibrary.wiley.com/doi/10.1111/j.1468-0289.1972.tb02176.x/abstract

involved in the construction of the infrastructure in question (being one of the main costs the acquisition of the area where this one frames) that, later, would recover, with the corresponding profit, across the tariffs cashing. Although the infrastructures need of an enormous initial investment, there do not seem to be insuperable obstacles so that the private sector harvests the capital necessary to support them: for example, the famous Eurotunnel that joins the United Kingdom and France across the English Channel was financed entirely by means of the flotation and bonds on the part of a consortium of private enterprises that received not even only one public subsidy although the entire cost was amounting to approximately 17.000 million current euros[28]. But tariffs won't be high if we allow competition to exist in the infrastructure market, as companies will increase their productivity and reduce their costs being more efficient and offering better conditions to consumers in contrast to the public sector.

Looking from the present perspective, one might be scandalized by the idea that the motorcars drivers should pay tariffs in all the highways they use, but the truth is that with the State highways these tariffs are already being subscribed, although in an opaque way: through the taxes that are paid in a periodic way and that are assigned to construct them partly and to maintain them. Also, to pay for the use of the highways is something very similar to the very socially recognized payment of the railroad services: we all understand that, in exchange for having used the railroad, we must pay for it (although it is at a subsidized price), therefore we should not be surprised of that the same principle prevails in the

---

[28] https://www.gov.uk/government/publications/retail-sector-in-the-uk-investment-opportunities/retail-sector-in-the-uk-investment-opportunities

highways (as it happens already today with the private freeways) keeping in mind, that it is the user, and not the taxpayer, who pays for benefitting directly from the service.

This would be, in fact, a very reasonable way in which every user internalizes the real costs of his displacement in a private vehicle: if for example, some citizens or entrepreneurs were considering to be excessive the cost of the tariffs of the private highways, the logical thing would be that they appealed to the most accessible (and sustainable for the environment) public transport (bus or passengers' rail transport); right now, nevertheless, the taxpayer is subsidizing necessarily the transport deprived of those people who make a more intensive use of the highways, destroying the civil public transport demand. In any case, we must also bear in mind that the toll of the main private highways would be significantly lower than the one of many current freeways, since the average cost of this type of projects with such a big initial investment (and therefore, the price that his owner has to demand to reach the profitability threshold) decreases with the number of users, and the number of users would be probably major in case of subsidized State alternatives not existing.

An economic agent with much relevance in the management and planning of infrastructures would be the governmental bodies of the private cities. First, because the urban highways and other municipal infrastructures (like the metro) would be common spaces managed or subcontracted directly by these governments, and second because even for the inter-city highways or the railroad lines it would turn out to be essential to be provided with the government's assent in order to connect the inter-city highway with the access to the city or in order to install the stations inside the city. In a certain way, the client of the big means of transport is the whole downtown that has been tried to provide with an infrastructure whose residents could possibly use (and not so much isolated and identifiable individuals who are always going to use it). Hence the representative of the interests of this downtown possesses a big negotiator influence on the final form that this one will end up by adopting. As a clear example of a subcontracted metro railway, we can find the London Subway, which is overall managed by TfL[29]

Deeply, consequently, it is a question of a scheme very similar to the one of the XIXth century — or to the one of the current new infrastructures of freeways — but developed without the interference of the public sector. In principle, nothing is, then, the big infrastructures that disqualify them so that they are provided by the market. And, nevertheless, this possibility has been submitted to very diverse criticism directed to the question of its viability and expediency; most of this criticism referring especially to the land transport, related to the highway or railroad since the limitation of the land seems to create an impassable barrier so that the market deals with it. On the contrary, it is usually not doubted that private sector could construct and manage ports and airports, since wide evidence exists on this matter: in the one hand, two-thirds of all the English ports are completely private; in the other, the Branson airport in the United States, the airport Mar de Cortés[30] in Mexico or the Karaikal airport in India are examples of terminals entirely financed by the private sector.

---

[29] https://tfl.gov.uk/corporate/about-tfl/how-we-work/corporate-governance/chief-officers

[30] http://www.grupovidanta.com/en/airport;jsessionid=8825DA99E417FF883868FC3EFB375DFD

COMPARATIVE OF GLOBAL COMPETIVENESS IN INFRASTRUCTURE:

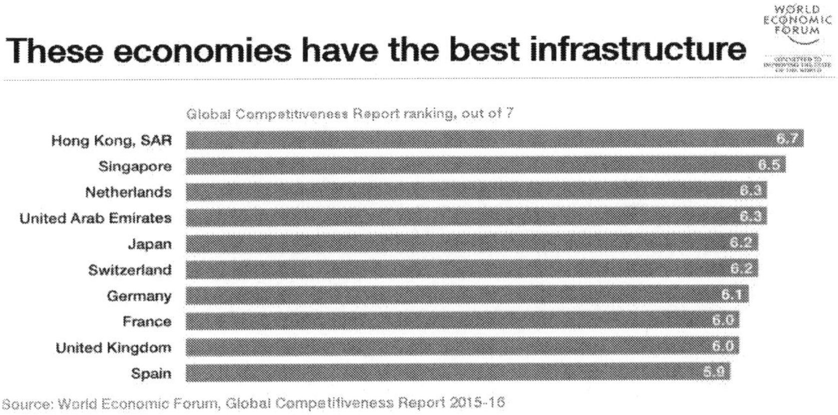

The biggest of the criticism against the deprived provision of infrastructures affirms that their construction would be simply impossible without the intervention of the State and, very especially, without his capacity of necessary expropriation.

It happens that, even if we were admitting how valid this argument is, it would not imply that the State should finance, manage and be the owner of the infrastructures: as we have already had occasion to verify, in the XIXth century the big communications routes were deprived but their holders were provided with the governmental privilege of being able to expropriate the necessary properties to execute its work. It is not a question, certainly, completely strange for us in Spain: since the middle of the decade of 1990 almost all the autonomous regions have regulated the figure of the "developer agent", who is only a private town-planning promoter who is provided with the right to urbanize an area even against the desire of its owners forcing them to support the cost of this urban development or, in its defect, to transfer part of their grounds with a payment (an indirect expropriation). In sum, the need for a necessary expropriation does not justify that the infrastructures should be financed by the public sector.

Everything seems to indicate that different strategies exist deprived to overcome the biggest disadvantage which conducts to not being provided with the tool of the necessary expropriation, namely, that any of the owners of the grounds that the promoter must acquire refuse to sell them to themselves with the target to obtain increases in price for them and that, due to this opportunist behavior, the investment in the infrastructure stops being profitable and is suspended. Obviously, nobody denies that the necessary expropriation should facilitate enormously the operation for the infrastructures promoters, but hence it is not concluded that its absence disables the negotiation with the owners. First, because an infrastructure can have many alternative tracings, in which case the land owners will compete between them for selling their grounds to the promoter of the infrastructure; second, because the promoter can maintain secretly his project and use dummies to acquire separately the areas (as it happens already at present on the stock markets when it is a question of being taking positions in a company); third, because the promoter can determine the definitive acquisition of the totality of the areas to which all the land owners bandage, announcing with anticipation that it will suspend the work in the opposite case; quarter, because, in projects of a great importance, the promoters might border on the denial of some land owners constructing underground stretches of the highway or the railroad (as if it was a metro); I conscript, because in many cases, the main benefits for the land owners will not come from the direct sale of a part of their areas, but from the revaluation of the rest of their areas as a result of the construction of the infrastructure; and sixth, because it might be the proper land owners who, as a cooperative, were constructing, were taking part in the co-ownership or were managing the infrastructures: without going further, two thirds of all the highways of Sweden are of private entitlement, being their proprietors cooperatives specially constituted for its management. Finally, it does not seem that the presence of the necessary expropriation is an essential requisite for the construction of big public infrastructures, even if, obviously, it constitutes an instrument that, violating the property rights of thirds, lowers the price of the costs of the infrastructure's promoters; on the contrary, the narrative in defense of the necessary expropriation seems to be a rationalization at a later stage of the despotic absolutist powers that, from his origin, already the State was arranging against the private citizens.

Any more beyond the necessary expropriation is not the only criticism that goes against the private infrastructures. A full argument appellant is that the highways or the railroad routes are "natural monopolies": since it is not possible to duplicate the number of routes, the ones that have been constructed first of all might receive the highest prices from the consumers. The reasoning seems credible, but the truth is that, in the one hand, there can actually be, of the same type of transport, diverse alternative routes to come to the same area (something that also usually happens when the infrastructures are public); and, in the other hand, there can also be diverse alternative transport means to come to the same place. For example, when the railroads were generalized in Great Britain, the tariffs that were receiving the channels had to go down drastically, and the same would be necessary to say right now in Spain when there coexist diverse routes of bus, plane, railroad or particular vehicles to come to the same place. Also, it is convenient to remember that, as we have already explained, the governmental bodies of the private cities would play a predominant role in the design of most of infrastructures (not only of the city's internal infrastructures like the metro, but of the inter-city ones that need the installation of certain stations or points of access in the city), which would allow them to redeem a notable counterweight role as "natural monophony" (that is to say, the municipal governmental body might be considered in practice by the only client of the monopolistic provider of infrastructures); for example, a certain urban government might negotiate discounts in the tariffs of an inter-city highway for its residents in exchange for authorizing its entry to the city and for transferring, during completed period of time, the necessary adjacent areas to be able to gain access to the same one.

Other one of the criticism that is usually directed against the private infrastructures in way for itself partly of the previous one: if the entrepreneurs refuse to admit that the infrastructures construction is a natural monopoly and they tackle a crazy career for making a profit, they will tend to construct redundant and unnecessary infrastructures that will condemn them to failure. The argument, despite departing from the false premise through which the infrastructures are a natural monopoly, comes to a true conclusion: the managerial error which is something omnipresent in all the industrial sectors and the proper economic progress provokes that past good investments turn into bad future investments (the railroad ended up by displacing the channels, and the plane displaced partly the railroad and the ships). But this criticism cannot obviate that the State is usually much more conducive to incur into this type of mistakes that the private sector. Not in vain, the network of infrastructures constructed by any modern State escapes to any economic logic and, ideally, it answers to considerations merely inquiries (in a lot of other occasions it is usually a way of making a profit for big construction firms that act as the lobby). The cost of numerous infrastructures can overcome very extensively the value of the services that it will go so far as to provide along all its life, without it having to be an impediment to keep on multiplying the quantity of this type of works and without nobody having defended up to the date that, due to these more than obvious duplicities and pouring of money, the State must stay apart from the infrastructures construction, as occurred in Singapore where nearly 75% of investment in infrastructure is done by the private sector[31].

In Spain, for example, it is famous the case of the lines of high-speed AVE. Our country has invested nearly 50.000 million euros[32] in railroad lines of high speed up to turning in the second country of the world (only behind China) into network's size, despite the very scarce use that is given to them: the Spanish lines of high speed --150.000-- are used by an average of 6.000 passengers per built kilometer, while in France and Germany 60.000 passengers patrol per kilometer as in Japan. This atrophied use of the AVE happens even though the tickets are subsidized in an amount not lower than 60 percent of their real cost, what means

[31] http://www.worldbank.org/en/news/press-release/2015/10/27/singapore-world-bank-group-agree-to-establish-major-infrastructure-and-urban-development-hub
[32] http://economia.elpais.com/economia/2015/03/26/actualidad/1427367930_711155.html

that the use that really would happen of this service in case of reflecting the totality of its cost would be very low. Not in vain, the Spanish lines of high speed do not even cover today the derivative variable costs of continuing in function. Therefore it is not necessary to think that the gigantic fixed costs of their construction are never going to be recovered.

KM OF HIGH-SPEED TRAIN IN SERVICE PER COUNTRY:

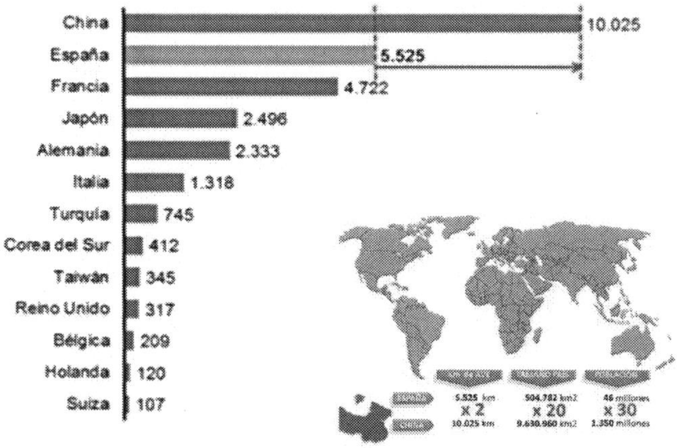

Similar comments might be carried out about the Spanish Aena airports: of the 49 in functioning[33], only seven are profitable. A finished silly thing that might never have happened in a free market on the subject of infrastructures, except in periods of irrational credit exuberance that, as we will see in the following lines, would tend to disappear in a frame of free investing competition. Also, even if episodes of bad investments could happen in infrastructures, what turns out to be obvious is that these would stop operating as soon as it was verified that they were not even capable of covering their variable functioning costs, unlike what happens

[33] http://www.abc.es/economia/20131221/abci-aeropuertos-rentabilidad-201312201606.html

with a public sector that keeps on squandering money of the taxpayers to conceal its past shameful mistakes.

Besides, we should not restrict our criticism against the nonsense of the public infrastructures to those projects that, like airports or railroad lines, we know are not profitable: in these examples we are conscious of being before bad investments (or good investments incorrectly managed) because there exist market prices that allow us to take into account certain income and expenses. But in other cases, like the ones of the State highways without toll, there does not even exist an income that allow to know which exceeds the profitability threshold and which constitutes in an absolute waste of expenditure, in the other hand: that is to say, in these cases nobody — neither the State — knows what infrastructures are profitable and what not. Exactly, the huge problem of the public sector is that it cannot make a correct economic and managerial calculation on the subject of infrastructures and, for it, its promotion and management should not entrust itself as it is necessary, to be afraid that many of these works with unknown profitability will end up being an absolute squander of resources.

The following criticism against the private infrastructures is exactly the inverse one of the previous: since the beneficiaries of the infrastructures are much wider than the direct users (profits exceed externalities), the profit of a private enterprise will end up by harvesting and will artificially fall, and they will encourage the construction of very few highways. But, again, if we attend to the historical experience, the shareholders of the companies of transport not only were valuing the profitability expected from the company, but not monetary benefits that could derive of the project was ending up by going out forward: sometimes, the actions were acquired by the land owners to whom people around were trying to construct the infrastructure to benefit from the foreseeable revaluation of their grounds; in others, it were the proper potential users of the routes who were helping to support them like investors, given that they were wishing that the project ended up being completed (this is the case of the Swedish model, where, as we were saying, two thirds of the highways are deprived); and, in others, the proper capitalists were satisfied obtaining profitability below the average in exchange for the social welfare that was waiting, that the infrastructure would generate for the community. Nevertheless, it is clear that there can be cases of externalities that can't be managed "internalize-ly", but the same can happen — in an even more marked way, as we have just commented — with a system of public infrastructures since: how can the State know with accuracy when doing the "social benefits" of an infrastructure overcome to its "social costs"? Simply, he is not capable.

Nevertheless, we will include a small annual budgetary endowment — of approximately 3.000 million euros, as it is exposed in Tim Marshall's book: *"Planning a Major Infrastructure: A Critical Analysis"*[34], accumulative in his not ready part exercise after exercise — inside our model of the minimal State if it was necessary to promote in an exceptional way some infrastructure (including, as then we will have occasion to develop, the scientific infrastructure: that is to say, the fundamental research) whose positive externalities were gigantic and were not coming to be internalized

---

34
https://books.google.es/books?id=sDUKfG7Gn8kC&pg=PA122&lpg=PA122&dq=3000+million+euros+infrastructure&source=bl&ots=j04r393J66&sig=v0X1krmMEZjxEYSYfjkE1T_OYko&hl=es&sa=X&ved=0ahUKEwjs4ImVoIvSAhXMAsAKHd9cBBIQ6AEISTAG#v=onepage&q=3000%20million%20euros%20infrastructure&f=false

on the part of any entrepreneur, being slightly extremely improbable that it would not serve as an excuse so the State was supplanting the free market in a task that the last one not only can be realized, but it can be realized much better.

As we have been able to see throughout history, public investment on infrastructure projects has only been used by governments to implement projects quickly and exalt their political support, encouraging external debt and forgetting about the future damage this effects can have on the economy. As always, once again, free markets and capitalism have stood over interventionism by proving that private investment on infrastructure is possible through a major attraction of FDI. By offering a diversified and accessible fiscal policy, international investors would be granted to come into our country, and in the absence of State funded highways, introduce money in that sector, looking forward to a greater demand, which they will be able to satisfy due to a lack of State interventionism and free competition perspectives.

4-PRAY FOR A LIBERALIZED LABOR MARKET

One of the most hyper-regulated markets that exist at present is the labor market. The Marxist rhetoric about an omnipotent capitalist class who cruelly exploits the working people has drawn strongly from the society[35], who has ended up by accepting submissively that the State interferes in the relations between working people and employers with the supposed intention of protecting the first ones of the "natural aversion" of the second ones.

The "protective" scheme that the State has designed consists on the whole jumble of labor regulations that demand that any employment should have stabilized a few certain minimal labor conditions: minimum wage, minimal annual holidays, limitation of the maximum working day at eight daily hours, minimal indemnification in case of lay off, etc. In fact, we can group the effect of all these imposed labor conditions saying that the State establishes a minimal cost on the work obligatorily.

The question that we have to settle, therefore, is if it is convenient that the State and its military arms — management and trade unions, as in Spain for example, more than 15% of workers are affiliated to a trade union[36] and participate actively in it, without taking into account the "worker's rights defense committee" which prevails inside companies the vast majority of the time— imposing regulatory measures over all the

---

[35] https://www.nyu.edu/projects/ollman/docs/what_is_marxism.php
[36] http://www.rtve.es/noticias/20110303/afiliacion-sindical-espana-mas-bajas-union-europea/413217.shtml

workers and over all the entrepreneurs a minimal labor cost in its very different declarations (minimum wages, obligatory full holidays, imposed severance pay, labor representation, etc.). The domineering popular thesis is that this minimal labor cost not only turns out to be suitable but essential to avoid the capitalist development: without labor regulations, it is usually said, the wages — and the rest of working conditions — would be supported at a level of mere subsistence. But: would it actually be like that?

The natural tendency of the free markets is that the remunerations of the working people constantly increase even if there do not exist State regulations that impose minimal wages (among other conditions). There are no governmental measures but those that increase the salaries, instead of the accumulation of capital and the competition between the entrepreneurs. The same way as the economies are accumulating capital; the work factor is becoming more scarce about its capacity of generation of wealth so the entrepreneurs prove to be ready and occur capable of paying increasing wages, although it is only because they must compete with them to hire the working people. For example: if recording to a worker the annual income of a company increases in 50.000 euros, his salary will not be able to stay anchored in 2.000 euros; having the need to overcome the minimum wage rate set at 707.60 per year[37], also established in an impeditive way by the government, for the long time, since the different entrepreneurs will fight for hiring him, increasing his salary up to levels near to the 50.000.

[37] http://www.datosmacro.com/smi/espana

The logic is not too different from how it is formed the remuneration of the electricians and the plumbers who repair the breakdowns of our houses. In a poor society, the tariff of an electrician or a plumber can only be very limited, since the incomes of his potential clients are very low. On the other hand, in rich societies, the tariffs of both professionals are usually very high (even giving an identical service as in the poor ones) because the purchasing power of his potential clients is superior. In these cases, the families that hire his services occupy the position of the "exploitative entrepreneurs", while the electricians or plumbers would come to be "that of the exploited labor"; and, nevertheless, it does not seem that in a rich society the families could impose on them these professionals "tariffs of misery". Simply, the competition between the families for hiring a limited number of electricians and plumbers raises their similar tariff if the country prospers. The same happens with the wages in a free labor market.

LEVELS OF UNEMPLOYMENT COMPARED TO THE GDP IN SPAIN:

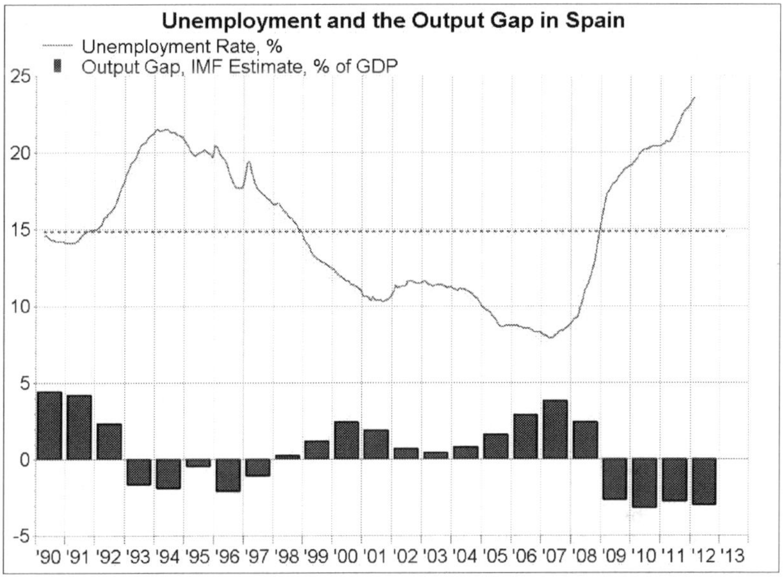

The same we can say with regard to the rest of labor conditions. The consensus among historians and economists supports that it was the accumulation of capital and the consequent increase in the productivity of the personnel what allowed to reduce the working day and finish with the kids laboring: that is to say, the progress of the standard of living of the proletarians did not come from the labor regulation of the State or from the trade union pressure, but essentially from the capitalist growth. In fact, even at our time a notable interrelation exists between the labor productivity and the number of hours employed at the different OECD countries, as in Spain workers are employed for 280 hours more than German's, implying our reduced labor productivity as the main factor for wages allocation[38]— to major productivity, fewer hours of work — that is to say, it is not the State regulations what allows reducing the number of

[38] http://economia.elpais.com/economia/2014/10/14/actualidad/1413280845_997503.html

hours worked without decrease in the wage income, but the top capacity of generation of wealth of the workers in the different economies.

A free labor market does not need regulations to achieve that the working people perceive in every time major salary or so that they notice a few every time better labor conditions. The more the companies invest, the scarcer becomes the worker with regard to the piled up capital and, therefore, the major remuneration he tends to perceive. Now then, it might be supported that, although the labor regulations are not essential to improve the standard of living of the workers, yes they might remain justified in those cases in which the markets present asymmetries in the bargaining power between working people and entrepreneurs: this is what is known as monopsony markets.

A monopsony market is the one where there only exists one buyer who, therefore, shows a big bargaining power over his sellers (the opposite just to a monopoly, where only a seller exists with big power on the buyers). If we understand that on the labor market the labor "sell" its professional services and the firms "buy" them, to characterize the labor market as a monopsony implies suggesting or that only a businessman exists in the whole economy or that the entrepreneurs are cartelized to reduce their working people hiring's and this way to pay lower wages than they would turn out to be pushed to paying if they hired in a competitive way.

In Spain, for example, there were in 2013 almost 3,2 million entrepreneurs[39] (adding 1,75 million of autonomous and 1,4 million of PYMES and big companies) opposite to a maximum number (in full real

---

[39] http://www.ine.es/prensa/np858.pdf

State bubble) of 14 million working people for a foreign account in the private sector. Namely, there are less than 4,5 working people for every businessman[40]. It turns out to be almost impossible that this 3,2 million people (and all the other potential enterprises which might enter the market) were agreeing in creating a demand cartel: almost as impossible as that 14 million working people would form another cartel of offer that was resisting the previous one.

It is a bad representation of the reality because the whole monopsony model settles on a slightly believable premise: the monopsonies businessman is unable to pay wages different from working people who give the same service (to know, he cannot practice the wage discrimination). At last, if the businessman is capable of keeping on hiring new workers without having to increase the salary of all his remaining employees, he will keep on hiring new workers while it keeps being profitable for him (in particular, until the full salary is equal to the marginal productivity of the last worker employed). To take up to date, it seems slightly realistic that the businessman enjoys a sufficient bargaining power as to fix wages but simultaneously insufficiently to discriminate through wages against his labor force. And once we leave the slightly realistic hypothesis of which he is unable to pay different wages for the same service, the predictions of the monopsony model are not already fulfilled: it is true that the employer will obtain in the short term extraordinary benefits, but he will do it without an industrial army of reserve (this is, will do it with full employment). Also, in these conditions to try to rise the salary, forced by the imposition of the government would

[40] http://www.ine.es/inebmenu/mnu_empresas.htm

tend to destroy employment (especially, if the agreed wages are not absolutely flexible).

It is a worse guide of the labor policy because, even neither in those cases in which the monopsony market model fit perfectly with the reality, nor the power of the company to impose wages would be absolute (since a company that pays wages below the marginal productivity of its working people will be a company with extraordinary benefits, which therefore will attract new national or international competitors who will bid for hiring the personnel raising their remunerations). Of the fact of which, sometimes, a businessman could be paying to an employee something less than he might go so far as to pay away from him. The conclusion does not seem that the State should regulate at all times the working conditions establishing by implication the labor costs of the whole economy, since the profit for the working people would be in any case exceptional (the reality usually does not fit with the model), scarce (the breach between the full salary and the potential salary cannot be too high, not even in markets that fit the model) and in the short term (in the long term, the salary would end the same way fitting), and the foreseeable damages of this State intervention will be very considerable.

The main problem of the State regulating the labor relations is that it raises the minimal cost of the work and, by doing it, it frustrates the positive effects that to follow says: a wide consensus exists in the economic concept about which, when the increases of the minimal labor cost exceed the productivity of the working people, the clear effect ends up by being a destruction of employment, especially between the least qualified working people, or a notable deceleration in the rhythm of new hiring, as occurred in Spain during the financial crisis with a destruction of 1.5 million jobs per year[41], hopefully, they weren't in government for a long period of the crisis. Moreover, the minimal labor costs imposed by the State to the hiring also tend to depress the least qualified income of those working people who preserve the employment (due to a reduction of the worn out hours), encourage a hasty abandonment of the studies (mining the productivity and the future salary of the working people) and they even go as far as to increase the number of poor families or in poverty risk, as raising the minimum wage will generate a fall in demand for labor, generating unemployment in a derived way. In other words, the labor regulations — and simultaneously the minimum wage — cannot "accelerate" the rhythm of growth of the remunerations of the working people: if they try to, unfailingly they will generate unemployment and poverty between those workers of the least productive labor force.

In spite of everything, it is usually thought that the minimum wage laws, although they can condemn certain stages of the population to the unemployment, at least manage to increase the salary of that small group of working people who, charging below the minimum wage, are not dismissed once the rate is increased. But, even leaving aside that it does not seem too fair to condemn to unemployment a few work people so that others see their salary developing, here, again, the most solid empirical evidence is obstinate: in general, this effect is nonexistent or even negative.

First, as we have just said, it is true that the salary increases for hour of not dismissed working people, but their entire income tends to fall

[41] http://elpais.com/diario/2012/01/28/economia/1327705201_850215.html

down because of the reduction of worn out hours or for suppression of their extraordinary gratifications; second, the effect of this legislative increase of the minimum wage tends to vanish with the flow of the years, since the entrepreneur chooses to freeze the optional wage rises of the least qualified working people, so that the minimum wage acts, ideally, as a temporary advance of future increases that the same way would have taken place (without minimum wage); and, finally, the wages that can tend to increase as an answer to an increase in the minimum wage are those of the moderately qualified working people who were already charging in advance over the minimum wage: before the wage rise, the enterprise tends to replace slightly qualified and relatively expensive work with more qualified labor and relatively less expensive, increasing the demand for this personnel and, therefore, their salary (in the end, the firm tends to mechanize the job getting rid of the slightly qualified and expensive employment).

MINIMUM WAGE IN SPAIN:

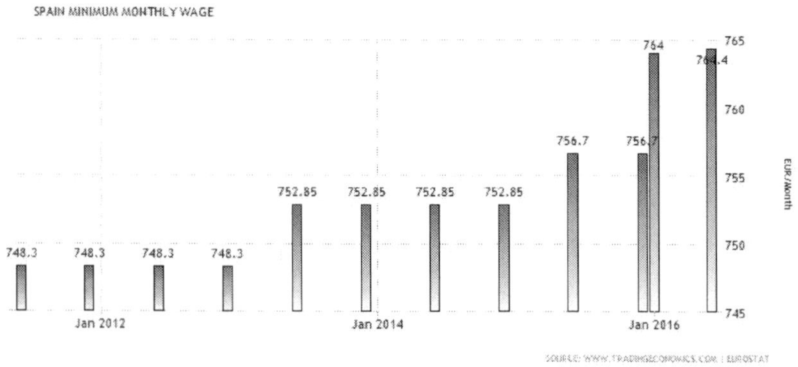

So, for us to make an idea to ourselves, the extra professional minimum wage in 2014 was 645 euros[42] a month, being of 707 euros in 2017. But this one was not greatly less than the minimal labor cost that a businessman was supporting to be able to hire a worker. First of all, 14 pays are the minimum wage in exchange for eleven months of work (due to the full holidays), what implies that the prorated monthly cost is 820 euros. Second, at this cost, it is necessary to add the tax pay to the Social security at a charge of the entrepreneur, what implies increasing the cost to 1.065 euros. And, finally, it is necessary to add other expenses linked to the worker (like the provision to face the temporary employee dismissal or the labor representation) that, at minimum then the labor cost to 1.100 monthly euros (paying the minimum wage!).

Consequently, in 2014 it was impossible to hire legally in Spain a worker to full-time for less than 1.100 monthly euros, as the vast majority of companies suffered from a minimum impeditive base from the Social Security of an average of 753 euros[43]. The situation, in fact, was worse than the one described. In practically all the economic sectors there exist collective agreements that fix minimum wages for professional category superior to the legal minimum, and fix them not only across the wage stage that contains the agreements but across a wide variety of bonuses (antiquity, productivity, annual wage rises, etc.). For example, if we apply the previous calculation of the minimal labor cost to III State Agreement of the sector of the daily press (signed in 2008), we will verify that this one was imposing a minimal cost for the least professional category (the correspondent, for example, to the cleanliness works) for 1.250 monthly

---

[42] https://www.boe.es/diario_boe/txt.php?id=BOE-A-2013-13764
[43] http://www.tiemposmodernos.eu/tablas-2014-cotizacion-seguridad-social-smi-iprem/

euros; a level editor, on the other hand, supposed to the company a minimal monthly cost of approximately 2.400 euros; and an editor-in-chief, 3.100 euros. Also, the agreement was imposing that these costs had to increase 0,5 percent during 2009 and 2010, what supposed ending up by increasing them up to 1.310, 2.510 and 3.250 monthly euros respectively. And so, the collective agreement was forcing to that a small writing of eight level editors and of two editors-in-chief had a minimal wage cost of more than 26.500 monthly euros (or more than 320.000 euros per year)[44], without being provided with all the remaining managerial costs of not labor character (rents, electricity, subscription to news agencies, computers, financial expenses, etc.). The highest minimal monthly invoice imposed just on the beginning of the biggest crisis that was going to suffer the sector of the printed press in all its history.

A frequent counter-argument consists on referring to everything pointed to countries of our environment where minimum wage laws exist much more aggressive that in Spain and where, yet, the unemployment is less. For example, in Belgium and Holland, the minimum wage is about 1.500 [45]euros, and their unemployment rate does not overcome 8 percent; however, what is not mentioned usually is that the medium-sized salary of these two countries reaches 3.000 euros (the double that in Spain). If we take a glimpse to the rest of OECD countries we will verify that their minimum wage usually represents 50 percent of their medium-sized salary: a number that only reveals that the richest countries (those countries where the labor productivity is raised more due to the big capital accumulation) are capable of supporting more aggressive minimum

[44] http://www.elmundo.es/mundodinero/2009/11/11/economia/1257956546.html
[45] https://www.government.nl/topics/minimum-wage/contents/amount-of-the-minimum-wage

wage laws without generating a high unemployment. For analogy, a minimum wage for 200 monthly euros would not also provoke necessary unemployment in Spain — since the capacity of generation of wealth of all the workers overcomes this level, even if it could generate it in other countries of our environment (for example, in Russia the minimum wage is about 130 monthly euros and in Bulgaria about 160)[46].

In sum, it is already not a matter of the State regulations that impose minimal labor costs being unnecessary to increase the remuneration of the working people, but of that which are tremendously harmful as they can condemn to unemployment to an enormous labor force quantity: in conclusion, or they do not supply effect (when the imposed minimal costs are so low that they do not affect anybody) or are harmful (when the minimal costs are sufficiently raised as to turn in certainly unemployable people whose productivity is lower than this minimal wage). The State should simply move back from the labor market and allow the labor contracts to be negotiated personalized between employer and employee, in the same way in that are negotiated the contracts of many other ambiances of the economy, freely.

This beginning of free negotiation between parts should also be supported for the case of the immigration: in the minimal State, any foreign citizen should be completely free to negotiate and to sign a labor relation with Spanish enterprises. The most common argument to be opposed to the no-restrictiveness immigration is that the immigrants' free entry would reduce enormously the national wages up to comparing them to those of the Third World. Nevertheless, the available evidence

---

[46] http://www.tradingeconomics.com/russia/minimum-wages

demonstrates exactly the opposite: the immigrants have a void or even positive effect on the wages of the nationals.

The theoretical error consists of supposing that the immigrants are substitute working people of the nationals when the immigrants are usually used for low qualification and the nationals don't (88,5 percent of the Spanish working people have a title of secondary or top education which the majority of immigrants lacks). This means that, for most of the cases, the immigrants are complementary and not substitute working people to the nationals: which is to say, that, on the one hand, the immigrants facilitate the creation of new workplaces (for example, on having lower the price of the domestic service, they have allowed increasing the women's participation in the labor market, as occurred in Spain after the dictatorial period and with the introduction of a new Constitution in 1978[47]); for other, an increase of the internal working people because of the immigration supposes, also, increasing the home demand for the rest of goods that the nationals had producing, what allows to increase their remuneration: it is not a question of a major number of working people distributing a given number of workplaces, but the additional expense of the new immigrants allows to support new workplaces (let's remember that between 1820 and 1914 the American population multiplied for ten and the real wages did it for four[48]). But the fact is that, also, the immigration might be beneficial for the national working people even in case the wages were diminishing: for example, constantly increasing the price of the housing (that is to say, creating economic bubbles due to inflation) and, therefore, revaluing the

---

[47] https://dialnet.unirioja.es/servlet/articulo?codigo=2380454
[48] http://www.cambridge.org/catalogue/catalogue.asp?isbn=9781107015982&ss=fro

patrimony that these slightly qualified working people could have. Also, there agrees to mention briefly that another typical argument against the free immigration — that it gets dearer the clear cost of the State for the nationals because the fiscal income increases less than the expenses — does not have any empirical support either: the clear fiscal effects of the immigration are usually void or lightly positives.

Therefore, there is no reasonable motive for restricting people's free circulation between countries appealing to its harmful effects on the labor market. The attack on the migratory freedom is only one more facet of the restrictive model of labor relations that tries to impose coactively the State, implied many times by old-fashioned political leaders applying to patriotism as the last refuge for protectionism. By allowing free labor markets to function, we are able to break up and dismantle a huge and historic number of utopias build up by extreme right or left economic policies all around the world through history.

5- THE IMPORTANCE OF MONETARY POLICY AND BANKING IN THE MARKET ECONOMY

The money has always been considered to be one of the basic infrastructures of every capitalist society, but not necessarily an infrastructure that should be provided by the State. Adam Smith, for example, described and defended in "The wealth of the nations" the monetary system of his native Scotland: a monetary system where the citizens had chosen the gold spontaneously as money and where every private bank was enjoying full freedom to produce its own notes.This monetary system, from Adam Smith's Scotland, lasted between 1716 and 1845[49] and turned out to be one of the stages of those that the planet has never enjoyed: practically all the English, French or German economists of the period were considering it to be a modality of excellence worthy of putting in practice. Its death was not linked by any means to economic problems derived from the monetary freedom, but by too difficult politic decisions: the progressive authorization of a monopoly on the notes emission in the whole United Kingdom to the Bank of England.

The case of Scotland, nevertheless, is neither unique nor exceptional. The successful examples of free monetary systems and not taken control by the State have been numerous in our long history:

---

[49] http://web.stanford.edu/~johntayl/Adam%20Smith%20Lecture--Taylor--2007.pdf

Canada between 1817 and 1933[50], Sweden from 1831 until 1901, Switzerland between 1826 and 1907, Chile between 1854 and 1898, Australia between 1817 and 1911, and this way up to sixty episodes on the whole world (you can consult it in the world's economic freedom classification). Against what might be thought, the reason for which the immense most of countries ended up by restricting the monetary freedom of their societies had nothing in common with the "macroeconomic stability", but with much more financial reasons: to guarantee to the government of revenues that were being lost from the monopoly of the emission of notes. It was not the well-being of the citizens, but the one of the State, what finished the market freedom in such an essential industry for the capitalist economies as it is the monetary one and the financial one.

Nevertheless, it is necessary to admit that, from a current point of view, it is hard to imagine how there would be a free monetary system in which the States could not intervene by any means. And the fact is that, for starters, it is usually thought that we would fall down inevitably in a monetary chaos: if every person was using his own money, in the same society one large number of different types of currencies would coexist in parallel, what would make enormously the most routine payments operations difficult. Also, it is common to admit that a free monetary system would stretch to be much more unstable than the regular one, supervised and protected by the State through the central bank. Both fears, yet, are inevitably badly backed up, both from a historical and theoretical point of view.

---

[50] http://www.bankofcanada.ca/wp-content/uploads/2010/07/dollar_book.pdf

There is no practical difference between what every bank offers as its own services of checking account (and allow to turn payment operations against the same one) and the production of its own notes or interest rates, so that if at present no chaos takes place for the fact that every citizen has his checking account in a different bank, it would not also be in case every citizen was using interest rates from different financial institutions, simply, we would have to concentrate on the money to which the currency is equivalent used to pay or to charge, as we do it today when we extend or accept a check to the bearer against the checking account of a bank.

The authentic question does not reside in whether a system with diverse payment means might work without enormous complications for the average citizen since the true thing is that "it is already working" whenever we use the debit or credit card or even the checks to charge at a different bank. The authentic question is, rather, if we might put ourselves all in accordance with the hour of selecting the "basic" currency and interest rates of the economy, that is to say, the money that the banks promise to deliver in its debts. Perhaps it should not be the State who, in any form, was putting us to all in agreement so that we were using the same currency, and overall with the same value?

In fact, no. The money is a free flowing tool that tends to be so much more useful all the more agents use it: it is enough that some perspicacious individuals begin to use a certain currency that possesses good properties to act like way of change or like deposit of value so that more and more agents are using it in their deals, as occurred with Chinese yuans throughout the period of 2013-2015, while the government thought that devaluating it by a 21%[51] in contrast to the Japanese yen would be a good strategy for increasing export levels. And this way, once a large number of people has migrated and has begun to use a certain currency, its use and widespread acceptance tend to be established through time, just as it happened in North America's history with the dollar, and just the opposite of what occurred with the euro.

This way, until the beginning of the XXth century, the economic agents chose in a spontaneous way the gold and the silver as money due to their excellent monetary properties (wide ornamental demand, resistance against external agents, big divisibility, ductility and malleability, easy to storage and transport, etc.). It was not necessary that any central bank was imposing their use on them since all of them chose them for expediency. Also, if we go back in history, we will verify that other societies chose the cattle, the salt, the cocoa or the copper to act like last way to pay the debts (like currency or exchange value) even cases had registered, as it happened inside the prisoners' fields of the second world war, in which the tobacco turned spontaneously into money, due to the large hyperinflation that Germany had at that period, when paper money was used for fires in winter.In fact, at present and without need that the States have stopped trying to monopolize the money provision, more and more economic agents are trying to migrate towards new forms of private money that have emerged spontaneously on the market; the most well-known case is that of Bitcoin: a created virtual currency that wasn't centered in a particular State and that has been already recognized as a valid trade currency in the United States and Germany.

[51] http://economia.elpais.com/economia/2015/08/11/actualidad/1439269139_483697.html

In sum, the doubt about what would happen with the money if there were no central banks is similar to the doubt of what would happen with the Spanish language if the Spanish Royal Academy of the Language had never been created: absolutely nothing at all, since the people did not begin speaking Spanish because the RAE was imposing it on them and they would keep on speaking it although this one was disappearing (in fact, in the English-speaking countries official academies of the language do not exist although they use published norms but not centralized for prestige publishing houses). The State, even if it could influence or even impose its particular currency, is not essential so that this one emerges, and neither it is in the case of the language. And so, if the monopolistic central banks and the laws of legal currency had never existed, the economic agents would have reached in a convergent way the money from which registering their accounting, to receive their credits and to pay their debts: the most probable thing, if we attend to the historical precedents, is that the currency selected by most of the planet was the gold and the silver, although perhaps some communities preferred other assets as Bitcoin. The key is that they would be the sovereign economic agents — and not the autocratic States — who would choose between a few possible money or others according to which it was assembling the ideal qualities to fulfill in a best possible way the functions that these demand to the money.

A free monetary system, where the society chooses decentralizedly and spontaneously the "basic currency" and where the banks express debit named in this basic money that, in turn, could be used to a more comfortable payment way, as occurred lastly with the introduction of the Bitcoin which since its introduction has been revalorized, reaching even in

2016 a value of 200 dollars per Bitcoin[52] , not having anything utopian, since it has happened in the most numerous occasions along the history. Perhaps, therefore, the question is if this free monetary system, without the harsh interventionist State that manages it, turns out to be preferable to the current one from two optical ones: first, if the money chosen privately by the market is preferable to the currency chosen coactively by the State; second, if the intervention of the State in monetary matter is necessary to minimize the financial crises that recurrently the capitalism endures.

As for the first question, the answer should be obvious: if the States have destroyed the valuable currencies that the economic agents chose freely it was not to improve it but to worsen it exceedingly. At present, in the euro zone the basic money is constituted in the notes of euro that the European Central Bank expresses and in the United States by the tickets of dollar that prints the Federal Reserve, which implemented a sudden expansion of monetary mass of more than 530% in the period of the financial crisis[53], from 2008 to the mean quarter of 2014. It is a question of a very suitable situation for the public sector, since, as it created the notes in monopoly diet, now the population feels forced to use them, it can finance part of their expenses resorting to the inflation: by means of the inflation the State steals from us part of the value of the money that it has forced us itself to use.

It is not complicated to observe that, while the dollar and the pound sterling were linked to the gold (to the select money as such for the market), they were capable of maintaining their purchasing power for

---

[52] https://www.redeszone.net/2016/06/16/bitcoin-crece-sin-control-triplicando-valor-ultimo-ano/
[53] https://fred.stlouisfed.org/series/BOGMBASE

almost one century with very light and decreasing oscillations (the only valuable fall in the United States took place during the War of Secession when, precisely, the gold standard gave in, which can also occur in actual free markets). Since 1914, yet, the governments were leaving the gold standard progressively and the subsidence of the value of the currencies — the inflationary theft — was gigantic: in 2012, the pound sterling and the dollar had lost more than 95 percent of its value from 1914[54].

Therefore: the money imposed by the State is much worse in the long-term that the currencies which are chosen by the market, and in the short term it doesn't offer excellent stability or predictability.

The second question — if the State regulation of the currency and the banking is necessary to resist the self-destructive tendencies of the capitalism in the shape of economic crises appellants —it certainly has a major juice, although it is to present a factor to add to the totality of the conventional knowledge: the economic crises are not a consequence of a private banking that enjoys too much freedom, but a private banking that holds too many privileges thanks to the State interventionism.

In particular, the private banking has the strongest incentives to receive capital through State managed short-term debt (deposits at sight, impositions to one month, bonds to six months) and, in parallel, to use this capital received to grant long-term loans (your mortgage to thirty years, managerial loans to five years, loans to the consumption of three years...). The advantages of this operation for the banking sector are clear: for the capital that it gives in the long term it can receive very high-interest rates. It is logical: in the financial markets, the usual thing is that

---

[54] http://www.miketodd.net/encyc/dollhist.htm

the long-term interest rates are much higher than the short-term interest rates (it is what is known as "a normal curve of yields", and not an "inverted yield curve", as which occurred in the USA during the housing market bubble, which produced interest rates to fall from 5.26% in 2007, to a sudden 0.13% in the mean period of 2012, and they were brave enough to call it still an "inverted yield curve"[55])

Nevertheless, it is very widespread and well known that bank operation is deeply not coordinated and distrained for the set of the economy. On the one hand, although the great majority of the people want to give some use to their capital in the short term, the banks are immobilizing it in the long term, so that the needs of the average people will end up by turning out to be frustrated: they will not have the capital that they need at the moment when they need it. On the other hand, thanks to this lack of coordination between short-term saving and long-term investment, the banks manage to reduce enormously the interest rates of their long-term loans, what encourages an enormous and artificial increase of the family and companies indebtedness with the target to increase their consumption and their investment in an unsustainable way. In the end, then, the economy experiences a period of "science fiction" prosperity (given that there grows the entire expense supported by means of the expansive indebtedness) which will be necessarily followed by a period of depression (the cheap credit comes to its end, and the false prosperity based on the untenable hyper indebtedness ends up by collapsing), which as John Maynard Keynes said, are the effects of the money supply inflation, that tends to occur when we have very low-interest rates in the long term, or otherwise explained, an "inverse yield

[55] https://fred.stlouisfed.org/series/FEDFUNDS

curve", which merely caused an increase in American public debt of more than 91% [56]during Obama's legacy; without taking into account the municipal and State debt.

An apparent contradiction exists, consequently, between the individual well-being of the bank (to maximize its benefits getting into debt in the short term and investing in the long term) and the well-being of the whole set of the community (macroeconomic stability); contradiction that, in opinion of many, would need an iron-fist regulation on the part of the State to avoid this one very "imprudent bank behavior of pernicious social consequences". Nevertheless, the reality is that a free market is provided with enough instruments to make citizens capable of controlling their own lives and managing their financial operations.

ECB BOND PURCHASES PROGRAMME:

[56] http://www.usgovernmentdebt.us/

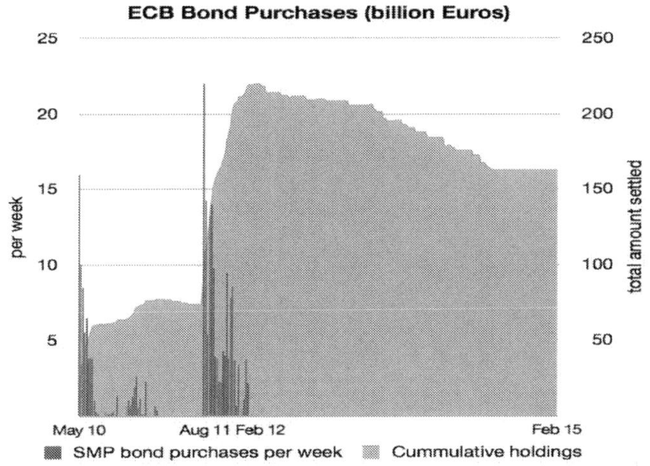

We just need to realize that a bank that owes a lot of short-term money and has its assets invested in excess into the long term will be inclined to fall down into payments suspension: being enough that several of its creditors claim their money producing that it has to close down or enter into a bankrupt process; this is what formerly is known as a "structural risk", which is one of the principal excuses that interventionist give to intervene the financial market. On a free market, the true risk of these panic devastators serves so that every bank declines to continue imprudent financing schemes (as it happened during most of the time in the historical earlier reviewed cases of free banking). We just need to foresee the perverse alliance between a few anxious banks to maintain their irresponsible but lucrative behavior and the State needed from the cheap financing that only the financial framework could provide it, which ended up by leading the last one to grant to the first ones a series of privileges designed to reinforce them of the risk of suspension of payments and, therefore, to give wings to their unbalanced an inefficient financial behavior.

The first one of these privileges was the creation of a monopolistic central bank entrusted to refinance the expirations of the short-term debt of the private banks. Since the central bank had monopolized the emission of all the State bonds of the country, also it was concentrating on its credit most of the gold reserves of the economy, which was granting a wide maneuver margin to extend profitable loans to those most undisciplined private banks that were close to the payments suspension. Now then, even the gold reserves of the central bank could have finished in case this one was choosing to provide financing to a too high number of imprudent private banks, which can be seen as the covered return of the public sector to the financial sector, which was to exempt the central bank of the need to pay its debts in gold: to resort to the current inconvertible paper money. This way, and as it happens nowadays, the central banks possess the aptitude to refinance without limit the private banking, so that this one is provided with more capacity than other financial institutions from other continents, never to reduce the interest rates and to expand the credit artificially, clearly generating a monetary supply inflation in the long term.

The second one of these privileges has been a regulation that was sold as protection for the depositors but that, in fact, is an indirect way of safeguarding the banks, through public investment. We refer to the "cover of deposits", an instrument of the State directed supposedly to protect the depositors of the losses that a bad bank management could cause them, as what occurred with the ECB policy of "I'll save it all" developed by bond purchases and external debt of State members, having invested, or otherwise wasted, more than 100,000 million euros in Spain since the beginning of QE[57], saving again; not even the contributors, but the government. The problem is that, thanks to this State guarantee, the depositors with ignorance of the administration, prudent or imprudent, of the entity in which they had deposited their savings, so preventing depositors from withdrawing their funds even when the institution was facing an economic recession, not generating a systemic risk, but at the same time reducing the value of investments and making consumption levels reach minimums; this way, the panic ones stop being a believable threat that restricts the behavior of the bankers and, consequently, they happen to behave in an even more irresponsible way for the sake of maximizing its short-term benefits (it is what the economists have named "a moral risk"). The logical degeneration of the cover of deposits that has been recently exposed in the major State rescues of the broken banks, where the taxpayers assume the totality of the losses of the set of the creditors deprived of the financial institutions (even of those who acquired State bonds from the banks), what obviously encourages an even more extraordinary risks assumption on the part of their directors. In sum, the second one of the privileges that the State instituted in favor of banking was thinking about how to rescue it permanently of the inexorable consequences of not worrying about safeguarding its solvency and efficiency, basically, preventing it from wasting money through extremely risky investments.

Finally, it is not a question of a free banking stretching to be more imprudent than the current one, but, precisely for being free and for turning out to be devoid of all the privileges that the State grants to it today, would become much more prudent and stable (since in the

---

[57] http://www.expansion.com/mercados/2016/07/04/577a8f0d22601d52228b45ef.html

opposite case it would turn out to be exposed to the bankruptcy), avoiding this way the manipulation of the interest rates that generates the economic cycles. The State regulation is not a valid alternative to the liberalization and suppression of the privileges which the private banks enjoy: if the bank privileges survive, the regulation will be insufficient to avoid the economic crises, as it has been throughout the XXth century; and just in the case the privileges disappear, it will be unnecessary to have State intervention into the financial sector, as it illustrates the historical experience on the subject of free banking. Even worse, nowadays the State regulation of the banks is only a morphine injection to the population who thinks that, tying in shortly the financial elites, their outrages will tend to disappear: what the same population does not seem to want to admit is that the political and financial elites are actually allied, that the State regulations are an only one way of concealing and camouflaging the State privileges, and that these privileges are the authentic problem of the financial society and the vast majority of its failures.

INTEREST RATES OF USA, UK, AND EU:

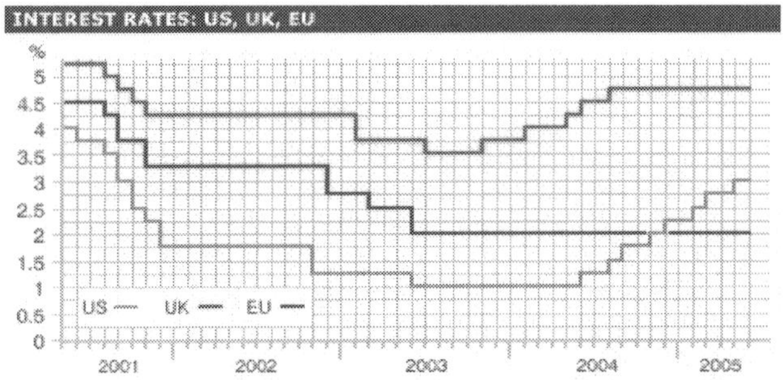

The monetary and financial system that Spain needs is, therefore, a free monetary and financial elite, where the State does not impose in a monopolistic way its exchange rates to steal the population by means of the inflation, and where the banks do not enjoy State privileges to make a profit manipulating the interest rates and generating consequent economic crises, created mainly by ineffective investment done by banks hyperinflated by the State, which only has in minds its protectionist interests. All this would imply closing the central banks and restoring the free bank competition: to the end, closing down the central banks does not mean that any of the necessary functions that at present they redeem in monopoly diet (interbank clearing organization or provider of liquidity in moments of unjustified panic, for example) should disappear; the only thing that would happen is that they would be exercised by other private banks freely created and regulated by competitive markets, driving to a higher productivity. The United States, for example, did not have an established central bank until 1913 [58]and it did not prevent along its history from arising private equities that were redeeming, without the need for State privileges, some of the typical functions that then the central banking would monopolize. There is neither reason of weight, nor

[58] http://www.let.rug.nl/usa/essays/general/a-brief-history-of-central-banking/federal-reserve-act-(1913).php

theorist not historical, to justify the unnecessary and exceptional privileges that the State grants to the bank industry, and which as previously said generates constant inefficiency in the sector, through investments as the 2008 real State bubble, or the enormous financial recession that it consequently lead to.

QE has never done what textbooks affirm it would do. And never will. Money shouldn't be introduced into the economy through public banking or even central banks. The ECB and the government do whatever they need to save just the euro and along with their reputation. I believe in the European project and unity of nations, but it seems than having scarcely recoated QE programs, Draghi would need another financial crisis to learn how asset bubbles work, and maybe then, he will discover the ghost of the economy. I said maybe. Because their argument can always and illogically be reinforced by some magic forces, called inflation and monetary mass. Maybe their ammunition ends, but their weapons won't.

6-HOW WILL BE RESEARCH AND DEVELOPMENT PROMOTED IN A FREE-MARKET ECONOMY?

The reason that the State usually adduces to justify its intervention in the scientific and technological progress of a community is that the social benefits of the innovations are superior to those private benefits that the investors are capable of capturing. In the end, the innovations, once open and spread, can be exploited freely by any other economic agent, without the need to remunerate the one who promoted them (cases of externalities, are normally called spillovers technically). For example, a certain invention can offer to the society a few global benefits for 1.000 million euros and, nevertheless, the profit the researcher obtains by means of its direct commercialization can remain limited to 10 million; in such a case, the efforts and resources that every person will tend to destine to the investigation and to the development will be less than the socially desirable ones.

The activity of the State in science and technology comprises two big classes of interventions: the first ones happen at the direct expense in R&D, already in the form of subsidies to companies, to public universities or to dependent organisms; the second one consists of increasing the profitability of the investments deprived in R&D, as we could be able to see when the Spanish State invested nearly 13,000 million euros representing 1.24% of the total GDP in 2015[59], paid already with tax benefits or, especially, with the patents authorization. The minimal State should neither spend straight in R&D nor grant a monopoly intellectual — clear — and both being deprived to increase their profitability artificially. Nevertheless, there exist more than logical doubts if it completes on the intervention of the public sector of science it might not condemn us to a new age of obscure and slow development and of technological deadlock. To appease such fears, firstly we will debate on if there would be R&D in the absence of public investment and, later, we will try to resolve the fact that there would be expense deprived in R&D without patents.

At present, the State investment in R&D is usually canalized across universities, dependent organisms and subsidies to the private sector. As we were saying, the target of these budget items is to compensate the supposed version of the private sector and to raise the national expense in R&D up to a level that reflects truly the social benefits that it provides: the fund thesis, obviously, is that the private sector would be itself unable to provide the ideal aggregate investment in research and development. This thesis, nevertheless, suffers from diverse problems.

The first one is that the State does not know which the social benefits of a certain investment are and, much less than an investment as uncertain as the R&D. Let's remember that no State has unbeatable problems of information to discriminate against the good ones of the speculative investments, but on the subject of science and technology these problems are absolute, as one of the major losses of Spain's public

[59]http://www.eae.es/actualidad/noticias/en-espana-se-invierten-13.000-millones-de-euros-en-actividades-de-i-d-i-un-1-24-del-pib

industry has been due to the AVE, having less than 100 passengers in 25% of the stations, and having previously invested publicly nearly 47,000 million[60]. Probably, the most resemble feature of the expense in science and technology is that, to a certain extent, the investor (every investor) goes in "blindly"; that is to say, good part of the discoveries have taken place in pure imagination or creativity, and afterwards have been developed, but always with the closed idea that yours is the best, and with desires of eating the world. Since it is logical, before carrying a scientific discovery out, we cannot know the content of the same one (or of its multiple and varied technological applications), by what the course of the investments in R&D can only be programmed in a very limited way, both in the public sector and in the private one.

In fact, the usual and convenient form that has the private sector of getting over this gigantic suspense about the final destination of the scientific investigation is through two instruments: the autonomous teams of investigation and the funds of capital risk. As for the first ones, the companies with big capital devote themselves to provide with a proper budget an open team of investigators so, with a high autonomy grade, it investigates those projects that it considers to be more interesting for the future of the company, but without imposing rigid guidelines on them: one asks them to walk, and the cross is drawn on the map, but they have hundreds of different ways to get to the same objective... profit. As for the second ones, the investment of the funds of risk capital is distributed, after the first initial investment, between an enormous quantity of different projects with the hope that few of them triumph and there allow to compensate the losses of all remaining others that was accepted from a

[60] http://economia.elpais.com/economia/2016/05/20/actualidad/1463758343_740934.html

beginning that they are going to fail, but were just invested in to generate competition with the powerful ones. In other words, the investment in R&D is a highly speculative investment, and with a few very uncertain results: the utopic idea that any expense in R&D is productive turns out to be tremendously naive.

It is convenient to have this unbeatable suspense quite clear on the basis of the R&D to understand that the argument of the spillovers has not a great sense. Surely any successful investment in R&D ends up by being lucrative for the set of the community once it spreads: but it is simply impossible to know how beneficial it will end up being. For example, a research project might give in today for ruinous and useless, but in fifty or a hundred years, once other complementary skills have developed the sufficient, the ancient invention or technological project might be the base of a gigantic creation of wealth. Does it have any sense to think that the States can know which is going to be in one century the social profitability of the R&D that they are supporting financially today? Obviously, no. Therefore, a number of entire expenses does not exist in R&D that is objectively ideal (already let's not say a number of R&D ideal for sectors and for research projects). When one appeals to the investment deprived in R&D due to the presence of spillovers one is appealing, simply and smoothly, to a faith utopia: what it is about to indicate is that, probably, it would go all much better if we were investing a little more in R&D, over the actually low investment level. But to reach this point, already it would have deleted any feature of rational management of the investment in R&D: any expense level can be considered infra-investment, in other terms... the scarcity of resources from the State or the private sector, which will make R&D growth much more difficult.

Of course, the public expenditure is not only assigned to the fundamental research, but to the development. However, in these cases, its importance tends to be even more irrelevant opposite to the private investment. In fact, in all those countries that spent more than a 3 percent of their GDP, as for example does the average of the EU in R&D[61], the public expenditure represented less than one-third of the whole; in Israel — the country of the world that had invested more in this rubric — did not even reach 15 percent of the whole[62]. On the other hand, in Spain, Italy or Portugal, where the investment in R&D was located concerning 1,5 percent of the GDP, the public sector managed between 50 percent and 60 percent of the whole; not in vain, Spain and Portugal were the OECD countries which public sectors were spending the most in absolute terms in R&D, concerning 1 percent of their GDP. In what sense, then, is the private sector unable to fulfill the public expenditure in R&D of Spain or Portugal when in the most advanced countries of our environment it is already investing two or three times more than our public sector?

Of course, the answer is negative: with other conditions and other institutional frame, the Spanish private sector might invest perfectly in R&D 2 percent or 3 percent of the GDP. This already happens in Israel, Finland, Sweden, South Korea, Japan or Denmark, turning absolutely redundant the current governmental expense. Of course, if the Spanish private sector was spending 3 percent of the GDP[63] in R&D, we might argue that the public sector should promote even top levels of expense (in an extreme case reaching even the hundred percent of the GDP, there

[61] http://www.abc.es/sociedad/20150702/abci-secretaria-europeo-201507021824.html
[62] http://data.worldbank.org/indicator/GB.XPD.RSDV.GD.ZS?locations=IL
[63] http://ec.europa.eu/research/innovation-union/pdf/State-of-the-union/2014/countries/spain.pdf

would always be margin to exalt this argument from a populist point of view); but, as I just said, this is a mere beginning request.

COMPARISON OF PUBLIC EXPENDITURE IN R&D OF SPAIN AND EU:

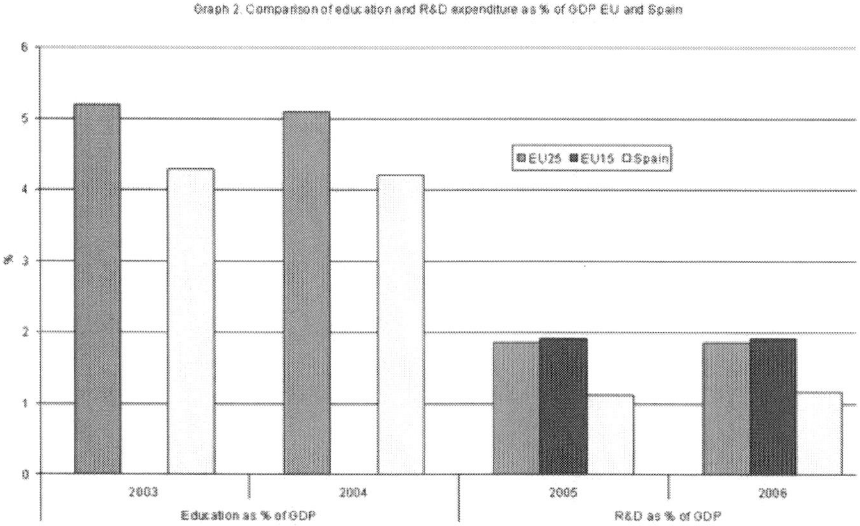

At the time of the truth, the investment in R&D will be more aggressive and intense for the simple reason of which it is profitable to do it: big part of the spillovers can be internalized across gradual and complementary investigations; for example, if the knowledge that a company develops generates its additional profit to another company, this one will result to invest and develop additionally this knowledge, which again will filter other companies that will increase their expense successively in investigation. The internalization will never be finished, for the simple reason of being impossible to know all the potential benefits of the R&D, but it will be in any case an expense in R&D much more rational and greatly more encouraged to the population's aims that a random funds share-out on the part of diverse government agencies.

In other words, a free market will not invest taking in consideration all nearly infinite potential future externalities, but the State would not work this way except if it was throwing enormous money quantities , or especially in investigative projects.The mistake and the incapability to do it belongs neither to the market nor to the State, but to the human knowledge: it is not possible to foresee our scientific and economic progress, even though there are many theories about both, but they are only that, theories, and nothing else. And if it is not possible to do it, it will not also be to gather at present the whole contribution of innovation expenditure in that absolutely uncertain scientific and economic progress.

Exactly because of this, the effects of the public investment in R&D are not so easy to annotate and to measure. The immense most of university studies highlight their kindness towards it comparing "good result" of the public expenditure in R&D with an entire major investment in R&D or with a major number of patents, but nothing of this means that the additional wealth generated by this major expense in R&D compensates the incurred costs; it would be so much as measuring the success of a company on the increase of its expenditure payments, or the increases in wages instead of focusing on the benefits from the firm. When, on the other hand, the studies are centered on analyzing the success of the commercialization of those private projects to which public support has been offered, whose results tend to be rather negative, even though some discoveries have been made an innovation might have succeeded, the account would still be registering red numbers.

In Spain, for example, the public university expenditure in R&D practically doubled in real terms from 2.750 million euros in 2001 to 5.200 million in 2011[64] and, nevertheless, the results have been rather scarce: the number of patents and models of utility registered in the Spanish Office of Patents and Marks has remained low and deeply concerning around the 6.000 per year and the value of these patents (measured by the foreign imports from similarities and revenues of the immaterial property) has suffered a little valuable real upturn during this period (from 410 annual millions to 580 million)[65], according to data of the Complutense University.

In any case, it might be thought that the public investment in R&D is to a great extent unnecessary but that it does not also turn out to be especially harmful except for the squandering of money of the taxpayers that it carries along. But, in this case, it is necessary to be quite sure that easily replaceable resources are not deprived by others, but highly specific resources and hardly substitutable: at last, a scientist who is working for a government agency will not be able to be investigating in a private project. In Spain, almost the three fourth parts of the investigators are employed or subsidized by public universities and organisms dependent on the State. Partly, consequently, the public expenditure on R&D has to displace by force to the investment deprived in R&D.

Certainly, the scientific conflict with the economic factors is ambiguous at this point, but the majority of theories seem to be that to shortly and medium term the public expenditure in R&D stretches to

[64] http://www.ine.es/prensa/np763.pdf

[65] http://www.forbes.com/sites/forbesleadershipforum/2013/06/25/how-to-tell-what-patents-are-worth/#2674137f6ac7

displace the private investment, especially if it rejects it in large numbers and the offer of the productive factors is very inelastic; in the long term, on the contrary, there seems to exist a light relation of complementarity that encourages to increase the investment deprived on the base of the public investment as a result of the spillovers existence. Now then, the long-term detected beneficial effects turn out to be quite doubtful: to the end, the private investment that is short-term displaced by the biggest public expenditure also would have generated spillovers that might have increased the private investment additionally. For example, historically in the United States, the percentages of public investment and deprived in R&D have constantly been moving in inverse directions.

PUBLIC EXPENDITURE OF THE UNITED STATES IN R&D:

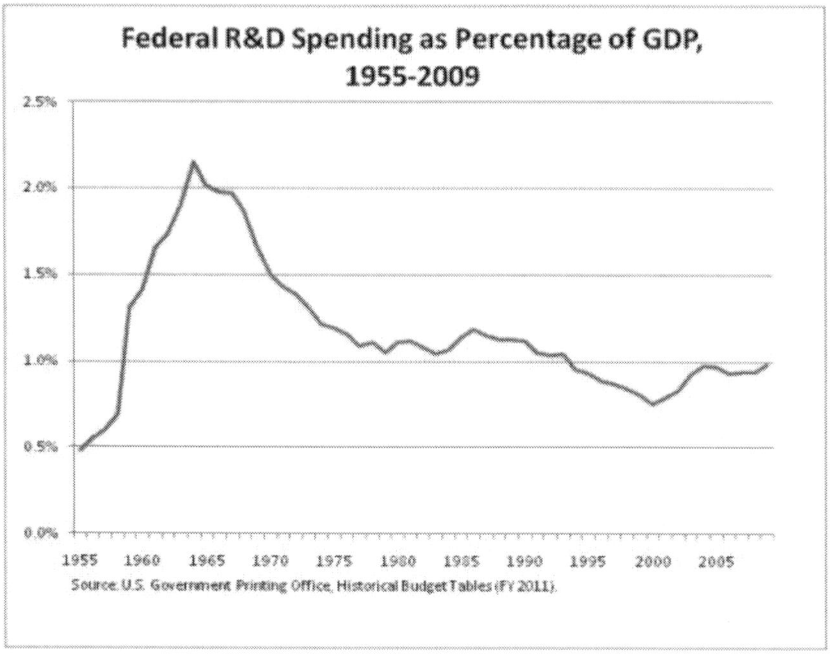

In addition, the public expenditure in R&D tends to displace a part of the private expense and to influence a bad sense to the other part. The spillovers existence does not justify in any case the support of the State to the R&D; not in vain, the national investment in R&D also carries along international spillovers that, on the other hand, have not led us to the establishment of the world State that they tend to invest in R&D. The private sector is enormously capable and desirable of managing the investment in science and technology — so, in fact, those countries that spend more in whole in R&D are those with a less relative weight of the public financing — and the State intervention, as in so many other sectors, tends to obstruct and to pervert more that to promote or incentive.

Nevertheless, since we might conceive the existence of some investment in fundamental research with a few overwhelming positive externalities and that the free market was not managing internally, we have included in our budget of the minimal State a fact equivalent to 0,3 percent of the GDP that will be able to be assigned, according to the needs for the exercise, or to physical infrastructures (highways, for example) or to infrastructures of the knowledge (fundamental research). One notice that 0,3 percent of the GDP is equivalent to the sum that today the government of the United States destinies to that purpose[66], and the United States is the country that invests the most globally in fundamental research; therefore, it is not a despicable total complain sharing a budget item with other infrastructures.

A totally different situation is, nevertheless, if another big intervention that the State carries out on the subject of innovation also turns out to be redundant or if, on the contrary, it constitutes a keystone of the technological development: making reference to the authorization of intellectual monopolies for the innovators across the patents system, which in many cases is wrongly used, and being allowed by the State, tends to generate monopolies, that later on will produce allocative inefficiency in the market.

A patent on public expenditure innovation, in contrast to private patterns, is only a temporary monopoly granted by the State over a few ideas. In particular, the patent grants the privilege of exploiting economically to the State; the exclusive innovations have taken the shape of the form of new products or of new procedures. Although it is habitual

[66] http://data.worldbank.org/indicator/GB.XPD.RSDV.GD.ZS?locations=US

to group the patents inside the category of "intellectual property", it is a question of abuse of the term "property", in the case of governmental patenting: the target of the patent is not allowing the inventor the use and enjoyment of his invention, but preventing coactively other agents from enjoying the same one making use of his properties. For example, if I discover a new medicine, the property right on the medicine should guarantee me that nobody prevents me from using it, from reproducing it or from commercializing it; but the patent does not try to safeguard my pacific enjoyment of the medicine, but to prohibit to others the possibility of being able to reproduce and use this medicine making use of its property (for example, reproducing the formula with their own ingredients). Namely the patent is a monopoly that grants the inventor (in this case the State, even though investments are from public expenditure) to itself to prevent others from being able to imitate his discovery inside their properties (therefore, it is a legalized violation of the private ownership), which prevents private firms from exploiting the discovery, even if the State is not going to merchandise it or develop it anymore.

As in any monopoly, the result of the patents is of increasing the profitability of the privileged monopolist at the cost of the well-being of the consumers — those who turn out to be forbidden of the offer of other providers — and at the cost of the benefits of their potential rivals — that turn out to be knocked out from the market—. In case of the patents, nevertheless, it seems that this wealth transference from the consumer and the competitor to the monopolistic producer might be justified like an incentive to be invested in R&D: since the necessary expense to discover a new product is usually the highest, it is necessary to guarantee that the inventor exploits exclusive during a time the profit that is related to his discovery, of course better than instead allowing any economic agent to copy it and to harvest fat benefits despite not having invested anything in the development of this new product, except if the inventor was the State, in that situation the story would get adverse.

Of entry, it is assumed that all the innovations need a gigantic initial investment that, consequently, takes a lot of time to refund. We tend to visualize the inventor as a genius who develops alone each and every one of the parts and stages of a new product. Nevertheless, in a world increasingly complex and specializing, this description turns out to be less and not very realistic: as we have already reported earlier, the innovations usually have a much more gradual character. Every inventor contributes marginal progress to the knowledge previously existing and, once many of this progress have accumulated, it is when seemingly a technological jump takes place, and in most of the cases, it is not the inventor the one who makes the initial investment, which justifies a second person to exploit the production of that new product, even though it was not his idea, but on the other hand it was his money, and it was this economic agent the one that took the real risk by financing the project.

The innovation process is gradual and much of having it decentralized carries along two implications of crucial importance to consider the social utility of eliminating the patents between investors and economic developers: on the one hand, the individual investment of every company in every project of R&D would be much more measured and gradually, for what its profitability would be much more rapid (technically, we would go on from a process of investigation placed in integral processes and closed to a period of investigation, while on the other way, with a second economic developer this process will be faster, generating higher benefits in the mean term, and allowing for reinvestment in the future); on the other hand, the fact that the main input of those investigators that look for gradual progress related to the previous innovations of other investigators, which means that without patents there would diminish enormously the costs of investigation (they would not have to pay for the patents that they want to use). Therefore, if the patents did not exist, we would move to a world where the fixed cost of innovation would be much lower and where, consequently, every company would be in a minor necessity of monopolizing or fixing cartels with other firms from the sector, with the only objective of reducing competition, overall over price. Sales will also have much less time to cover the amount of the initial investment, through financial help to reach the refund.

Eliminating the patents, then, does not finish with innovation: it simply modifies the way in which this one materializes, as reducing partially patents will raise production levels of technological firms, due to a decrease in price by a greater competition, leading to a much more efficient allocation of resources. Not in vain, the scientific innovation did not even begin with the implantation of the patents, and merely in the last three years they have increased by more than 40%[67], in Asia, not even the reinforcement of the monopoly of the patents has ever gone tied to an intensification of the technological development: on the contrary, the rule has always been the inverse one, namely, first an industrial sector was developing without the protection of the patents and, later, the State

---

[67] http://www.asianscientist.com/2016/08/topnews/thomson-reuters-emerging-research-and-innovation-hub-report-asean/

included it under the umbrella of the legislation of patents without it helping to increase the innovation with regard to the previous period (any sectors, like the one of the fashion, are not even protected today by the patents, without their innovative capacity being reduced). In this sense, we have abundant evidence of which, the same way as they have been extended or hardening the protection ambiances, even of the patents in those sectors where innovation and capital exist, the level of technological innovation has not improved.

Now then, although it seems clear that the investment in innovation might through circuits and that the patents bear numerous costs without associated benefits; it is legit that the doubts survive: what would happen with those innovations that could not be privatized or be decentralized but, by force, needed the strongest initial investment? In such cases, the patents clearly seem to be necessary in order to exclude the competitors until one manages to recover the enormous initial investment. The most famous and illustrative example probably is that of the medicines: the highest costs of the pharmaceutical investigation need of a few long patents to promote them. The intellectual monopoly of the patents, hence, might remain justified for these special assumptions.

PUBLIC PATENTS IN SPAIN:

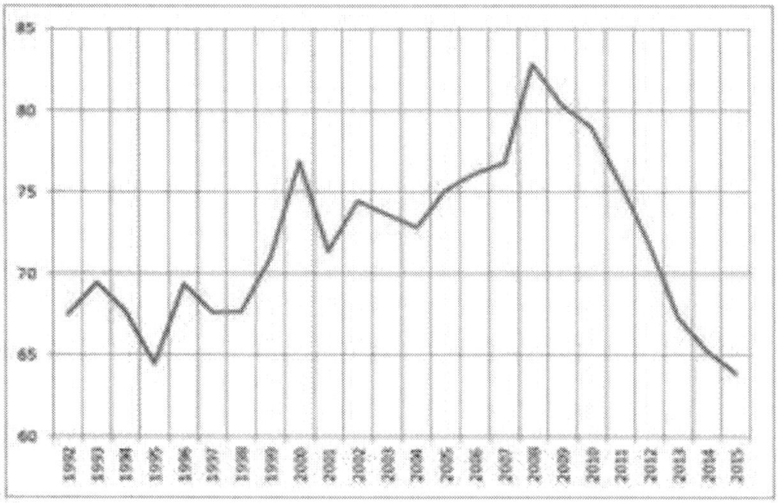

Nevertheless, the patents are not the only way of protecting the inventions in an opposite and interventionist way to the competition. In the biggest survey realized to innovative companies on the motives that they were leading them to invest in R&D, the main mechanism that explored companies emphasized to manage the promotion of their investigation and discoveries. This is, their aptitude to keep the newly acquired technical knowledge in secret, as patients represent a 36.22% of new innovation projects in Spain[68], required mostly by regular and large companies. The patents were relegated to the last place by the computer

[68] http://www.oepm.es/es/propiedad_industrial/preguntas_frecuentes/FaqInvenciones37.html

industry and by the technological sector and there did not even reach the silver medal between the pharmacists, who highlighted how more important the economic advantages that it transports to be the pioneer in commercializing a product, but not the only one supplier, as competition over this product much more spots will be invested into R&D. Only for the biotechnological ones, the patents of certain importance turned out to be, although with a subordinated role that of the industrial secret, what reflects clearly that other mechanisms exist, so is it more effective than the patents? To recover with profit the attacked investment. In fact, the same survey was reflecting that the main motives that were leading the companies to patenting their new products were openly monopolistic intentions (the reasons of "the copy prevented" and to block the entry of new "competitors" were quoted by 95,8 percent and 81,8 percent of the market share by different sectors) or strategies to be protected preventively opposite to the possibility that their rivals were patenting it in the future (the reasons of "avoiding interventionism in this model" and "to use the patent in negotiation processes" they were quoted by 58,7 percent and 47,3 percent of the companies[69]). On the other hand, the motives that might justify the social benefits of the patents — their use as a measurement of the proper yield or their employment for the cashing derivatives of their use on the part of third — were scarcely mentioned.

But we shouldn't judge a book by its cover. First, because the innovations are both present on goods that are going to be sold to the consumers, but also in production processes that can help to lower the price of the consumer goods and that can remain secretly inside the company for a long time. And the second and main, because the

[69] http://is.jrc.ec.europa.eu/pages/ISG/patents/mitra-kahn-New-insight-into-firm-level-innovation.ppsx

information transfer is not an immediate and free cost process: the simplest example but simultaneously the most illustrative will probably be how, more than one century after the commercialization of the Coca-Cola, its formula keeps on being secret. Applying it to the case of the R&D, this time of advantage which-which the company enjoys its pioneering innovation opposite to its competitors - copiers allows him to improve and develop its initial technology prematurely, so that when its rivals have managed to emulate it finally, it will be able already to offer to the consumers an improved version of the product, with major quality, reliability and quantity of services or simply cheaper (it is what is known as first mover advantage). The advantage of being a pioneer allows you to go, therefore, always two steps ahead of the competition, and obtain a benefit through the larger aggregate demand of this competition.

From this point of view, the investment deprived in R&D takes a much more social profile: it is the whole set of the society the one that, in a decentralized but complementary way, helps to make progress through knowledge and innovation, so there is no reason to grant a temporary monopoly on the economic use of a certain innovation to any agent. Let's imagine that two companies invest high sums of money in developing the same product in two separated ways, but one of them develops it one day before the other one and manages to patent it. What is the reason to that the first one should obtain all the profit derived from the same one? None, as the second company has also invested all the money into production. Also, having two companies producing the same product will be food for the economy, in the sense of higher economic growth through an increase in GDP levels, as occurred in Spain after the privatization of the electric sector, which became a private oligopoly; having more than

73%[70] of the markets share between the three biggest firms; which will be mentioned and discussed in the next chapter, due to the fact of State domination of the electric market: Iberdrola, Endesa and Gas Natural after having been an obscure and demoralised State-owned monopoly, a change that leaded to larger efficiency in the market. And the same is necessary to observe and analyse concerning the social interrelations of knowledge and technical progress that lead ultimately to a specific innovation: in certain grade, all the present innovations are offspring of the advances spent in the knowledge, so that there does not seem to be reason so that the State guarantees extraordinary profitability to any company for the progress carried out on the base of this socially piled up knowledge.

Also, the patents system generates, as we have already commented, the whole series of inefficiencies and redundant costs that get paid by both companies through the same investigative process and that, obviously, would be absent in a free market without patents. In the case of the pharmacists, the case of the calls is quite well-known: medicines are only reproductions of other patent medicines but with enough changes, bordering the cry zone of the patenting law to be able to produce the same or a cloned product without being fined. In general, the changes do not suppose any extremist progress, so, from an economic point of view, patents for many products as medicines are mainly just a barrier to economic growth and a competition murderer in the market. The only motive for which they keep on developing them are merely the distortions that introduce the patents: since those companies with a patent medicine can receive the highest prices for the same one during

[70] http://economia.elpais.com/economia/2013/05/06/actualidad/1367838934_683741.html

the validity of the protection, frequently it keeps on being profitable to develop the same medicine again for another ten years (or modifying the compound lightly) to be able to remain with part of this juicy cake called monopoly. The problem is that the magnitude of the squandering is not small: 75 percent of the whole expense of R&D of the pharmacists go to develop these redundant medicines. Without patents, there would be a few resources that the own pharmacists might destine to other much more useful investigations for the society.

Finally, there is no motive of weight so that the State maintains the privileged protection of the patent innovations, that is to say, there is no motive of weight so the State maintains a monopoly on the ideas. The private sector is provided with sufficient means as to manage to promote its productive investments in the absence of State-owned patents, and being in need of a private system of patent management, where companies are able to trade and commercialize their rights and their projects: far from, without leaving away the expense in R&D, the intellectual competition would drive to low the price of the costs and of the innovation, to direct the investment to socially productive activities, which will be much more profitable to the overall economic system in the long run. Once again, the State is just one more obstacle in our way to a freer and prosperous society.

7- A LIBERALIZED ELECTRIC MARKET

The energy constitutes one of the essential productive factors of any economy: having a cheap energy turns out to be fundamental to increase the productivity and the economic growth the other way round of what would seem foreseeable, as we have been able to see during the last year how cheap oil prices have risen production levels by more than a 5.4%[71] as an example in the Canadian manufacturing sector — the energy efficiency allows to obtain important savings in its consumption — a cheaper energy allows to promote many managerial projects that were not viable with excessive energy costs and, on having done it, it increases the entire energy demand.

Or to be said in a more resumed way: cheaper energy supposes larger growth, and more growth generates, in turn, a major energy demand. The main sources of primary energy of the world are the oil, the coal, the natural gas, the renewable ones and the nuclear energy. Their use goes to produce fundamentally heat, also for transport and to generate electricity. To a greater extent, the problems relative to the primary energy sources fit inside the analysis carried out previously on other chapter about the environment and the presence of externalities inside a city: the energy production will be regulated according to the

71 http://www.parl.gc.ca/Content/HOC/Committee/412/FINA/WebDoc/WD7864616/412_FINA_ILOPCE_Briefs%5CCanadianManufacturersAndExporters-e.pdf

rights of individual and communal private ownership assigned on the deposits in which these primary sources are, and their use will have to be designated with the property rights of a third as they could carry along external denials (pollution, heat, etc.).

In fact, the use of the energy sources would occupy in the first place to produce heat or for the transport, as it does not seem to imply too many complications beyond the already mentioned externalities and management of communal goods. Different is the case of electricity: the generation and distribution of large-scale electricity usually repute an activity in which the State must exercise, for diverse reasons that I'll explain in the next lines, defending a very direct intervention of the government, but just in this sense! Many economists as Paul Kaufman consider the electrical system to be the paradigm of the "natural monopolies," which is to say, how a type of industry must be cornered by a State monopoly or by a private monopoly hard regulated by the State. Considering the critical importance that implies having cheap energy, and much in particular a cheap electricity, for the economic development, it is convenient to analyze to what extent a free electrical market should exist in Spain.

Any electrical system can be subdivided into three activities: the generation of electric power in a head office, its transport and distribution up to the final consumer through the network electricity company, and the intermediation work (or commercialization) directed to coordinate the offer and the demand for energy. As an example of the energy sector liberalization, we can look proudly at Spain, which after Aznar's reform was able to reduce its costs by 3.63% since 1997[72].

The main distinctive note of this market is that its goods (the electric power) are not storable in practice, so that its marketers have to be provided with the skill of adapting themselves instantaneously to a demand that can go so far as to vary very much: in particular, the marketers have to be capable of supplying the extraordinary demand peaks and managing the continuous changes in the prices of electricity (given the changeable final demand, the price of the electricity on the wholesale market changes constantly).

On the one hand, the logical way of facing the first one of these two problems is to be provided with a certain excess capacity from the side of the generation, so that the marketer could resist a sudden increase of the demand of its clients with a few major great consumers to the generating head offices. Now then, as this generation excess capacity it will be distributed among a big number of head offices (normally with the head offices installation that only enter functioning during the hours of major demand) it will be necessary to be provided with a very interconnected electrical network, so that a marketer could acquire electricity in a flexible way within a variety of head offices and even to face to the interruption or unexpected congestion of some circumstances of the network.

On the other hand, to settle the second one of the problems — the management of a few very fluctuating prices — the marketer is provided with the possibility of acquiring on the future market the volumes of electricity that its clients will most likely demand, which causes electric

[72] http://www.celfosc.org/biblio/consum.estalvi/unesa.htm

demand to rise in Spain near to 11.4%[73] in the last two years, and predominantly in the periods of deep winter. This way, the generating power plants promise to supply them at the agreed moment with the offer of energy agreed at a fixed price closed in advance: as soon as there was closed the price of the wholesale market during the next months, the marketer can already offer a stable price on the retail market without being exhibiting to any risk. Another option to settle this problem would be that the marketer was advising to its consumers any fluctuation in the prices that was happening in the supplying process in the market.

Consequently, on a free electrical market we would observe multiple models of providing electricity to the consumers: some companies would choose to integrate vertically, managing their own generation and commercialization of electricity, as well as their own electrical network, in contrast to the previous Spanish electrical monopoly which was established before the reform having a market share of 73%[74] of the total electric market. Others, on the other hand, would limit themselves to act like generating head offices that spill and sell their production to the electrical network according to the demand of independent marketers, being the network a private ownership of one or of several companies, or even of the proper generators or marketers by means of forms of communal property. Some of them might even decide in favor of their enterprise to consume their own electricity through, for example, solar panels. The excellent thing is that, as in every environment and context the ideal way of generating electricity can change, the different economic agents would have the option to experiment in a

---

[73] http://www.ree.es/es/sala-de-prensa/notas-de-prensa/2015/07/la-demanda-de-energia-electrica-aumenta-un-5-4-en-julio

[74] http://www.iese.edu/es/files/energy%20report_Esp_tcm5-54915.pdf

variable way which one of the methods is more efficient of producing and distributing: the traditional models would compete with the disruptive innovations that were developing to undermine them, promoting a dynamic progress of the quality and the cost of the service.

Also, since the property rights on the environment would be assigned entirely, the head offices would not have any more remedy than internalizing the totality of their costs (the nuclear power plants should take charge entirely of the cost of their insurance and of managing their residues; also, the thermoelectric head offices should support the cost caused by their contamination), so that the energy mix that was resulting from the decentralized production process, and the investors would be completely compatible with the preferences and needs of the economic agents.

The free electrical market, nevertheless, is not provided with too many defenders between the economists and the public opinion. And the fact is that, due to the previously exposed factors (high initial investment even in excess capacity, managing network for the high interconnections, not storable goods with the consistent possibility of manipulation of prices), two obnoxious suppositions are carried out usually about the foreseeable evolution of a free electrical market: the first one is that it would degenerate into a monopoly or natural oligopoly where a few companies would plunder the consumer by means of high prices; the second one, that the frantic competition inside the electrical market would degenerate into a chaotic electrical system infested with blackouts, managerial failures and manipulated prices.

The first idea, that the electrical market tends to degenerate naturally into a natural monopoly, departs from the base of which not only it is cheaper to generate and to distribute the electricity with only one operator that with many others (what technically is known as "sub-activity of costs"), but also the presence of enormous initial costs of investment turns it very complicated that new competitors could bring in on the market before the presence of manipulations of prices, due to enormous economic barriers and high set up costs on the part of the competitors towards the monopolist. The idea turns out to be absolutely false for the matters of generation and commercialization: there is no founded motive for supposing that all the head offices of generation and the whole work of intermediation will manage in a more efficient and accessible way for only one operator that for multiple; an investor might possess a head office or a group of generating head offices and sell energy to their break-even cost, generating competition with the rest. In fact, as then we will remember, this way it has often happened along the history and this way it happens today in most of the Western countries, that the electric market tends to be a pure and solid monopoly, charging prices much higher than initial production costs, and producing in an inefficient way, which carries along with it an enormous amount of externalities such as pollution, and everything due to the lack of competition in the market, as was Mexico before its liberalizing reform of 2016, due to an increase in the pollution level, getting over the 100 points[75], caused by the inefficient production of the electric monopoly.

Different is the case of the networks of transmission and distribution, where there seem to exist founded reasons for supposing

[75] http://aqicn.org/map/mexico/es/

that they fulfill the characteristics of a natural monopoly. In case of the transmission networks — the transport at long distances through lines of high voltage of the electricity from the generating head office up to the electrical substation — the laws of the physics impose, on the one hand, the presence of important externalities in very interconnected transmission networks: the electrical flow across the transmission networks does not flow on as previously predetermined, but through a route which offers a lower resistance, what can end up by affecting to the networks of transmission of other enterprises or even to the effective attitude of other generators to spill electricity to the network and be given to its clients. On the other hand, the increase of the capacity of transference of an interconnected network does not depend on the capacity of transference of the isolated network that wants to be added, but on its effect on the set of the preexisting elements (there can happen the case of an increase in the size of the network ending up by reducing its transference capacity), by what the incremental investments in the network must be carried out of way planned by the set of its owners, studied along with physicists or engineers, to protect the profit margins. Also, the operators of the transmission sector need to maintain constant the frequency and the voltage at any point of the network to avoid damages of the service.

In the case of the distribution networks — those that transport the electricity at short distances from the substations up to its final users — it turns out to be slightly viable that in the same city or in the same industrial park coexist several distribution firms to which a family or a company can hire their services or be disconnected according to the tariffs which are different depending on the owner's consumption load. The logical thing, rather, is that only one company provides this service, avoiding costs and duplicities.

Well, being true all the technical considerations on the networks of transmission and of distribution, none of them implies that the electrical network constitutes a natural monopoly that should be stabilized or regulated closely by the public administrations. At last, the problems associated with the networks of transmission are problems of externalities and we have already analyzed in the previous chapters how such problems were settled: firstly defining individual private ownership rights on which negotiating the internalization of these external effects or, when the costs of deal linked to this internalization are very large, by means of the constitution of a communal private ownership. The case of the network of transmission is not different: an option would be that the diverse owners of networks of transmission were agreeing on some mechanism to share costs and then they were proceeding to assign transmission rights inside the network to the generating head offices; another option would be that the owners of the different networks were sharing a communal governmental body being in charge simply to manage the externalities that take place between them, redistributing their costs and benefits by means of agreed mechanisms. Not in vain, even between State systems of networks of transmission where there already exist communal governmental bodies that do not spend for the constitution of a public monopoly: it is the case, for example, of the European Network of Agents of Networks of Transport of Electricity. (ENANE)[76]

[76] https://ec.europa.eu/energy/en/topics/infrastructure

Also, let's not forget either that, even if the whole transmission network was a property of the only company, it does not imply that it possesses aptitude to impose any prices on its clients: not in vain, every time prices are increasing fast, just as much as the distributed or decentralized generation of electricity (for example, the cogeneration or several forms of renewable energies) that supposes generating the electricity in head offices very next to the final user that, therefore, can do without the transmission networks at long distance, exercising this way a potential and permanent competition on those owners of the network of high voltage who were daring to increase disproportionately their tariffs , and reducing costs for the supplier company.

Also, the difficulties linked to the existence of a network of single distribution for every city or managerial center do not turn out to be significant either. It is true that in appearance the owner of the distribution network will dominate a monopoly, but not for having the power to impose his prices unilaterally. To the end, the authentic client of the distribution network is not every user of the electricity individually considered, but the set of the community deprived of owners who, by means of their governmental bodies, accept or push back that a certain distributor provides a similar service to them. From my point of view, then, the negotiation does not take place between a monopoly and tens of thousands of dispersed clients, but between a monopoly (the only offered: the owner of the distribution network) and a monopsony (the only claimant: the government of the private city), from which no bargaining power presumption stems for the first one. It is only necessary to imagine how threatening it would turn out for the distributor of a city like this one, in a joint way, to be threatening in spite of stopping hiring his services (the proper city even might finance, by means of an extraordinary apportionment between the co-owners, the construction of their own network of distribution).

In the United States, the State regulation of the electrical markets did not begin in most of the States up to well brought in the second decade of the XXth century, although to a rhythm opposite to which it would be necessary to attend on the theory of the natural monopoly: those States that earlier regulated the electricity were exhibiting — before the coming into effect of this regulation — a few prices levels 46 percent less (and the electricity companies a margin of 38 percent low benefits) to those other States that later regulated it; circumstance that seems to indicate that the political motivation of the regulation is not necessary to find it in the pretext of avoiding the development of the consumers, but perhaps in another part.

Where? In the interest of the proper electrical companies to regulate the market with the intention of closing the entry to new competitors who were forcing them to lower prices. Finally, the origin of the State regulation of the electrical market derives rather from the excess of competition that was pressing to the fall of prices in favor of the consumers and was reducing the margins of profitability of the placed companies. There wasn't any track of natural monopoly until the State intervened. A clear example of regulatory impositions which rises the electric prices, converting electricity into a scarce good for many people, is in Spain, where 55%[77] of the total bill's price are State taxes.

[77] http://www.consumer.es/web/es/economia_domestica/servicios-y-hogar/2013/01/14/215327.php

But precisely this stage is the one that, in the opinion of other economists, justifies the intervention and regulation of the electrical market on the part of the State. In this case it is usually argued that, as the fierce competition between the generating head offices pushes them to sell their energy production to a marginal cost that scarcely allows recovering the very high initial expenses, there will not be incentives to be invested in excess productive capacity to attend to the demand peaks, what will degenerate into allocative inefficiency or even electricity scarcity for consumers. Also, and derivative of the previous thing, during these demand peaks the generating head offices will have a powerful incentive to restrict artificially the offer to achieve disproportionate increases in prices and extraordinary benefits, without these benefits being sufficient to attract new investment in capacity of generation which allows to increase the offer and lower the prices (since we remember, it breaks off the base of which in times of normal demand this additional capacity is not profitable, as there would not be economies of scale intervening in production costs).

In fact, this second apocalyptic stage has not also too much sense, since it is based on a slightly credible premise: that the whole electricity buying and selling is carried out at a single moment, given that the clients have not signed supply contracts with the electrical companies in which they represent fixed prices during a certain period of time and where responsibilities are established by the interruption of the service. Once the markets interfere in term inside the electrical system, it eliminates any apocalyptic stage derived from the free competition.

Otherwise, an electrical supplier can receive from his clients a fixed price over his marginal generation cost, including in this price the called "guarantees of potency" (payments directed to remunerate the ideal capacity available for facing the demand peaks). If such contracts include, also, an indemnification for the consumer of the interruption of service that proves sufficiently high as for disincentive opportunist behaviors between the marketers (as it might be, for example, charging the client for a guarantee of potency of the one that in fact does not prepare to maximize profit), the investment in excess capacity will be able to be carried out without too many obstacles, everything without governmental intervention.

The habitual complain about the previous argument is that the markets in term cannot work appropriately in the electrical system: although to big features it is possible to estimate with reasonable reliability the electrical demand in the nearby future, even though it turns out to be impossible to do it with absolute precision, so that it will keep on being necessary that the prices are regulated by a daily market and enclosed circles, where the offer fits exactly the real demand of the moment. Discarded the possibility of markets in term as an economic agent, the electrical system remains again exposed to the prices manipulation on the part of its operators, who can artificially limit the provision of energy offer before the extraordinary demand rises to obtain fat benefits and where, also, it is not possible to agree with the supplier on fixed and stable tariffs.

But, again, this rejoinder is erroneous: so that it exists a future electrical market is not necessary that they enclose in advance and with absolute precision all the offers and future demands of electricity. The normal functioning way is articulated through financial intermediaries: the marketer buys it (future energy actives) to a financial institution a future energy quantity at a price fixed in advance; the financial institution on its part, will devote itself to fulfill this commitment with the marketer buying every day the energy on the market, and will do it at the current price at this moment according to the offer and the demand of every moment. If the price of the market to which the financial institution buys the electricity is low compared to the price to which it has compromised to sell it to the marketer, it will gain money; if it is top, it will lose it. Therefore, it is perfectly viable that future contracts exist on the electrical market that allows including an increase in price on the marginal cost of producing electricity in this way to promote the existence of overcapacity with being able to attend the demand peaks.

Again, the available evidence is illustrative in this point: according to the historical statistics of the United States (Governmental Statistics), the electrical potency installed in private power plants went up from 1,2 million KW in 1902 to 8,9 million in 1917, and the electrical production increased from 2,3 million kWh to 25,4 million[78], that is to say, an increase of 650 percent and of 910[79] percent respectively in fifteen years. Undoubtedly, it might happen that, despite this one very significant increase, the electricity companies were limiting the energy offer artificially to get higher its price, but it does not look like a too probable existing account, as in the same period the tariffs decreased their price by 41 percent in economic terms.

---

[78] https://www.eia.gov/

[79] https://www.washingtonpost.com/graphics/national/power-plants/

Far from what it is usually believed, the case of the USA does not illustrate why the free market does not work but, rather, why the governmental interventions in the electrical system can be tremendously variable. Exactly we are going to dedicate the following section of this chapter to it.

The main problem of the State monopolizing or regulating closely the electrical market is that this one does not end up by answering to the needs of the consumers but to the interests of the planners. On a free electrical market, it was the demand of the consumers the one that was determining the offer of the producers, while in a stabilized system the offer is the one that is imposed on the demand.

Just like we have seen previously, once internalizing all the costs thanks to the allocation of rights of property on the environment and the cities, those head offices capable of generating electricity at a lower cost will be, for definition, which better cover the needs of the consumers. If, for example, the citizens of a territory affected by the activity of a head office detest enormously any type of contamination or do not want to have any negative externalities, under any possible indemnification, to the risk that represents a nuclear accident, the construction of thermoelectric or nuclear head offices will not be viable in this territory; if on the other hand, the residents accept fewer compensations for the contamination or for the risk of nuclear accident, these head offices might be possibly profitable. It is exactly like that, through the competence of experimentations decentralized in very diverse organizational scales (family, municipality, prime, big corporation, etc.), how the ideal electrical mix is discovered for the citizens, and decided by the citizens and not by governments, which in most cases only take care of their benefits.

On the other hand, in a stabilized electrical system, the politicians (or the "technical staff" designated by the politicians) are the ones who in a centered way decide what the ideal electrical supply is for the whole population, without bearing in mind the needs for the set of the citizens. For example, in 2014 France had 59 nuclear power plants in functioning, which supplied more than 75%[80] of their total energy output while Spain only 8[81]. Does it mean that the Spanish were much more adverse than the French to the risk of enduring a nuclear accident? It is doubtful: specially, because to a greater extent the Spanish are also exposed to the risk of a nuclear accident in France, without similar cost having been internalized by the French government (compensating the Spanish citizens). The most reasonable interpretation is that the Spanish politicians have decided unilaterally their "energy policy" and the French politicians their own without none having kept in mind the needs of the affected population, and the results of it in the national income levels.

ELECTRICAL MARKET IN THE UNITED STATES:

[80] http://www.world-nuclear.org/information-library/country-profiles/countries-a-f/france.aspx
[81] http://www.unesa.es/phocadownload/centrales-nucleares-2013-en.pdf

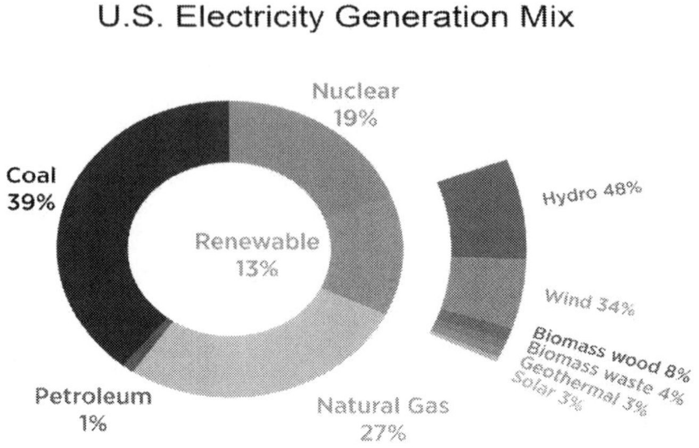

2014 preliminary data from U.S. Energy Information Administration, *Electricity Power Monthly* (February 2015).

The example should serve, also, to reveal the erroneous but habitual association between, on the one hand, the defenders of a free electrical market and the nuclear energy and, for other, the defenders of the electrical statist and the renewable energies. The defenders of a really free electrical market do not promote any type of energy in particular, but simply that one that minimizes the production costs, once they have of course internalized all the costs (included the environmental ones). If in these conditions the renewable head offices are more competitive than their alternatives, so much better for all the economic agents. But, for identical motives, the same would happen with the nuclear power plants. In spite of everything, there is convenient to notice in parallel that the alliance proves on behalf of the defenders of the renewable energies with the State when, first, the States have been the main promoters and developers of the nuclear power plants on the whole planet; not particularly in Spain (for the route to all its costs set on themselves on the population without internalizing them); and, second, the distributed generation of energy by means of renewable head offices is a paradigmatic case of the functioning of the decentralized free market. A clear example of the free development of energy and electrical markets in Spain were all the inefficient subsidies given to renewable energy during the period of the financial crisis, "donating" green firms nearly $548 billion[82] while representing only 19% of the total global production. The fact that the followers of an electrical free market are not favorable to impose by the force the renewable energy and to prohibit by the force the nuclear energy, even though if companies do internalize does not mean all their costs that they are hostile of the first ones and followers of the second one: simply it means that they are opposite to the State planning the supply of energy production.

And there it is because, for the same motives for which it is impossible to plan in a centralized way the whole economy, the electrical sector cannot also be planned to respect the real preferences of the citizens. More here it is also suitable to clarify an habitual misunderstanding: that the State could not plan with success the electrical sector does not make necessary that a sector stabilized is going to exhibit retail prices more expensive than a liberalized market. If the publicly controlled electrical system does not internalize all its real costs (this is, if these costs are socialized across the State coercion), it is completely probable that it supplies the energy at a price much less than it would sell in a free market. For example, if the State provides a subsidy of 80 percent[83] on the price of the sale of the electricity, for example in India, being obvious that it can manage to reduce it artificially at the cost of using the coercion on the taxpayers. In the same way, if the State imposes

[82] https://www.iisd.org/gsi/renewable-electricity-subsidies
[83] http://panchabuta.com/2013/05/16/tamil-nadu-to-provide-80-subsidy-to-solar-powered-irrigation-pump-sets/

coactively the construction of a head office that generates gigantic externalities on a territory without granting any indemnification to the residents of this area, it will also be reducing its price artificially at the cost of the citizens of this land. The problem, clearly, is the fact that in such a case, few citizens — the consumers of electricity — will be exploiting to others — the taxpayers or the residents of the territory that suffer from externalities.

Consequently, an electrical free market is not a guarantee of that the price is necessarily going to fall down with regard to a State situation in which big part of the costs was not internalized. What obviously tends to obtain is, first, an alignment of the electrical offer with the preferences of the consumers; and, second, a minimization of the price of the electricity once there are really internalized all the costs (as it happened to a great extent before the States began to regulate and control the electrical systems).

It achieves both laudable targets by means of the decentralized experimentation of numerous agents on which the best and most efficient methods are in every case employed to produce the electricity.

Nevertheless, this conclusion seems to occur repeatedly, with reality very near to the Spanish: the supposed liberalization of the electrical market initiated in 1997 has only achieved that the retail prices of the electricity in Spain have experienced very superior to those of the rest of Occident. It happens that, as we will explain in the latter section, the vision it had on the "privatized" Spanish electrical system is so distorted like the one that was the American one, during Reagan's mandate: in fact, very considerable rises in prices have been a consequence of an omnipresent State control and not of a genuine freedom of market.

According to Eurostat, the nominal prices of the electricity in Spain before taxes have doubled between the year 2000 and 2012 both for domestic and industrial consumers[84]. It is a question of an increase without precedent in Europe that, in spite of everything, does not even reach to cover the entire costs of the Spanish electrical system (Making clear exaltation for the one that, both in 2012 and in 2013, kept on accumulating the called deficit tariff: the expenses excess on income owed the Spanish electricity companies). Since in 1997, with the approval of the Law, it started the supposed liberalization of the electrical system, the top or end of this fiasco seems clear: the freedom of market that has degenerated into an oligopoly dedicated to plundering the Spanish with continued increases in price for the major luck of their shareholders. Nevertheless, the authentic devastating factor is not a nonexistent market freedom, but an extreme State control that has not stopped intervening actively in this sector, up to the point of having varied in any more than 30 occasions the Law from its coming into effect

Of three stages of the electrical market, the two supposedly liberalized in Spain are the generation and the commercialization; the transport and distribution do not even try to be liberalized since even the legislator keeps on including them under the rubric of "regular activities." More in particular, in these two regular activities, the public sector does not only demand previous authorization for the construction of new networks of transport and distribution, but it forces the owners of the

---

[84] http://www.inega.gal/descargas/enerxia_galicia/precio_tarifa_electrica_castellano.pdf

same ones to allow free access in exchange for the tariff fixed by the government: it is as if, having constructed a new stretch of the network a private investor, authorized by the Administration, the State was nationalizing the new stretch of the network in exchange for a periodic compensation, in the shape of tariff, to this investor.

Consequently, on the subject of transport and distribution, it is the State the one who must authorize the construction of new networks, who determines the conditions of use of the same ones and who fixes the price of their service. The difference with a completely State electrical network is, therefore, very scarce: in fact, 84 percent of the transport networks in Spain keep on being a property of Electrical Network of Spain SA[85], controlled company by shareowners for the State across the State Society of Industrial Shares (SEPI). Bearing in mind that about 20 percent of the entire costs of the Spanish electrical system correspond to these two activities, and that between 2002 and 2012 their costs more than duplicated it (as a result of the enlargement of the network), probably it turns out to be premature to blame exclusive the free market, and not the State interventionism, of the explosive evolution of the prices of the retail market, generating nearly hyperinflation in the electricity production and commercialization market.

But, despite the appearances, the interventionism of the State is not less than in other two "liberalized" activities. On the subject of generation, from 1997[86] it is not the State who, across National Energy Plans of protectionist character, plans the enlargement of the potency installed by

---

[85]http://www.unesa.net/unesa/unesa/transporte/ficha4_2.html

[86] https://www2.deloitte.com/content/dam/Deloitte/global/Documents/Energy-and-Resources/gx-er-market-reform-spain.pdf

means of the construction of certain types of head offices: in principle, any Spanish that has enough capital assembled can invest in the construction of a power plant. Nevertheless, already from the beginning any plan deprived of investment needs of authorization previous to the diverse competent administrations, so that deeply they keep on being the politicians (and not the citizens and entrepreneurs) who have the last word on how much power it settles and where it settles: if some administration wants to paralyze the construction of some head office refusing some of the necessary authorizations, it has the power to do it.

Over the previous thing, being serious and flexible, there is not the main factor that truly perverts any attempt of liberalization of the sector of the electrical generation in Spain. Since we have already said, at first it is the managerial initiative the one that impels the construction of new head offices of generation and, as we have exhibited previously, on a free market with all the costs entirely internalized, there would be the market prices those that would guide the decisions of the entrepreneurs. The trial of privatization of the Spanish electrical system was not continued by any internalization cost process across the market yet: since there was no intention of assigning property rights on the environment and on the common spaces of the cities, neither market nor any price exists for the externalities that were provoking certain types of energy power plants. To exalt this situation and to try to simulate what might have happened in a free market with the externalities internalized, the legislator resorted to the taxes and subsidies to encourage the installation of certain types of head offices that in a seemingly minor way were implying externalities denials (less contamination, essentially) or major positive externalities (like jobs creation), and all this companies were of course private, from where we can denote the efficiency of the nearly invisible period when Spain had an attempt of a privatized electric market, which surely didn't carry on : there were the called head offices of "special diet", as there can be those of cogeneration or the renewable ones (the wind and solar, fundamentally).

.ELECTRICAL MARKET IN SPAIN:

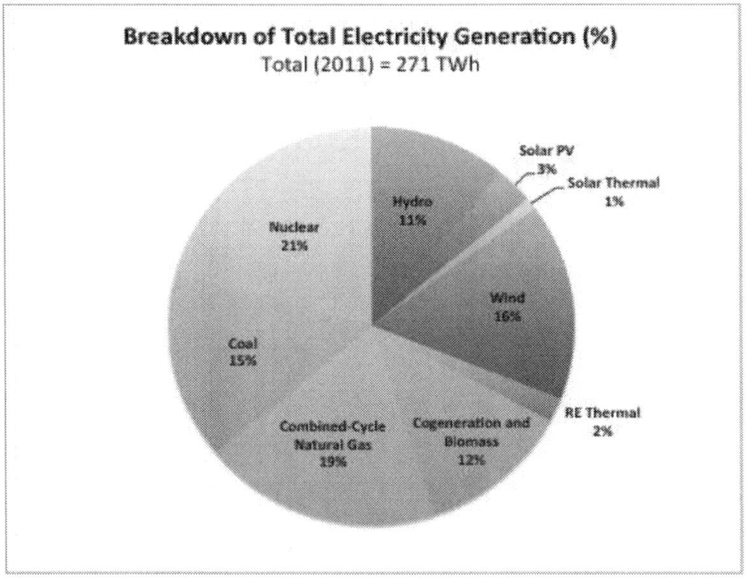

It is enough to point out that at the end of 2012 Spain was provided with an installed power network of 108.148 MW, of which 44.327 MW was installed before 1998 (data from the Industry Ministry), under the instrument of direct State planning of the National Energy Plans. Others 63.821 MW[87] settled, in fact, from 1998, under the normative frame of the supposed freedom of the market. Now then, more than half of this new

[87] http://www.minetad.gob.es/energia/balances/Balances/LibrosEnergia/Energia_en_Espana-2012.pdf

electric network installed from 1998[88] (in particular, 34.580 MW) corresponds to head offices of special diet, this is, head offices encouraged and totally provided and supported financially by the State by means of the establishment of enterprise which guarantee extraordinary profitabilities and foreign competitiveness to the market. In other words, almost 75 percent of all the current installed potency (that, for more in, in the year 2012 was the fact in charge of more than 85 percent of 283.071 GWh of clear generation) correspond to State planned head offices (National Energy Plans) or by implication (occupying first place to the energies of special diet) to the State.

In the only case, then, a small part of the head offices constructed between 1997 and 2012[89] (in particular, the head offices of combined cycle) might be considered the market to be liberalized. Anymore, in fact, it is not even necessary to refute them in such a way. Firstly, because there was no internalization of all the environmental costs in Spain, so that, on it having prevented, we might think that the State was granting a secret subsidy to them. And second, because their installation was the irrefutable result of the State politics of promotion of the State financed energies: since these were head offices of very irregular production (the wind ones only generate electricity when there blows the wind and the photovoltaic ones when it is sunny), it was turning out to be necessary to assist their supply with head offices of more flexible and stable provision, as there are the head offices of combined cycle. Therefore, there were the State incentives to the power plants of special diet those that determined

[88] https://www.boe.es/buscar/doc.php?id=BOE-A-1998-18795
[89] http://www.energiza.org/979-centrales-de-ciclo-combinado-en-espa%C3%B1a

the profitability of investing complementarily in head offices of combined cycle.

But the State interventionism on the subject of generation does not end there. The State also influences the way of functioning of the coal head offices, giving priority to the use of the most expensive national coal opposite to the foreign coal; it grants a very important barrier watched to the nuclear power plants limiting to 700 million[90] their indemnification responsibility in case of accident (the rest of indemnifications would run in charge of the State, which is to say, the taxpayers would socialize losses between them); it socializes the lowest costs of generation of the Iberian peninsula with the highest extra-peninsular costs of generation (Canaries, Balearics, Ceuta and Melilla) with the target to reduce the invoice of the light of the above-mentioned (when they should be its residents who were answering to the biggest generation cost consuming less or being more efficient in its consumption); and until the year 2006, the Spanish electricity users were forced to indemnify the electricity companies harshly for the supposed damages derived from the liberalization of the market across a few variable Costs of Transition to the Competition, in summary, the costs of the electricity bills increased over the 1995-00' period of time.

In the year 2012, the citizens paid subsidies of special diet and the extra-peninsular compensations were representing a third of all the costs of the Spanish electrical system: more than 16.000 million euros[91], opposite to less than 2.500 million of the year 2002. Said otherwise,

[90] http://documents.worldbank.org/curated/en/885921468760526393/text/multi-page.txt
[91] http://www.elconfidencial.com/economia/2014-04-22/el-sector-publico-reparte-mas-de-16-400-millones-en-subvenciones-pese-a-los-recortes_119244/

adding transport, distribution and the costs of the direct intervention of the State in the electrical generation, we come to that more than 55 percent of the entire costs of the system are straightly attributable to the State interventionism.

Precisely, the last famous intervention of the State in the subject of electrical generation has been to institute the called "toll of support" to keep on receiving this 55 percent of entire costs[92] (that comprises, between others, the transport, the distribution and similar of the special diet regime, which basically is the State support given to the electric market making it much more inefficient) to those head offices of personal consumption that remain connected to the network. Personally, those economic units that, remaining connected to the network, decide to generate and consume their own electricity, even if they do not use for it the electrical network and do not consume the energy generated by other head offices of special diet, will have to pay the same over cost for kWh consumed that the rest of users who do use the networks of the system and stock up, partly, with the head offices of special diet. Certainly, the mere fact of being connected to the network implies a series of costs to which of course they should pay the State for its providing, but it does not seem that these costs are the equivalents to be assumed for all the auto generated energy that uses the network of transport and distribution or that they have an obligation to remunerate a few head offices of special diet which generation they do not consume except exceptionally.

For clear motives, to the support tool also it has been named "tax to the sun," since the main affected ones are the personal consumption solar

[92] http://www.elespanol.com/economia/empresas/20170120/187611240_13.html

power stations. The nonsense of the State interventionism in this head office, then, is maximum: in the first stage the State devoted itself to remunerate in a disproportionate way the installation of photovoltaic head offices inside the derivates of special diet under the declared target to promote their proliferation; some years later, and existing account of the over cost owed during several decades by way of this similarities, the State has chosen to harm and get dearer very significantly the solar personal consumption, braking overland the new installation of this type of head offices that might suppose a truly disruptive competitive innovation opposite to the traditional model of the big electricity companies.

Clearly, only from a sarcastic point of view, we might affirm that the sector of the electrical generation in Spain is the ideal one of a free market: neither its structure of production nor its cost structure have been determined by the decentralized experimentation of entrepreneurs and investors but by the centralized planning of the political power.

Something similar happens with the stretch of the commercialization. Since we know, the task of the marketer is coordinating the electricity offer on the part of the generating head offices with their demand on the part of their clients: their operative one consists on buying electricity on the wholesale markets (where they sell the generators) and to offer it in the retail markets (where the final users buy), obtaining profit across the prices differential. The logical thing, therefore, would be that the price loaded by the marketer in the retail market was serving to cover its costs on the wholesale market, so much the linked ones to the generation as the related ones to the transport and the distribution. Nevertheless, the Government decided to intervene in the prices of the electrical market, altering the coordination between supply and demand deeply.

This way, until 2009, the consumers could take refuge in the called "integral tariff" that was only a State fixation of the price of the electrical supply on the part of the government: there were the proprietary companies of the distribution network in every territory, and those who were in charge of providing to the user the electrical supply at the price marked by the State. From the year 2009, the State supposedly liberalized the prices of the retail market, allowing to be the competition between marketers what determines the retail price. Now then, even after the "liberalization", the State keeps on setting most of the final retail price: and the fact is that it is the State — and not the marketer — who establishes the so-called tariff or toll of access (the one that remunerates the costs of transport, distribution or the premiums of special diet), which tries to cover between 60 percent and 65 percent of the totality of the costs of the system, as also occurs for example in the UK electric market[93]. The problem did not come only from this governmental fixation of the prices, but so much before 2009 (fixing the "integral tariff") as from 2009 (fixing the "tariff of tax of access"), the total prices of the retail market were turning out to be artificially low, that is to say, they were covering not even distantly the totality of the costs of the system. As a consequence of it, the electricity demand on the part of families and Spanish companies did not fit to its real costs: it kept on increasing and increasing with charge to an underlying debt that the proper families and companies will have to repay in the future (the called piled up deficit of

[93] https://www.ofgem.gov.uk/electricity/wholesale-market/gb-electricity-wholesale-market

tariff or pricing debt). To practical effects, it is as if the State had forced families and companies to get into debt against their will to keep on consuming a light much more expensive than they were ready to pay (instead of not allowing them to get into debt and reduce their light consumption).

The persistence during more than one decade of the pricing deficit — that is to say, integral tariffs or toll of access were artificially increased — preventing the marketers from developing the work that they should have executed on a free market: to coordinate supply and demand. On the contrary, the fixation price policy which has discoordination of supply and demand, favoring an overload of both to a few ludicrous costs: in the last decade, the average of Europe, not only has doubled the electric network installed in Spain but also the nominal prices of the electricity. Would the demand have grown so much as to have to duplicate the installed potency in case the prices had reflected from the beginning the authentic underlying costs? It is very doubtful: before the increase of the retail price, the demand would have fallen down and the exuberant construction of new potency (and of new networks) would have been postponed. But nothing of that happened as a result of the State intervention: circumstance which reflects again that in the Spanish, enclosed electrical system after its "liberalization", it was not the users, but the politicians, who determined the electrical mix and the cost structure... as it happens in any sector belonging to the State.

Finally, the essential features of the Spanish electrical system are those of a sector controlled nearly fully by the State and under hyper-regulated control: the transport and the distribution keep on being activities planned by the public sector; the generation is still determined in most cases by the remunerations fixed by the State in the Official Bulletin of the State and not by the remunerations determined by a free market that internalizes all its costs; and the necessary coordination of electrical supply and demand that the marketers should have developed has been sabotaged deliberately by means of integral prices fixation until 2009 and by means of fixation of most of the tariff since then.

It is possible that the operators of the Spanish electrical market are private agents, but that does not mean that we are less capable to have a free and competitive market, which is just what we need to achieve an electrical provision compatible with the preferences of the citizens and more possible sale: that is to say, Spain needs to eliminate the whole system of remunerations (subsidies) and political restrictions to the free competition at the same time that it internalizes all the costs assigning property rights on the cities and the environment. In any other case, we will not be able to speak about a free electrical market, but about systems with a grade of more or less direct State interventionism (In case of electricity and energy production and distribution, the State controls fully 55-60%[94] of the market share, considered as a governmental monopoly)

The way that the legislator found of encouraging the construction of the head offices of special diet was really diverse, but the problem is that the State had to find it! State interventionism in the private sector of electricity generation has only caused gas emissions to be higher than they would have been if 50% tax wouldn't have been imposed on them.

---

94 http://www.ieee.es/Galerias/fichero/OtrasPublicaciones/Nacional/2014/LibroPDF_SectorEnergeticoEspanol_AportacionSociedad_2014.pdf

People dying in the streets because of electricity scarcity would be fewer and more protected because prices will be lower and electricity more accessible. The government, as always, should have a neutral point of view on electricity generation and the various types of energy, letting the market and consumers form themselves which kind of model of production is more desirable for the. As always, let the market decide.

8-HOW DO COMPANIES GROW IN A TOTALLY FREE-MARKET ECONOMY?

It is frequent to confuse capitalism with corporative spirit. “Capitalism is a system based on the capital accumulation and on the free competition directed to satisfy the sovereign consumer inside a respected frame to the private ownership and the voluntary contracts”- as Adam Smith said[95]. The corporative or corporate spirit, on the other hand, is a form of State interventionism directed to transfer revenues of the taxpayers to the related entrepreneurs who are friendly to the regime. Of course, the corporate spirit never appears as such, but it usually camouflages as "industrial policy" faced to promote the growth of certain companies (the called "strategic sectors" o "national leaders") under the pretext of which these will be capable of competing in the international markets and generating employment inside the country. The corporate spirit is deeply anti-liberal and really harmful to the interests of a free and prosperous economy since it is based on the State development of many by the suffering of a few ones.

In a system of free competition, every company might try to promote its business plan faced to generate value for the consumers. To achieve it, previously it should be capable of attracting to the productive factors necessary to implement it: for example, it would need sources of

---

[95] http://www.economicsdiscussion.net/capitalism/capitalism-meaning-features-merits-and-de-merits/14124

financing (thrifty people who share with it itheir capital), working people at different levels of education, providers of raw material, energy, and intermediate goods, etc. If the promoter of a business plan achieves to get on and unite with the productive factors that he needs, he will be able to begin to make those goods and services for those that he believes that an intense demand exists between the consumers. If he is capable of supplying the offer at a price that allows him to cover his costs, he will gain money; otherwise, he will lose it.

Nobody knows beforehand what goods and services must take place in every moment not, especially, how he or she must take place: the technologically viable projects are in fact infinite, so that the companies must discover, by means of experimentation based on test and error, how the business plans could be relatively more valuable for the consumers.

At present, nevertheless, we do not live in a free managerial market, as Spain is positioned in the number 43 in the international classification and 20 into Europe[96], but in one controlled and regulated by the State. In this sense, the State usually privileges some entrepreneurs in two ways: transferring to them straight the money of the taxpayers (for example route subsidize, State rescues or public works), which is considered as corruption, or granting them regulative privileges normally directed to limit the competition and to create sectoral oligopolies (licenses, tariffs , patents, etc.). Both types of interventions should be eliminated.

The general principle or value in a free market economy has to be that those companies unable to generate value for the consumers by their

[96] http://www.libremercado.com/2016-02-10/espana-sigue-estancada-en-el-indice-de-libertad-economica-1276567403/

own means must transfer their space and their resources to others that could do it, in give back of an accorded payment, which is known as productive commerce. Unfortunately, the Spanish State has been characterized historically for promoting aggressive politics of transferences of revenue and of restrictive regulations of the competition, as tariffs set up during Franco's dictatorship of nearly 20% of the original price for more goods, and non-tariff measurements as quotas were also imposed[97] in favor of certain managerial elites, most of the cases, Spanish oligopolies.

In the last decade, the Spanish Public administrations have destined about 2 percent of the GDP[98] as a grant to the private sector subsidies and help it with investment, a number that should be eradicated in its entirety. The minimal State does not have to prevent harsh monetary violence or its money to any company, as it comes from the taxpayers to deliver it to companies that have not done anything to obtain it for voluntary means on the market: they are the taxpayers, in their role of consumers or investors, who must decide if the goods and services that offer them the different managerial plans are deserving, or not, of their capital. If they were, the State would be unnecessary to attract them to come to these funds; if they were not, the public sector would promote an inefficient allocation of the economic resources against the needs of the citizens.

It is usual, nevertheless, to argue that the companies might not develop and grow without the active support of the State in the shape of subsidies or favorable regulations: this is what is named sectorial politics, faced to promote the development of the agriculture or the industry.

---

[97] http://www.ehu.eus/ojs/index.php/HC/article/viewFile/4267/3813
[98] https://www.boe.es/buscar/act.php?id=BOE-A-2015-11644

Inside the European Union, for example, they have acquired throughout the last decades a very notable importance, as the Common Agricultural policy (directed to guarantee the self-sufficiency and the competitiveness of the internal agricultural and cattle production, as well as to encourage a sustainable rural development) and the European Energy Strategy (destined to achieve a competitive supplying of the energy compatible with the environmental sustainability).

The problem of the sectorial politics is double: on the one hand, they subsidize inefficient production methods, so, instead of being replaced by other superior ones which have been discovered across the competitive pressure, they are perpetuated in the time under the protective umbrella of the subsidies; for other, the subsidies are not granted usually free, but they are associated with the whole series of regulations and governmental guidelines that the politicians believe that they help to improve the productivity or to reach another series of not economic targets.

The result of all these State interferences on the free managerial competition is the consolidation of agrarian sectors and inefficient, slightly competitive, stagnant industrialists, without creativity, addicted to the subsidy and that, for more inri, suppose a slowdown for the rest of the economy. It is convenient to stress the importance of the latter effect, since the consequences of the State interventionism on an industrial sector end up by contaminating all the resting sectors that somehow are related to him: for example, the industrial policy of promotion of the steel developed by the United States between 1975 and 2000 has reduced the competitiveness of this raw material by almost 5 percent[99], but the decrease of the competitiveness of those other sectors that were using the steel intensively as a productive factor has become of 50 percent[100]. Of course, one might conceive an industrial policy that was turning out to be successful, but this low success probability would make necessary to conciliate it with all the remaining sonorous defeats to which with more frequency it usually give place and even with those private industries that do not go so far as to be born because the capital that they needed has been forwarded to the State to promote its "national champions": in general, the empirical support for the industrial policies is very weak.

In the case of Spain we also find notable and deplorable examples. Inside the primary sector, 30 percent of the income of the Spanish field come from the subsidies of the PAC[101], what has condemned the sector to a finished stagnation: although the set of the economy expanded 163 percent in nominal terms between 2000 and 2012, the agrarian sector "decreased" 3,5 during the same period[102], up to the point of which today it scarcely represents 2,3 percent of the GDP[103] and occupies 4 percent of the population. Opposite to this interventionist disaster, we are provided with the case of New Zealand: in 1986[104], this country liberalized its agrarian sector, suppressing of fact all the subsidies (at present, less than 2 percent of the income of the farmers come from the subsidies and these

[99] http://www.forbes.com/sites/beltway/2011/05/31/antidumping-reform-crucial-to-u-s-competitiveness/#54366f6f70ba

[100] http://www.tradingeconomics.com/united-States/steel-production

[101] http://www.fega.es/PwfGcp/en/accesos_directos/consulta_de_beneficiarios_de_ayudas_de_la_pac/consulta_de_beneficiarios_2015_presenta.jsp

[102] http://www.ces.es/documents/10180/3828741/Cauces_31_pp67-71.pdf

[103] http://economy.blogs.ie.edu/archives/tag/estructura-del-pib-por-sectores-economicos-en-espana

[104] http://www.stats.govt.nz/tools_and_services/data-archive/data-collections/industry-sectors/agriculture/agricultural-production-census-1986.aspx

link to the R+D) and, thanks to it, the agrarian activity between 2000 and 2012 120 percent expanded more than one, its contribution overcomes the GDP today 5 percent and occupies 7 percent of the labor force[105].

As for the energy policy, the price of the electricity for domestic consumers has increased in Spain a hundred percent between 2002 and 2013 according to Eurostat, while in the United States it has only been done by 50 percent as the EIA[106] (Energy Information Administration), being in 2013 almost the half that in the present year.The subsidized promotion of the renewable energies constitutes the main cause of this increase, which has provoked the destruction of more than a hundred thousand workplaces in the rest of the economy. Nevertheless, as we will study in a subsequent chapter, the authentic problem of funding the Spanish electrical system is much more serious: the nonexistence of an intervened electric market that such a name deserves.

Therefore, as the general norm is necessary to think that the sectorial politics stretches to be always a disaster. In fact, not even in such a mentioned case of the Asian economies (in which, seemingly, the guessed right industrial policy of a few very efficient governmental bureaucracies managed to promote the most rapid economic development in these countries), it is necessary to affirm that these were truly successful: the evidence on the results of their industrial policy points, rather, that the promotion by means of cheap credit and subsidies of certain industries transported costs quite superior to the harmed benefits, which the capital was assigned incorrectly in most of the occasions, and for which the balances of their banks were contaminated

[105] http://www.teara.govt.nz/en/workforce-composition/page-1
[106] http://www.eia.gov/todayinenergy/detail.php?id=25372

by unpaid credits, which managing teams were created with scarce culture and skill to compete in the free market, which resources moved incorrectly from the sectors that were experiencing a major growth to those that were already entering phase of slope, where too risky projects were encouraged and which, in many assumptions, the industrial policy ended up by being captured by the lobbies on their own and exclusive lucre. This way, for instance, the studies on this matter show that the industrial policy of Japan was irrelevant (or even harmful) for the development of its electronics, biotechnological industry and of the engine, that the attempts of the Malaysian government of favoring the development of the car industry, of the aviation or of the plywood were a costly defeat, and that the Asian Southeast wasted large numbers of capital on having promoted the metal, chemical industry or the transports.

Obviously, the sectorial or regional politics do not have reason to fail always, and along with the previous fiasco of the Asian economies, also some successes stand out in South Korea, Japan or Malaysia. The basic criticism is not that this one would always fail, but the politicians do not have better information not better incentives than the entrepreneurs — normally, much worse than the second ones— to develop the business models that better fit with the preferences of the consumers. The only route which they have to be right is the test, the error, and the rectification, as any businessman does it. But if, as we have already exhibited, the free market is the excellent frame of the decentralized experimentation: what might be the motive of appealing to the governmental experimentation annulling the much more decentralized and dynamic variations and volatility of the markets? Moreover, as the sectorial politics usually contaminates regulation and through interventionism the whole economy or the whole industry, the errors of the political planning occur much more extensive and deep than those of a particular businessman (the one who starts by operating in a small market with a small shop and, only if he is successful, grows and is capitalized), what gets us to score to the productive model in a certain wrong direction from which it can take a lot of time in failing (it is what is known as "dependence effect").

In sum, the sectoral economic policy implies a lot of more risks than potential benefits: it is not a question of a politician being able to be always right, but he will tend to fail rather for not being provided with the information, the incentives (of profit and reinvestment) and the feedback of those that usually arrange the rest of entrepreneurs who risk in a competitive way their capital in the frame of a free market. In most cases, then, the sectorial politics simply will constitute a massive masked ball to redistribute the wealth from a part of the society (consumers and efficient entrepreneurs) towards another part of the society (inefficient entrepreneurs and lobbyists), provoking in the process a clear destruction of the entire wealth, and reducing consumption and consequently economic growth.

Deeply, the conditions that favor that the companies prosper and develop in a free economy are quite simple and they have not anything in common with the subsidies and the State privileges: juridical safety that guarantees the private ownership and the fulfillment of the contracts; few regulations that allow a high degree of flexibility and autonomy at the time of developing the business plans; plenty of saving and capitals (never provided by the State) to be able to finance the new managerial ideas; not abusive taxes imposed that do not steal from shareholders and entrepreneurs the wealth that they are generating; largeness of markets in which to commercialize their goods; quality infrastructures that facilitate the interconnection of the different industries in their sectorial and marketing search; and availability at competitive prices of productive factors (work, human capital, raw material and energy).

The minimal State that we have proposed would unite all these conditions, as essential sectors for the management of businesses (like the infrastructures, the education or the energy) would stop falling down under the ambiance of the State planning and would happen to be an object of the free coordination and managerial cooperation. Namely the entrepreneurs of a sector who needed certain infrastructures or of working people at certain levels of education would not have reasons to think that the interventionist and bureaucratic State should realize for them, should approve and should implement the investment in these factors correctly, but they would be other entrepreneurs those who, with the biggest possible space, would locate these business opportunities and would attend to the needs for the rest of entrepreneurs.

Finally, a free market does not need of a State that plans the vectors of the economic growth, since nobody knows with certainty which is going to be these vectors: it is up to it to discover it to the decentralized experimentation of multitude of entrepreneurs in the permanent rivalry. The State only has to limit itself to without interfering and corrupting this healthy process of test and error, this is, it has to limit itself to without interfering and corrupting this healthy process of test and error that takes place inside a competitive frame. Until now we have developed how the

State intervenes negatively on the markets in three fundamental aspects for the generation of wealth inside a company: the labor, the electricity, and the technological innovation. Afterwards, nevertheless, we will make an effort ourselves to look at the properties with which this frame of free competition must be provided so that it should be really effective and how the State interventionism tends to undermine these properties, and as always backing it up with facts, which for disguise of many expose the reality.

MAIN FINANCIAL SOURCES OF PYMES IN SPAIN:

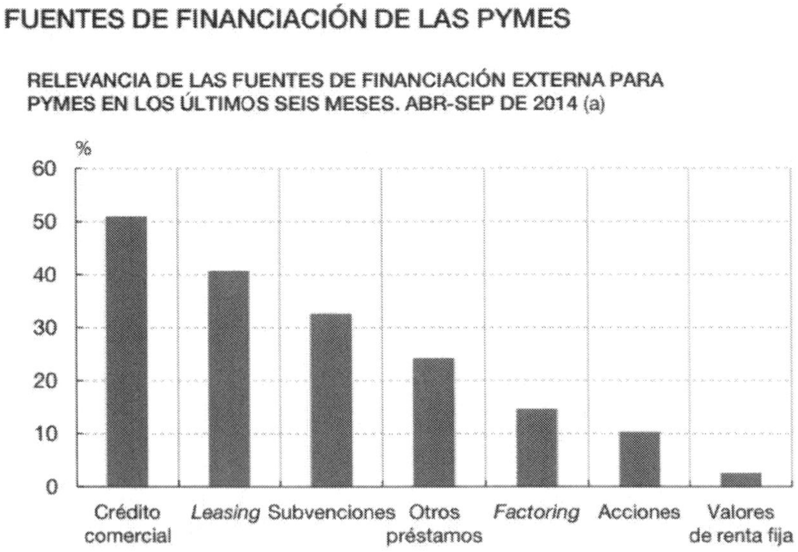

The State does not only intervene in the managerial sector transferring funds to certain companies at the cost of the rest of the society but regulating the conditions under which the competition develops. These regulations can split into two big irregular groups among themselves: on the one hand, the State says to guarantee the competition in all the sectors avoiding the formation of "monopolies" or "oligopolies"; for other, the same State limits the competition in many ambiences by means of the licenses authorization, normally in sectors where they tend to provide all the offer through public expenditure. None of these two interventions is by any means well-taken. A clear example of economic reforms towards enterprise creation has been the sudden increase in number of PYMES and small firms due to the financial crisis, having more than 3.110.522 small companies nowadays[107].

For what represents to badly called politics "in defense of the competition," the States get obsessed with that no company grows too much and is capable of imposing its conditions unilaterally on the consumers. In our society there usually reigns the idea that the very big companies or multinationals end up by turning into monopolies that exploit the consumer and the worker, preventing from prospering the competition. Now then, before the so-called "Courts of Defense of the Competition" promoting an aggressive State intervention directed to divide this big company and the autonomy of their business plan, we should discuss how it is possible that a company maintains in the time a prime line position on the rest if he does not enjoy any State privilege.

And the fact is when a company prospers on the remaining facts and obstacles up to the point of surviving with the practical totality of the market, it is because it possesses a competitive advantage that the others are not capable of replaying. Although we could believe that the possible

[107] http://cincodias.com/cincodias/2015/09/02/pyme/1441206221_324356.html

competitive advantages are varied, in fact, they all can gather together in five essential points: real differentiation of the goods (the company offers a product better than the competition, even if it is because it possesses an advanced technology or because it offers a product which quality, as it happens with the social networks, increases with the number of users); perceived differentiation of the goods; also called "brand factor"- as for example in the phones market Apple versus ZTE, having surprisingly 90% android phones in Spain with data registered from 2016[108] (the products of the company, although they are technically equal to those of the competition, possess a reputation and a prestige of mark that do that the consumers prefer them); less costs of production (the company can sell cheaper its goods because its production cost are lower thanks to its really efficient business plan or the existence of economies of scale, due to its consequently increasing size); loyalty to the client (the clients are unwilling to change company because they have worked for a long time a relation of confidence and of mutual comprehension with their provider and in the short term rivals might not enjoy a similar integral service in other companies, as clients are treated better with the first supplier); aptitude to exclude the competitors (across governmental licenses), even though this point reflects the barriers set up by the government to prevent competition in many cases.

In fact, that a company grows in size for any of the first four competitive advantages should not be a motive of worry: its growth is due to the fact that it offers a product with a few characteristics of predominant quality or a more competitive price than those of its rivals.

---

[108] https://www.statista.com/statistics/260419/market-share-held-by-smartphone-operating-systems-in-spain/

Moreover, the existence of these competitive advantages stimulates the rest of entrepreneurs to design novel plans of business that incorporate innovative mechanisms to compete with the placed company, generating this way new types of goods or new alternative productive processes that end up by displacing it, as they will require lower input and reduced expenditure.

The type of "competitive advantage" that should constitute a motive of deep worry is exactly that resultant from the State intervention: the artificial limitation of the competition by means of the licenses authorization. To limit the competition always bears pernicious consequences: deeply, the State prohibits a businessman who is considered qualified to open a business, even though he has presented a plan that improves the life of the consumers to be able to try to do it, and perform his business. Certainly, it is not easy to find good reasons that justify it and, in fact, in most cases the real intention is simply of assuring to an already placed managerial oligopoly a few extraordinary profit to at the cost of forcing the consumers to receive a worse or more expensive service than other entrepreneurs without license might offer them, as the State will be able to charge high taxes in monopolies or oligopolies because the demand (PED) will be much more inelastic, converting goods into a necessity.

Nevertheless, to backup is convenient to remember that, in general, the governmental licenses usually justify themselves under three types of pretexts: the first one, to give time to the entrepreneurs who are inside the sector to develop without the pressure exercised by the fierce competition; the second one, to guarantee that the service is performing or producing under certain conditions, of course previously established by the State; and the third one, the need to distribute the competition in a sector where the maximum number of suppliers is technically limited, as said before... an oligopoly. Again, none of these excuses turns out to be convincing.

The first justification of the licenses is evident especially in defense of the tariffs and taxes against the foreign trade, that is to say, in the limitation of the local demand for foreign products with the intention of favoring to the local industry. Fortunately, an absolute consensus exists between the economists — even between those who keep less sympathies towards the free markets — concerning the benefits of the international free trade: the tariffs or the quotes to the import do not promote the development of the local industry in general, but the development of that local industry in which the country lacks competitive advantage and in which, therefore, it is possible to generate less wealth for the set of national and foreign citizens. The restriction of the international free trade is only a way of transferring revenues from the consumers and the efficient local producers towards the inefficient local producers. The appellant does not even turn out to be a valid argument that the tariffs and taxes which are necessary to promote the development of an industry in its first periods of life (the called "nascent industry"), that is when a firm is firstly launched, since their effect tends to be the opposite: the organization of an industry in inefficient and unable business models to compete with the foreign industry but effective to maximize the short-term pillage of the consumers.

Finally, some economists usually rise that the licenses barrier is essential in that business where the number of suppliers is inevitably in excess, needing an intervention of the quotes in the market, generating technical limitations in production. The typical case is that of the telecommunications: since the radio-electric space of a country is limited and not the whole world can establish a company of telecommunications, it must be the State who distributes licenses on its use. The reasoning, nevertheless, settles on a unjustifiable excuse: as all the resources are limited, any sector has some limit at the entry of new providers, without it justifying that the State should regulate and distribute licenses to act like businessman, and be otherwise the competitors through product differentiation the ones that lay out other competing firms out of the market.

GROWTH OF COMPANIES IN THE EU:

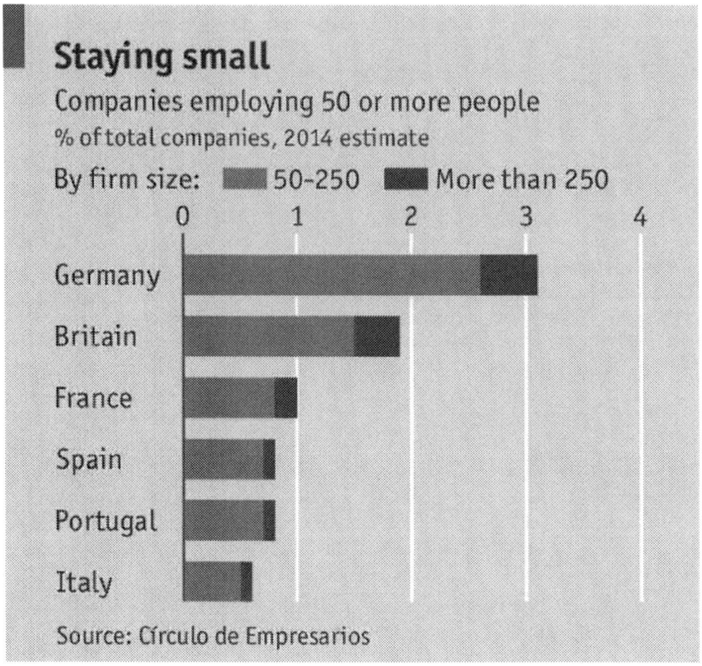

In this graph we are able to observe how countries with a freer and more dynamic economy are able to hire more workers in average per company, like Germany for example, having more than 2.5 million[109] firms employing between 50-250 workers, while Italy has just 500,000 companies with more than 50 workers in it.

Finally, the only monopolies of those that we should worry are those that result from the State regulations on the subject of licenses. Solid economic justification does not exist with the objective of the State trying to destroy those competitive advantages that have emerged naturally on the market as a result of the value supported that they generate for the consumers, but finally the State imposes artificial competitive advantages with the intention of preventing from appearing

[109] https://issuu.com/yousufali0/docs/the_economist_-_august_15_2014

new enterprises which, on having created new value for the consumers, remove the inefficient entrepreneurs previously accommodated, and treated with preference by the State.

Even though it is more beneficial for the economy to have a private than a public monopoly, the best solution for a faster and consistent level of economic growth, is an intense and efficient level of competitiveness in the market, with a market open to international trade, and with no barriers to entry, generating growth through competition over time. With no barriers, and of course with a minimized State.

9- EDUCATION, ONE OF THE PILLARS OF THE MARKET ECONOMY

Fortunately, at current times, there exists a wide range of ideas in which the education constitutes one of the basic pillars of any society. The progress of our knowledge of the continued formation allows us a better comprehension of the world where we live and this way it facilitates our decision making and our personal self-fulfillment. Consequently, the education purposes, on the one hand, have a clearly instrumental intention: the better-formed individuals are capable of generating a major wealth for themselves and for the society; but, for other, the education is also turning into a target on itself: more and more people want to increase their formation for the mere cultural use. It is not a coincidence, therefore, that a clear parallel relation exists between expense in education and wealth: really only the best formation of a society allows it to generate more wealth; the fact is that the richer a society turns, the more it wants to spend on education, to be able to raise its formative level.

The controversy, then, cannot turn if the education is important (it obviously is), but concerning who must be the manager of deciding how much we spend on education and what type of education we receive: whether the State or the normal citizen, who should decide? Namely the question that it is necessary to raise is if there turns out to be preferable a diet of public education or a system of private education.

The almost impulsive reasoning of most of the population is that the education must be regulated, controlled and provided by the State "because it is a very important area of our lives." Nevertheless, starting from the true premise which says the education is very important, it does not justify the conclusion of why the education should be public. On the contrary, in this chapter, I will try to prove how, precisely because education is so important, it should stay under the control of every particular person, and not of the State, in order of election of knowledge and not of economic support.

The education comprises two facets: the transmission of knowledge — what we might call "a subject" — and the transmission of values. When someone defends that the State must take charge of the provision of the education (be already with public schools or with mixed and regular schools) one is defending that the State must control some of these two matters (or, generally, the two simultaneously); that is to say, in inverse sense that person is defending that there are neither the parents nor the students who possess the last word at the time of determining what values and what knowledge must be transmitted: the State control of the educational offer implies that the centers of education are not formed according to the preferences and needs of their clients (parents and students) but according to the expediency of the politicians and the bureaucrats, and the lessons taught depend on the colour of the government in turn. The risk of this model is more than clear. For the side of the transmission of values, the leaders can be tempted to indoctrinate the population to keep them into their values and gain votes in the future. All the totalitarian systems have monopolized the education to handle the minds of the new citizens from the tenderest infancy, and only for it should already be prudent at the time of leaving this face in the hands of the State.

Certainly, the modern democracies are distant from being very much a reply of the totalitarian dictatorships in educational matter, as Hitler's Nazi Germany, or Stalin totalitarian Communism, which spent nearly 15.8%[110]of their GDP in education in the Nazi's case, but the manipulation risk is always present inside a system that gives away the educational monopoly to the State. Not in vain, the different political features, as well as the lobbies that from them, try to arrange the classrooms to inculcate their own pre-formed values to the Spaniards. The typical debates as if Religion has to be taught in the schools or on what the content must be in Education for Citizenship, or on which does it have to be the primary language of the classes, they can only happen in a system in which the politicians impose the only solution for all. On the other hand, on a free market where every center of education had autonomy to form its own educational offer, there might be schools of all kinds as the specific demand of parents and students: schools that were not transmitting religious values and schools that were doing it, laical schools and religious schools (of all kinds, also: Catholics, Protestants, Muslims, Jewish, Buddhists... etc), schools with Education for the Citizenship and schools without it, collectivist schools and individualistic schools, schools in Spanish or schools in Catalan, English, French, German, Chinese, Hindu, etc. Just trying to represent and fulfill the widest moral

[110] http://assets.cambridge.org/052166/2915/sample/0521662915wsn01.pdf

values[111] plurality which exists in society, and it should be every family or every student — and not the politicians escaping out of lobbies — who could choose those educational centers more according to their particular scale of values.

But the importance of the private education is not only linked to the free election of centers as the values to which they are assigned, but also to the configuration of the instruction, as this will reduce the public expenditure on education by almost 2% of the GDP from the 4.3%[112] the Spanish government is spending right now; that is to say, of the curriculum and of the pedagogic methods of every school. After all, there exists not even a curriculum that is objectively superior either to the rest or a teaching method that always beats the others. Again, it is not a coincidence that one of the most habitual political affrays happens in the field of the education: every government tries to impose "its" educational reform because it believes that it is better than the rest. Some governments give more importance to the classic and humanist matters (philosophy, history, Latin, Greek, etc.), while others to the linguistics (languages) or to the scientific skills (mathematics, physics, chemistry). Also, some governments think that the ideal way to learn is to memorize, while others put the emphasis on the comprehension; some of them believe that the teacher must enjoy an irrefutable authority inside the classrooms, others that he must act as partner of the students; some of them believe in the control of the learning process by means of the achievement of final examinations, others are more confident in the continuous assessment even without examinations; some repute in a

[111] https://revistas.ucm.es/index.php/RCED/article/viewFile/RCED9898220101A/17334
[112] http://datos.bancomundial.org/indicador/SE.XPD.TOTL.GD.ZS?locations=ES

really important the homework, while others exalt the effort and compromise it carries along with it; some defend the implantation of formative itineraries, others push it back; some try to extend the school schedule, others to reduce it; some would like to move all the classes to a modern teaching area, different ways but they all attend for the same, which is a large expenditure on education; right now of 4.4%[113] out of the global GDP, and taking into account emerging economies; with the unique objective to seem the most friendly government you can find, and assure that you re-elect them the next time you go to the ballots.

In sum, the whole world is thinking about knowing how and what way it should teach the students, but in fact, it is quite doubtful that the only and universal answer exists for these problems. Considering the variety of interests, skills, and capacities of each person, the reasonable thing should be that every individual (or his parents, while his is on their charge) could join to those profiles and educational processes that he considers to be ideal for his formation. And the fact is that only through the competition between educational centres we can discover what education methods are better or just different (for example, across the trajectory of their pupils): when in a country there only exists a curriculum and a teaching method, it is impossible to confirm its merits in contrast to its possible alternatives. Far from tending to an unique and centralized schools system, we should advance towards one decentralized and with predominant variety of autonomous school which compete among themselves: autonomous schools to select the school schedules, the textbooks, the teaching curriculum, the teaching methods, the criteria of evaluation, the election of the director, the selection of the teaching labor

---

[113] http://datos.bancomundial.org/indicador/SE.XPD.TOTL.GD.ZS?locations=1W

and of not teaching workers, the wages, the incentives and the responsibilities of the teachers and of the rest of the employees, etc.

This way the educational offer would tend to answer and to adapt itself to a much more realistic way to the real needs of the students, who in turn would try to visualize what type of formation is the one that allows them to generate a major value for the rest of the society, and to accumulate wealth in the future for themselves. As then we will exhibit, one of the facets of the education is that of contributing to the formation of the called "human capital", which actually in Spain is formed by 23.3 million[114] citizens, representing the formation of one more productive factor inside the economy: a few quite formed working people allow a country to increase its productivity and to specialize in goods of high extra profitable margin, increasing the standards of life of the whole population. Nevertheless, so the human capital could form correctly it would be necessary that the educational offer adapts itself to the last needs of the consumers, and only trusting it to the teaching institutions to the demands of the students one can achieve this complicated social coordination; when the centers are financed at the cost of the taxpayer, they do not turn out to be by any means motivated to satisfy his demand. In this sense, the State had helped to reduce competition and efficiency in a teaching method with a curricular content adapted to centuries away times— when it was thinking about how to alphabetize and discipline the working people in the resolution of a series of very mechanized problems — but not to the modern times — when work people need the companies with managerial spirit, this is, with an open mind and not tight that it is

[114] http://www.ine.es/dyngs/INEbase/es/operacion.htm?c=Estadistica_C&cid=1254736176918&menu=ultiDatos&idp=1254735976595

capable of thinking out of the box one that the teacher provides him, and being able to form his own opinions, just as myself in contrast to my teachers, to give a fair example.

In fact, even in systems of State education, it has been proved that the decentralized schools work much better that the centralized ones, as for example in South Korea, named as the best education system in 2015, and which has 41.4%[115] of its schools being of private holders and independently managed. The educational decentralization (from the central government to the municipality or even to the school) is usually prepared with a progress in the results of the pupils, with a better managing team and with a better selection of the teachers: there exists a profuse evidence of which those public schools autonomous and tight to the competitive pressure of the private schools obtain systematically better grade or qualifications in The Report of the International Program for Students (PISA). The famous Finland's educational system — that, in spite of everything, obtained results almost identical to those of the Spanish private and compound and mixed school in PISA 2012 — bases good part of its success on the autonomy which the municipalities and the educational centers enjoy to establish the formative curriculum and the evaluation methods of every school; also, the South Korean educational system, which in many aspects overcomes the Finland, owes its excellence to the supplementary education that provides the private academies to which most of the students assist. Nevertheless, if the private decentralization and the extra-curricular work, given that they adapt the educational offer slightly to the specific needs of the student, we should not be sufficiently satisfied with a shy decentralization and a partial

[115] http://wenr.wes.org/2013/06/wenr-june-2013-an-overview-of-education-in-south-korea

privatization of a system — the State one — in centralized in itself, but we should advance towards the same system in itself decentralized and deprived: an educational free market.

Now then, as we were saying earlier, an education free market does not come down to the private schools managing the educational organization as it exists today, but there could appear multiple models which compete between them to end up by discovering this route which turns out to be preferable for every user's profile. The previous thing does not only include changes in the teaching methodology that could use every school but even the possibility of educating the pupils out of the schools. This is what is known as homeschooling or education at home, a method of educating the pupil radically different to the one it imposes the State schooling (given that the student receives the formation of his parents, private tutors, academics, or professionals of the sector) and that, nevertheless, it usually generates spectacular turned out results where it is applied. In the United States, for example, 4 percent[116] of all the children are educated at home and they obtain a few qualifications in reading, natural sciences, mathematics and social sciences, as economics that, as it comes up, they are superior to those of 96 percent of the population[117], even fitting the results for the different socioeconomic profile of every student. The prohibition and restriction of the homeschooling usually justifies itself under the argument that it makes the socialization of the children difficult, but, again, the evidence proves simply that the grade of interaction and socialization of the children educated out of the traditional school system is very superior to that of

[116] http://www.businessinsider.com/why-kids-should-get-homeschooled-2016-8

[117] https://pjmedia.com/lifestyle/2014/2/15/8-reasons-homeschooling-is-superior-to-public-education-2/

the children educated inside it (also, if the authentic reason for which the States prohibit the homeschooling was the absence of the socialization of the pupils, they would not also prohibit the flexible schooling, this is, the schooling only partially at home).

Obviously, it is not a question of suggesting that the ideal thing would be that every pupil is educated at home, but simply showing that at present the State prohibits or bans educational alternatives perfectly valid and even presenting exceptional results, as we have been able to see in Spain where homeschooling is illegal but more than 4,000 families[118] already practice it. And it prohibits them without another reason except for the monopoly of the education system to be guaranteed. There should not remain big doubts that an enormous progress potential exists through the decentralized experimentation of new formative models, and the only way of exploiting this potential is allowing the free entrepreneurship and the free competition between different educative models, as much those that exist already like those which might go so far as to exist in the future. Actually, and in my opinion, the only truly effective way of experimenting is privatizing and liberalizing the offer of educational services.

The knowledge that the education transmits possesses a double side of measuring: on the one hand, we can consider it to be a consumer item that satisfies the direct needs of the student (the necessity for learning); for other, we can see it as a good of investment that allows us to comprise and to relate in a better way with our environment. To be characterized in this way, the education is useful because it reveals something that many more classical visions of the education usually

[118] http://www.elmundo.es/espana/2015/02/16/54e0cf70e2704e6c038b4586.html

forget: if the knowledge is a consumer item or an investment good, its demand cannot be infinite. And it cannot be infinite because the production of all good implies a cost, and nobody is ready to support infinite costs, as it is what happens with State supported education nowadays.

Certainly, the idea of to that to increase the expense and the resources destined for the education is always slightly socially positive can turn out to be very attractive, but it is completely false, as Timor-Leste is the country with the highest expenditure on education globally, with 16.8%[119]of their GDP, but are not even into the top 100 educative systems worldwide[120]. To spend more in education supposes spending less in other matters: for example, health, pensions, housing, highways, etc. If always having to spend more in education would turn out positively, we would come to the absurdity of immobilizing hundred percent of our revenue in educational activities, remaining without resources to feed or to dress. Therefore, the ideal expense in education — just as in any other activity — has its limits. But: which are these limits? As consumer item, the people demand education up to the point at which it stops being useful to them as regards other alternative consumptions. We can notice that the use of the term "education" in its wide sense: not only courses ruled in schools and universities but also the acquisition of books or of another material of learning, can also be taken into account as a private or consumer good, entering into market competitiveness. It corresponds to every subject, consequently, to set in what moment he wants to stop acquiring more education goods and services to begin to acquire other consumer goods: it

[119] https://en.wikipedia.org/wiki/List_of_countries_by_spending_on_education_(%25_of_GDP)
[120] http://hdr.undp.org/sites/all/themes/hdr_theme/country-notes/TLS.pdf

is each particular enterprise who better knows when he reaches this "saturation'' demand level.

But the education is also a good of intangible investment in a double facet (invisible trade): on the one hand, it is an investment directed to acquire major knowledge to turn us more productive and help us to generate more wealth; for other, it is an investment directed to acquire a certificate (or title) that gives an expert opinion of us to prove others our capacities and professional skills, hard-working and disciplined behavior. The one who studies engineering in the MIT obtains this active double: first, a technical formation of the first level; second, a socially recognized certificate of which a person is the sufficiently competent active as to have graduated in the MIT.

Being the education such an extremely profitable investment, it would seem suitable to destine to it so many resources as it is possible: the more we spend or invest today, the richer we will be tomorrow. From this vision, it even might even look like a logical thing that the State was stimulating it or was forcing to expand the educative system: with the simplest conclusion that more is always better. Nevertheless, there exist two powerful reasons for which this exposition is a clear mistake.

PUBLIC EXPENDITURE OF SPAIN IN EDUCATION:

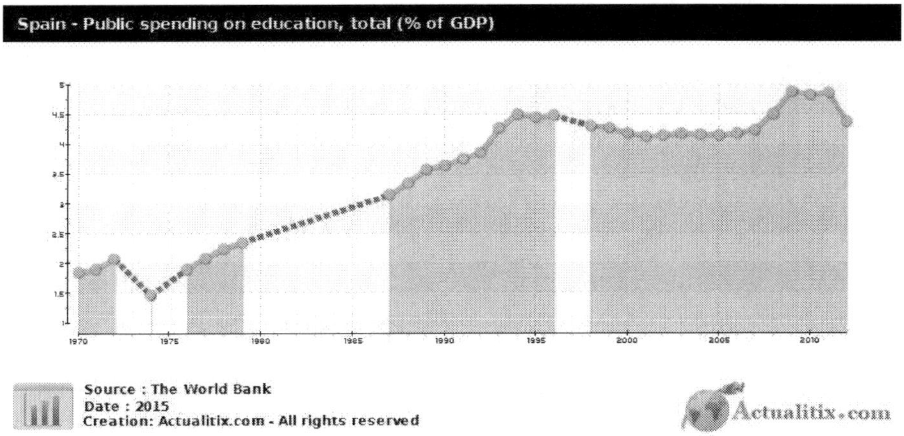

The first one is that, as it happens with the rest of investments, the education in its private sense is in general profitable, but it does not mean that in all the particular cases it is. For example, in the last two hundred years the American stock market has provided average profitability of 7 percent, but that does not mean that for investing blindly in the shares of a company, in particular, we are taking a good decision, as the volatility factor is always present; on the contrary, the habitual thing will be that in such a case we are wrong and end up by losing part of our capital. That's why, as we would consider a madness investing any capital quantity blindly on the real estate market or in that of variable revenue, also we should consider it this way in case of the education market, as in Spain financial education is not even a curricular activity, and is only taught in scarce cases. A clear example of this type of education rejection was a study done in the USA where 87%[121] of the people supported financial education, while in Spain, with the same inquiry, 72% rejected it. The investment in human capital is an investment much more valuable than all

[121] http://www.fundssociety.com/es/noticias/private-banking/los-colegios-deberian-ensenar-educacion-financiera

the remaining ones: every investor should compare the extra income derived of reaching a certain formative level with the costs necessary to reach it and, from this private calculation, to decide if to invest in education or not to do it. Nobody is in a better situation than every subject to know his favorable attitudes, weaknesses, opportunities and threats and, from here on, to consider the benefits and the costs been expected for deciding to invest in certain elements.

The second reason is that, as we were saying, the investment in education is not an only one way of acquiring new knowledge that return more productive to the subject, but also a way of acquiring a title that offers signs to the market of which you are an intelligent, hard-working and disciplined person in comparison to the rest of individuals who do not possess this title. And so, the high derivative profitability of advancing in the formative stages includes so much the profitability harvested for being more productive; with an special need in Spain for an increase in productive levels, being now of a depressive rate of 58,815euros[122] per worker, while in Ireland, having the highest one is of 164,711 euros per year, which implies profitability harvested for differing from the rest of working people by means of an educational title. The problem of the above mentioned is that, all the more people who possess a certain title (for example, the baccalaureate title), less useful turns out to be this title to differ from the others, as the labour differentiation factor is reduced, so that a competition starts between all the individuals to differ from the rest acquiring qualifications superior to those that the others possess: in these cases, to have a title keeps on being individually profitable, but socially a waste, on case it doesn't allow you to find your desired job. Said

[122] file:///C:/Users/Usuario/Downloads/INDcap06.pdf

otherwise, in such cases any more education would not involve any more productivity for the set of the society, but the same productivity, even though it would be credited in a much more expensive way. In economic slang, we would say that the overinvestment in education has "negative externalities," in particular, to get more efficiently the mechanisms of social transmission of information.

And so, the more we spend in education is not always the better: it will be only true when the cost of acquiring new knowledge is lower than the utility or than the additional wealth that this new knowledge provides. And, as we have already exhibited, nobody is in a better situation to know if every individual is already consuming or investing too much (or too little) in education that each of the individuals who consume or invest in his education. One notices that, even in such conditions, the set of individuals might invest "too much" in education during "too much" time (if it is that its motive for investing in education is only of differing from the rest), but in the long term this situation will end up by reverting the costs: the excess investment turns the education like a differentiation mechanism, fewer individuals will be ready to (or they will be incapable to) pay the high prices of the superfluous qualifications, and the set of people will begin spontaneously not being able to invest in this portion of education that does not work to increase their productivity. What does not make sense is that the State prolongs artificially this demand subsidizing the education or even turning it free for the user at the cost of the rest of taxpayers, instead of providing education checks for the privatization process, and with the same public cost.

To the end, let's repeat that the State cannot offer "free" the education from the moment in which it has to pay away from the teachers, away from not teaching personnel or away from the providers of the center of education. What in fact does the State that proclaims the cost-free status of the education (will be already offering places in the schools from public or subsidized to private schools) is not to charge "straight" to the student for the educational services who receives in exchange of forcing the taxpayer (who will be the proper student, through his parents) to support them. Nobody gives anything away: simply, the costs of the system move on a person who not necessarily has to coincide with the beneficiary of the service or who, even in case he coincides, cannot give up receiving the service in exchange for the cost saves for himself. The problem of this false cost-free status that detaches the perception of the benefit with the assumption of its cost is that it links to over-dimension the demand of educational services, so much in its slope of consumer item as of good of an investment.

As for consumer item: what would happen if, for example, the State would increase the taxes to turn "in free" a basic educational material as they are the books (not only manuals, but also novels, and not only in the educational sense)? Since that the books demand to a cost for zero euros would be very superior to the current one, generating an excess of demand, which won't be in absolute profitable, would this be an expense that the citizens wanted to do? No, because at the current moment they are not ready to spend a major percentage of their revenue on acquiring books, since the additional utility that brings to them a book does not compensate the cost of acquiring it. Into what would change it, of course, if the State will force them to incur this cost? In summary: simply, the citizens would turn out to be forced to acquire more books than they need at the cost of resigning from other goods that turn out to be more valuable for them.

As for investment good, the analysis cost - benefit that every student should realize to decide if it is convenient for him, or not, to confront this expense, remains completely distorted. In a previous example, we saw that an individual would be clearly ready to study a university education with an annual cost for 5,878 euros per student in Spain's public university[123] , following data of 2012, and if it was providing an annual extra pay for 12.000 euros to him up to his retirement. Let's imagine that this annual extra pay comes down to 2.000 euros: for example because it is a question of a career where there is postgraduate saturation, and the entrepreneurs are not ready to pay a valuable extra pay for this formation. Should this person study the career? No: it would be a ruinous investment and the investor would lose money. In this situation, the social and personal incentives are quite aligned: there is postgraduates' saturation and there diminishes the number of students of this career for its poor profitability. But: what happens if the State subsidizes this career and it only costs 7,861[124] euros, which is the actual price in 2017 per student in the public university per year to the student (taking into account the financial crisis effects)? Since that the rational decision of the students would be that of studying it because, in fact, it would provide to him average annual profitability of 7 percent. The State, therefore, is out of line with the personal and social incentives on having kept on expanding the unnecessary expense in education.

---

[123] ww.mecd.gob.es/dctm/inee/indicadores-educativos/mapa2015/2015-f2-gasto-por-alumno.pdf?documentId=0901e72b81e3a3af
[124] http://www.teinteresa.es/educa/alumno-educacion-publica-colegio-elite_0_994102504.html

However, in fact, the problems of the State socialization of the educational expense are even major. As we saw already, the education is a sector very inclined to the unnecessary waste: since the educational qualifications are differentiation hard-ware, and the temptation to initiate totalities of competition is very big. This way, all the more qualifications possess each person, more qualifications it will have to possess one to stand out from the rest, independently if these qualifications are useful inside the productive process or if they are not. The only natural counterweights that exist opposite to this widespread resources waste are, on the one hand, that the educational centers are the sufficiently flexible and creative as for, at the time that the prices raise for pure effect of the market, also they raise the quality of education offered (rebounding to a better human capital); for other, that the private sector discovers new differentiation mechanisms for the working people much cheaper than the qualifications of reputable institutions; and, ultimately, that does not go out already for the student on account to incur such a disproportionate expense and accent of thinking about how to differ for this route. The problem is that when a good part of the expenses of education are subsidized and controlled by the State, these natural brakes whether do not go so far as to enter functioning or do it in a much more later way.

Consequently, the State not only cannot force the citizens to decide when they want more education, or to be already like a consumer item or as a good of investment, but the most common effect of the public expenditure in this rubric will be of turning into an enormous subsidy to the resources squandering to prolong the sterile competition for the differentiation between titled working people, AMD not providing education expenses in the form of a private check for citizens.

As a quite approximate indicator of the expense in education we obtain it across the working people estimations overqualified, that is to say, of working people who have a level of education superior to that of the employment that they are redeeming. What is the intention of investing information more necessary thing to occupy work? Certainly, there can be good reasons that do not happen for the mere squandering: it can aspire to promote one in the future, or one can be interested simply in acquiring new knowledge. But, in general, a few high over qualification evaluations indicate an excess of investment in education. In Occident, these over qualification valuations are usually placed over 20 percent[125] (in Spain, almost the double), what indicates a notable and superfluous overinvestment in education; overinvestment to which, certainly, have contributed significantly the multiple State subsidies (in the shape of "free" education or much subsidized for the user).

Finally, the demand for educational services will only tend to the reasonable use of the resources if the beneficiary of these services is, in turn, who supports its costs entirely, that is to say, when they do not tend to socialize costs (public education) and to privatize benefits (private extra pays): that's why the State should not subsidize it.

In fact, the argument most extended in favor of the public education is not based that is more efficient than the private education, but its biggest equity: in the widespread fear of that, if the education was deprived, "only the rich ones might study", exalting the social promotion and consolidating the inequality inherited from revenue. But: is it true that with a private education, immense most of the population would turn out

[125] https://www.oecd.org/eu/EAG2012%20-%20Country%20note%20-%20European%20Union.pdf

to be turn out completely to depend on the State aids to be able to educate their children? No, not much of them, even though State subsidies are necessary for many situations and reasonable in many countries.

Already of entry it is necessary to point out that it was not the public and obligatory education the one that extracted Europe of the educational system but, on the contrary, the extraordinary wealth that generated the Industrial Revolution and that allowed, among other things, the families to be able to be allowed to educate their children and buy books (until then, luxurious goods for the popular classes).

In sum, during the Industrial Revolution, the private education did not remain restricted to the base population, but it was of benefit directly to the popular classes, while the public education had scarce or void influence at the time of extending the literacy to these popular classes.

Second, the private schools were provided with many better infrastructures than the State centers. In the following table, we can find the percentage of private and public expenditure that in the USA, which was provided with a certain basic service for the education; between parentheses there appears the percentage of public centers that were provided with the same service.

PUBLIC EXPENDITURE THE UNITED STATES IN DEFENSE AND EDUCATION:

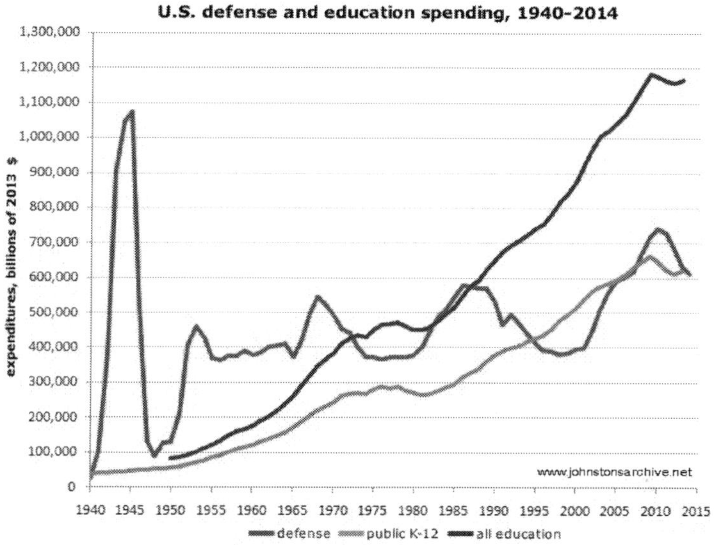

Hence the private education turns out to be accessible to almost the whole world, with independence of whether we are in a rich country or in a poor country (or in a poor epoch as the Industrial Revolution or in a richer epoch as the current one): in the poor countries the wages of the citizenship are much lower than those of the rich countries, but for the same motive also the wages of the professorship are much lower (and, therefore, also are the registrations in the private school). The education only becomes inaccessible when the average wages of the teachers move away enormously from the average wage of a country and when the pupils ratio for teacher stays rigid, but this only happens when these conditions are not determined by the market (that is to say, its clients) but the State.

But, why a few better-prepared teachers do not provide a better education? Obviously, a very bad remuneration of the teaching sector has negative consequences so much in short as long-term: in the short term, a few teachers very badly full end up unmotivated; in the long term, the low wages would only attract to the educational sector those less productive and worse formed working people. Consequently, it is obvious that obviously, some relationship exists between wages and quality of the education. Now then, also it should result from common sense that, from a certain level, the biggest wage increases, either do not improve the quality of the education, but there are simple "completing of revenues" on the part of the teaching personnel. In other words: that teachers should be quite prepared does not mean that they should be extraordinarily well paid in contrast to other professional categories. As normally they generate much lower tangible benefit. In fact, the evidence indicates us that, beyond a minimum, very little interrelation exists between the expense per pupil of the school and the academic results.

But, especially, the decisive reason for which the costs would get cheaper is of supply motives. Big part of the current costs are destined to regulative bureaucracy that forces to that, even the completely private schools, provide the education in a specific way: for example, all the pupils have to be educated obligatorily for six years for five days and 25 weekly hours in classrooms with a maximum of 25 pupils and where the teachers have to develop a program absolutely ruled by the State. What would happen with regard to the costs if we were allowing every educational center to modify by its own, and in free competition, the hours and school days, the number of pupils in the classroom, the subjects to be given or the methods with which they are given? For example, what would happen if the school days were coming down to the half, or could be given partly (or in their entirety) through the Internet, or some subjects were suppressed, which the parents consider not being important for the formation of the pupil?

It is difficult to make an exact calculation, but we can make ourselves an idea attending to the previous graph in reference to the private cost of what is properly the school basics (suppressing, therefore, all the compliments and out-of-school activities): in all the cases — included the primary education — it is located in half of the current costs in the public one and in some cases — like the secondary one — practically in a third.

With all this, we might be speaking about an average price for school square lower than 3.500 euros per year; a cost that vaguely would even stay out of the mean of the majority of Spanish school system expense. Let's remember that the most common salary in Spain is 15.500[126]euros and that the average taxes paid by a modal salary overcome 9.000 euros[127]. A couple where the two parents are working for 15.500 euros would be paying more than 18.000 euros in taxes, would be able to face loosely to the schooling of their children in a cheaper private system, due to a higher competition (the children average in Spain is 1,3 [128]for woman); if one of the two was not working, then he might adopt some of the formulae of supplying the educational offer about which we have just spoken (for example, the flex-schooling or the on-line education), reducing, even more, the cost.

In sum, it is a myth that "the private education is only for the rich ones." It is the State — its regulations and its high taxes — those who

[126] http://www.payscale.com/research/ES/Country=Spain/Salary
[127] http://www.advoco.es/hot-topics/107-spanish-income-tax-rates-2015.html
[128] http://data.worldbank.org/indicator/SP.DYN.TFRT.IN?locations=ES

prevent the immense most of the Spanish taxpayers from being able to be allowed to take their children to the schools deprived of their election. But nothing is in the nature of the private education that turns it inaccessible to most of the population: even between the poor of the poorest countries, as their objective is mainly to reduce their prices to attract more demand and increase their benefits, which they can't do due to high set-up costs and State barriers.

Of course, the previous thing does not mean that there could not be cases in which even this very accessible private education stays out of the budget of many families, but cost-reducing mechanisms exist for these exceptions (I insist on noticing that they are the exception and not the rule inside a free market).

On the one hand, the proper educational institutions or other private charitable institutions can be in charge of granting scholarships to their best students. For example, the main universities deprived of the world awarded a scholarship in 2012 to about half of their pupils, covering like an average between 40 percent and 50 percent[129] of the whole of the registrations (what means that many pupils could study in a completely free way). The reason is not only the reputation that grants to these universities counting from prestige, but the scholarship can remain a subordinate to that the pupil works or investigates during part of his day for the university (let's bear in mind that an increasing portion of the income of the private universities comes from private and public research projects in which they need to be provided with good professionals). In a certain way, then, the scholarships are like a long course of learning

[129] w.thebestschools.org/blog/2012/12/04/50-best-colleges-united-states/

financed by the company to receive excellent work people, in a certain future.

On the other hand, the same student can get into debt to gain access to his university studies. After all, as we have already seen, the education are assets (human capital) that provide high profitability (of between 10 percent and 15 percent per year)[130], so that it should not turn out crazy that the pupil would get into debt for some years to 4 percent or 5 percent of interests to face to this investment. The investment in education should not be seen as anything very different from acquiring a house: nevertheless, although the cost of the education is less enough to that of a housing and its very top yield, most of the accepted people as a normal and reasonable practice being mortgaged to buy a house but it would seem like something aberrant getting into debt to pay the studies to someone... why? And what's more important?

And, finally, we have already mentioned that in the budget of the minimal State there will be a part instead of being of "social work," which might be used to settle subsidized and limited (probably nonexistent) students' cases with few resources that might remain excluded from the system.

The education is, certainly, an economic good which is very important, but more important than different production resources which are already an object of free agreement and cooperation inside the market (like the food or the clothing). Although decades of statist propaganda have ended up turning into dogma that the education must be provided or controlled by the public sector, as there is no good reason

[130] https://www2.deloitte.com/us/en/pages/human-capital/articles/introduction-human-capital-trends.html

for it and there are very powerful motives so that it turns out to a completely free sector and not regulated : the private school tends to be much cheaper than the public one, as the competition between entrepreneurs of the education adapts with flexibility the educational offer to the changeable and particular needs of the pupils, as the student, through his effort, tends to minimize the expenditure in education, due to higher profitability in the future.

But, especially, an education out of the claws of the State is a much freer education: it is a system where anyone (any educational institution) can offer its particular instructional program, and anyone can demand it without censoring or inquisitions on the part of the new settlers of the educational programs or systems. People have to be free to spend their money on what they want, and the State shouldn't prevent it from happening. The scholar check has been proposed several times in Spain by free market supporters from many different atmospheres, but it has always been rejected. As always, interventionists prefer the Father State taking care of them, with a false mattress underneath. The fable of the stick and the carrot repeated. Again.

10- SAY YES TO CULTURE... BUT WITHOUT (PUBLIC) SUBSIDIES

The intellectual and human progress of a society does not only depend on the level of education that it receives but on the cultural production that it develops. In a certain way, the cultural heritage might be reputed like the esthetic face of society, like its highest and lasting expression that allows the members of a group to be identified and to be recognized as such, and as members of the same nation our group with any relation. It is not a small group the ones who think, in fact, that the culture in its diverse forms — literature, art, music, movies and even, for some, you won't even know, but still receive subsidies from the State — which in many passions unites the society and ennobles to the human being, but only through representative and primordial aspects of a culture. There exists, consequently, a reason to consider the production of cultural arts and the cultural diffusion as positive declarations of a healthy society.

Now then, there are great economists and even philosophers who, paradoxically, think that the culture cannot be left "in the hands of the society" (or as some interventionists wrongly usually express: "in the hands of the market") and defend some type of State intervention that protects it and promotes it, with Spain as an example, with a government that "donates" from our taxes annually more than 1,5% of the GDP[131]. The motives are diverse but they might split into two big groups: on the one

[131] http://www.mecd.gob.es/dms/mecd/cultura-mecd/areas-cultura/industriasculturales/plan-fomento-industrias-2016.pdf

hand, there is that they think that the free market does not remunerate sufficiently the artist, so that culture of the pointed one will tend to be generated less; for other, there is that they believe that capitalism subordinates the artistic production to the direct link with money, corrupting with it the cultural ideal.

In sum, the thesis or general idea of both groups is that the free market is unable to generate a culture in a quantity and with a quality sufficient and that, for the sake of resisting this mark, becomes necessary that the State takes control to provide financial autonomy to the intellectuals or artists (so much so that they are independent at the time of producing cultural assets as so that they are provided with the means enough for it). In this sense, two types of favorite interventions, and what next we will analyze, are the subsidies to the culture and the establishment of copyrights, without a profitable frontier in mind of the State. But first it is convenient to tell why, against the opinion of good part of many great and admired economists, the free market capitalism constitutes the ideal frame for the flowering of the different cultural forms, and in many cases with subsidies provided only to the profitable sectors or by the private market. As a defender of bullfighting in Spain, I strongly reject all subsidies given to this sector annually which altogether are more than 564 million euros[132]

Any intellectual and artistic production is a fruit of the work of artists or groups of immerse artists in a certain social and cultural ambience. The motivation of these people can be diverse — money, reputation, self-fulfillment...-, but all of them develop their activity

---

[132] . http://www.20minutos.es/noticia/276608/0/fiestas/taurinas/millones/

thinking about how to establish some type of relation with their public. The relation between the producers and consumers of culture is polymeric and complex (some producers answer passively to the cultural demand of the consumers, others try to face and undermine their tastes, and some of them think about how to receive simply feedback of their public to keep improving), but they all try to establish it somehow: the art and the culture cannot be understood without the communication between the producer and his public. Namely for the cultural flowering activities and trends it is necessary so much that the artist has the required material to be able to make his work seem to be capable of turning it accessibly for his public. In this sense, capitalism encourages so much the conditions that allow an increase of the material means in hands of the intellectuals or artists, as the enlargement, specialization and development of the cultural demand.

As for the availability of material means, capitalism provides both material resources and financial resources so the author could prepare his work. The technological progress and the capital accumulation have allowed reducing enormously the cost of creation, storage and reproduction of the cultural events: let's compare simply the cost of writing and reproducing a book, in contrast, to hand a book before the invention of the printing with the current cost of writing it on the computer, distributing it to the Internet to all the corners of the planet and reading it in electronic devices. It is clear that the proper technology and the accumulation of the capital of capitalism lower the price of the availability of material means to create a culture and that they allow, today, almost any individual to be able to try to turn into an artist. In a certain way, the capitalism has acted by delivering the fire of the cultural creation to the current man.

But also, capitalism provides the cultural creator of financial resources to be able to dedicate time and struggle with rear effort to his production. Of entry, without a wide division of labor it is simply impossible that it turn out to be an intellectual that enriches our cultural heritage: in those societies where everybody has to devote himself to, for example, the food production, nobody has time to specialize in writing poetry, painting a picture or directing a movie; only when a society turns so rich that it can "exempt" part of its citizens of the responsibility of being employed at the satisfaction of its most immediate basic needs, it is when this part of the citizens can devote to explore their aesthetic sensibilities. Without division of labor and without capitalism (the one cannot exist sustainably without other) there might be no type of art, except which it was instrumental to develop its occupations (like the music related paintings). Now then, the artist does not only want to have the option to develop his ingenuity and original idea, but he aspires to do it in an autonomic way, and for that he needs to be provided with sufficient means, as funds how to survive while he conceives his work. A clear example of private funding of culture can be private banks investing through investment funds on pieces of art as paintings or sculptures; having a demonstration in the US with *Anthea Contemporary Art Investment Fund*[133].

Again, capitalism promotes through diverse routes an increasing financial independence of the artist, so he is not tied to the only patron

---

[133] http://www.privateartinvestor.com/art-finance/art-funds-survey-2015/

who tries to control and direct his creativity, which normally tends to be the State: first, the reduction of the number of working time allows the existence of high-level artists or part-time professionals, which allows them to generate wealth from other activities. Second, the saving and the increase of the hereditary wealth of the families favors that the children could not only study for more years but dedicate this formation time to teaching like artists; and third, the capitalism multiplies the capital reception options, appealing even to the proper final consumers of the cultural material (for example, the called crowdfunding by which in short term many articles are supported by video games or the sale for fascicles of a novel).

In spite of everything, the latter financing option will not be able to satisfy many artists, whose target is precisely of changing, and not of bending, the conventions and tastes of the current society, to adapt their offer to the actual demand, and not as in Spain where the cinema sector registered losses near 700 million[134], with overloaded effects due to film hacking. Besides, exactly in this point, the free market helps to extend, specialize and increase the sophistication of the cultural demand and, on having done it, it extends the round of options available for the artist: the globalization and the extension of the distribution networks as they facilitate enormously that every author could look for his own nucleus of consumers to whom to speak initially to then influence other people. Said otherwise, the cultural creator already does not need to satisfy the taste of the masses to be able to finance his work (unless the cost of this one is disproportionately high, as the super cinema productions of Hollywood), but there can be faced a relatively small group of dispersed consumers by

[134] http://los40.com/los40/2004/06/09/actualidad/1086732000_276294.html

different regions of the planet. Probably, any artist of medium-sized quality can find a group of several thousands of followers between several thousands of million people (even if it is a minimum percentage of society) and, on this limited initial base, he can establish his influence on the rest of the society. In fact, thanks to the wealth that generates capitalism into the free market, the number of people capable of appreciating the specific art (literacy and increasing education) and to be interested in the culture (with free time for it) also is on the increase.

In sum, capitalism offers the suitable conditions so that there booms up a diverse, expansive and independent culture inside every society. This does not necessary mean that the artists who emerge inside this institutional frame are going to be successful at the time of developing quality art: it simply means that they are provided with the ideal conditions to do it. Nevertheless, the general perception of most of the upper economists, in contrast to my opinion, is that the capitalism is incompatible with the cultural progress and that every time the art is formed in less quality. To what is cultural pessimism of big part of the economic atmosphere nowadays, or what events have been shown to prove their theory? The motives are diverse, and to a great extent they depend on every person in particular, but certainly common peaks exist.

Firstly, the human being is educated in a certain culture that has ended up being domineering due to diverse historical circumstances, and cultures, while the new artists usually try to spoil the established cultural order and traditions partly: it is normal, then, that the established cultural elites observe with suspicion, displeasure, and incomprehension the new cultural tendencies that they repute like direct competition of what they represent; also it is usual that these elites despise the popular culture that emerges of the masses, even if part of this popular culture could end up by turning into culture of the elite (a famous case is that of the jazz or even the rock and roll during the 30-40s).

Second, many artists tend to fall down in the error of comparing the price or the commercial success of their works with their integral quality, therefore they distrust the judgment that expresses the market assigning monetary values to the diverse currencies, which is one of the values of capitalism: leaving aside the case of arrogant artists that create members of an intellectual or artistic oligarchy with natural law to obtain profit over the rest of citizens, it is true that the market must not be understood like a court that judges the quality of work, but on the other hand represents their monetary value. At most, the market offers an approach of what the social perception is at a certain moment due to work: but the social perceptions not do not only have why to be always right, but the tastes and parameters or even artistic and design rules change along with the time. For example, acquaintance is that Van Gogh did not achieve to sell a single picture during his life but that, at present, some of the most expensive pictures of the history are his: the quality of the work of the Dutch was the same at the end of the XIXth century that now, but the social perception changed, which made the monetary value of his works increase consequently, generating an increase in demand due to the trend factor. If the artist is, in a certain way, a revolutionary, he should not be surprised of that to the beginning few ones recognize his art or intelligence, but this will be independent of the economic organization in which he is immersed, as the value starts from 0 and will not decrease any more, always going up, and normally due to a large flow of years.

Finally, capitalism provides the frame adapted for the cultural progress: it multiplies the material and financial means at the disposal of the artist and raises the profile of the demand for having improved the access of the public to the education and learning on that particular work. More, ultimately, the success or failure of the intellectual and artistic development will depend on how the artist uses his ingenuity and creativity to generate quality works, with higher funds and economic support than in a planned economy.

The criticism against the frame of cultural freedom represented by the capitalism has led many people to defend the direct participation of the State in the promotion of the cultural development. It is usually argued that the artistic development possesses externalities stamped on the education of the society and that it is a question of a legacy that the current generations donate to the future ones. Supposedly, then, the State intervention in the culture, subsidizing it, maintaining the museums, preserving the historical patrimony, creating public mass media or granting art monopolies (public copyright) to the artists, would remain justified to encourage the artistic production.

Nevertheless, the State interventions in the culture tend to generate perverse incentives that fossilize the artistic progress. On the one hand, the subsidies to the culture undermine the real motivation of the artist to develop quality works, degenerating into mere financier functionaries that live off the government for the fact of producing any work, but now being controlled by profit, which is the main capitalistic value. For other, the State subsidies tend to reduce even in 80 percent the donations deprived to the art, displacing the appreciation and courage from the citizen to the politician: The Americans, for example, donate ten times more money to support the art and the culture than their Spanish pairs.

SUBSIDIES IN SPAIN TO THE CULTURE SECTOR:

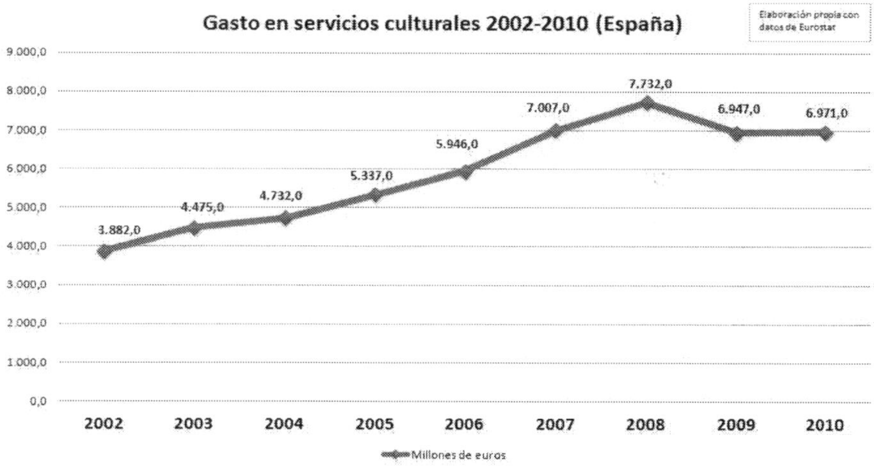

The intervention of the State is also considered to be indispensable for the conservation of the called historical patrimony of a country; especially those places qualified Patrimony of the Humanity on the part of the UNESCO[135]. Again, our intuition seems to suggest that the State must get adapted to a predominant role at the time of protecting the historical patrimony, but the problem is that, in fact, the historical patrimony can be so disproportionately wide that not even the politicians can guarantee an entire protection, so their task diminishes, rather, to deciding what hereditary assets funds receive for their conservation and which do not. And there does not seem to be good motives so that it is the politician,

[135] http://whc.unesco.org/en/list

instead of the society, who chooses what patrimonies to preserve and which not to.

The idea of that the owners would allow spoiling their valuable historical patrimony is equivalent to think that it would allow spoiling their municipal infrastructure or even their houses: as well as the citizens and the tourists value their history (and they do it, as actually, it indicates the strongest cultural tourism growth), the patrimony will survive. For example, National Trust of the United Kingdom — to which we have already referred to its protection work of the environment — also devotes itself to the safe-conduct of the British historical patrimony: in particular, actually its domains contains more than 200 historical buildings[136], 50 industrial monuments, 12 lighthouses (as rural houses)[137], 19 castles and churches[138], 57 villages, 25 medieval palaces and more than 830.000 books, manuscripts, paintings, sculptures, furniture or photos; all of them properly taken care, restored and opened to the public. It is not the only case: another foundation which is also entirely private, National Trust for Historic Preservation of the United States, devotes itself to receive funds and volunteers to rehabilitate historical places of the country (in 2013, they handled nearly 50 million dollars[139], and they were provided with 750.000 members and 30.000 volunteers)[140].

Another form through which the State tries to influence the cultural development of a country positively is the establishment of public mass media. In Spain, for example, there are more than 30 channels, costing

---

[136] https://www.nationaltrust.org.uk/houses-and-buildings
[137]https://www.nationaltrust.org.uk/features/lighthouses-in-our-care
[138] http://www.britainexpress.com/national-trust-properties.htm
[139] https://savingplaces.org/
[140] http://www.nationaltrustjobs.org.uk/our-stories/our-volunteer-numbers-hit-a-new-high/

187 euros[141] per family a year, of television and some other radio stations dependent on the Central government and on the autonomic administrations with a budgetary cost superior to 1.000 million euros per year, just protected by the annual BOE[142] justification. The justification of this horrendous financing of State mass media paid by the part of the taxpayer is usually double: on the one hand, it is supported that these channels have the mission to promote the language or the regional culture, by what, by definition, their public objective will be reduced, and they will not be able to develop without the help of the State; for other, and perhaps more important, many insist that the private media does not offer quality programming, but only junk TV. Deeply, then, what is indicated is that the public media have to re-educate the citizens, "teaching them" to appreciate quality programs that turn especially about the proper culture, but those programs that the politicians accept as ″cultural″, instead of those really demanded by the population.

The argument can have its apparent logic, but it continues without being sufficient to justify the devastating financing of mass communication media (including the public subsidies to the private means). First, because if a group of people wants to re-educate their citizens, what it must do is collecting itself the necessary funds and starting up its own thematic channel: if the sector was liberalized (as it should be), to create a television or a radio would be very accessible, as it illustrates the legion of local televisions that existed for the whole Spain before the "analogical blackout" (increasing intervention of the State in the economy) was having to close them down, as the multitude of illegal

---

[141] http://prnoticias.com/television/20145446-cierre-televisiones-publicas-coste
[142] https://www.boe.es/buscar/act.php?id=BOE-A-2006-9958

radios who today keep on operating the administrative control. With the Internet, also, these emission costs come down to an almost marginal total (especially in the case of media focused on the transmission of certain values or of a certain culture, which should not need the most expensive costs of set-up and production). Second because, even if a public channel offers to program "of quality", the people simply can choose not to synchronize it: if from the beginning the citizens were not wishing to watch this programming "of quality", which will generate boredom in certain occasions (hence no private businessman was throwing himself to the adventure of offering it), it does not seem probable that they begin to do it for the fact that a State branch offers it; that is to say, the citizens can keep on sheltering simply in the "junk TV" offered by the private sector, refusing to be "re-educated" this way by the State bureaucrats. Third, because the term "quality" towards which it is necessary to re-educate the people is quite subjective: are the Olympic Games (or the sport) a quality programming? And the animal documentaries? And the Spanish movies? And the American series of entertainment? And the programs on new technologies? And the transmission of a regional dance? And any content that is expressed in the local language? Everyone has his own concept of quality and what some acclaim like a cultural achievement, others detest it like an offense to the culture (precisely if there consists the cultural competition that we have already analyzed). It does not have, then, very much sense to force a citizen to pay for a few programs that are judged like "of quality" for other citizens: most of those who claim public quality means to re-educate the masses deeply simply, as they want that their masses, those who are subsidized and what they understand for quality programming; that is to say, they want not to support alone the cost of the mass communication media (in terms of time of advertisement or of quota of subscription) that only they like.

But, also, a last and worrying argument exists against financing public televisions that think about how to re-educate to the masses: the line between re-education and indoctrination is extremely thin, especially when the television is in the hands of the State. Must we entrust a few politicians, anxious for being supported by the power of the voters, the duty to re-educate the masses at the cost of the population? We are provided with enough experience on this matter in totalitarian or authoritarian countries (even in democratic countries) as to distrust the deliberation of this measurement. It is true that there are great economists and thinkers who hope that, with the due constitutional rights, the State mass media could be independent of the political manipulation and that, therefore, they should be useful not only for culturizing the population, but even to offer an information "objective", independent from the interests of political parties and of managerial lobbies. But again it is a question of an ingenious justification of the State mass media. First because it is usually confused between the term "independence with objectivity": that a public way is independent (which is managed by irremovable officials, for example) it does not imply that it is objective; if the working people have an ideological hint — and they all have it, in a sense or in other — the information that they will transmit will be leaked by this ideology; in other words, it is possible to create a television independent from the interests of entrepreneurs and politicians, but it is not possible to create a way independent from the interests of its working people. Second, because the really important thing is not that public institution is objective, but the viewers are conscious of that is not objective: that is to say, they doubt everything to what they listen to knowing that all the information has been previously arranged to taste of the issue; to create the objectivity sensation when it neither exists (can exist in many cases by employing experts in the matter) such an objectivity supposes anesthetizing the critical thought of the spectators and pushing them so that they submit to the "official" message of the State way. And, third, because nowadays, thanks to Internet, any citizen who wants to be informed arranges of the most abundant sources variety where to contrast, to compare and to refute all the information to his opinion; to collect and compress the informative revolution of last decades in article or bulletin that would be synthesized, from a public way, exposing "the objective truth" that the citizens have to learn and comprehend, not only is an imposition and dangerous strategy but condemned to the failure of society, as to pay for culture's promotion and 30 public TV's in Spain mean people and workers are suffering a mean income tax rate of 18.50%[143]. Is it really worth?

Despite what it could be thought, there does not exist historical evidence of any of the implantation of the copyrights — or their different extensions in term — that have helped to increase minimally the cultural production of the authors: in the United States, for example, it is believed that the last extension of the duration of the protection of the copyrights in 40 percent scarcely helped to increase the income expected from the author in 0,33 percent and, obviously, the number of registered works has not experienced any change, with 88%[144] on mean of media consumed

[143] http://www.spainaccountants.com/rates.html
[144] http://elpais.com/elpais/2015/03/10/inenglish/1425997747_249854.html

illegally due to piracy. In fact, in some fields, like that of the classical music, the evidence demonstrates, and through available data indicates that the number of composers contracted after the expansion of the copyright license.

PIRACY IN SPAIN:

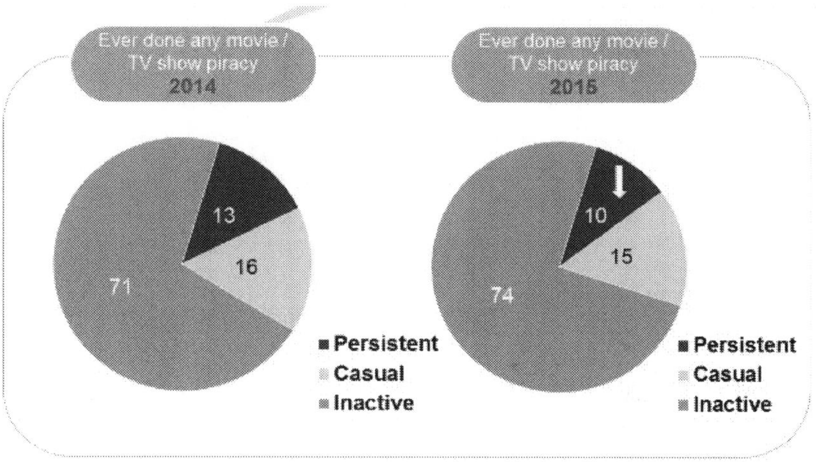

Finally, the copyright is one more example of intellectual monopoly that praises and makes the access to the culture difficult for the popular masses (this one gets dearer the price of the copy and, also, it turns it less available when the monopolistic publisher decides to outrange it) and that disables that other authors use this baggage to increase their own intellectual production (the compilations of histories or of essays or, of course, the creative imitation are not possible without the assent of the original author).

To end up, it would seem logical, then, that the State was not adopting two conflicting politics: on the one hand, to subsidize the access to the culture; for other, to get dearer artificially its cost granting the artist a development monopoly on its work. But the State answers to targets of contradictory lobbies and, for it, it adopts contradictory politics. As in the rest of sectors, it should not intervene in the culture either, as through copyrights prevents culture from developing, but in contrast through subsidies tries to revitalize it in an artificial and false way. The State shouldn't subsidize culture, but neither agriculture, manufacturing nor even the financial sector. But why? Culture is another mean activity in the market and it should be left alone for a correct capital allocation of resources. If costs are high, prices consequently will be, and people won't demand. As everything. As anywhere. This is the jungle. Culture can't expect to be protected from predators by the State eternally. Let's liberalize the cultural sector.

11- HOW TO MAINTAIN PENSIONS IN A FREE-MARKET ECONOMIC MODEL

Together with the education and health, the pensions constitute one of the basic branches of the called State of Well-being. For many citizens, it turns out to be incomprehensible that the State could ignore the situation of the elders and, consequently, they defend a State pensions system. Nevertheless, the alternative to the public pensions is not that the people with the lowest income turn out to be condemned to the poverty, but a society where the saving and the personal capitalization constitute the base of the future prosperity for all the people.

The energies and capacities of the human being are expanding the same way as it ages. The attitudes for the living of the revenue that one is capable of generating with his own work end up by declining unfailingly. But, except unforeseen accident, this slope does not take place for improvisation, but it is a constant of the economic cycle of the human being since the world started. Hence the individuals have the aptitude to plan their retirement: since we all, without exception, will end up by seeing how it deteriorates our capacity of generation of wealth, as we retire or leave a job for personal reasons, it seems logical that we all, without exception, try to prepare ourselves for this moment.

The prudent way of doing it is through personal saving: while the human being is productive, he can separate a portion of the revenue that he generates with the intention of saving it for the future. Now then, since one can begin to save decades before the moment of his retirement, it turns out to be slightly advisable to invest in a checking account the whole capital that it is safeguarding: the intelligent thing seems to be to use this retained capital to generate with it additional wealth that could save itself in turn and that increases our future patrimony. In other words, the habitual way of preparing the retirement is that of saving while our skills and energies allow us to generate revenue with our work, invest this saving and re-invest the profits of this financial movement: an operation that financially is known as a capitalization of our revenue or our saving, which the State can do without any problem, to generate the capital of its funds independently, putting a lower fiscal weight on the working population.

The capitalization of the saving resolves to clear advantages for the individual: not only, given that to it allows to enjoy a large patrimony and a few valuable revenues at the moment of his retirement, but because this patrimony also serves him for other business, increasing consumption, and converting economic growth into sustainable, maintaining constant or upper the GDP levels. On the one hand, the worker would enjoy autonomy to retire earlier once it had accumulated capital that seems sufficiently to cover his needs; even some voluntarily unemployed use their savings to consume during which reinforcing or redoing their formation. For other, the patrimony would act like insurance opposite to the most diverse accidents that could bother them along their labor life (illness, accident, loss of job, devaluation of its human capital, etc.). And, finally, as soon as he would be a holder of the saved patrimony after his death widower might diversify it to his spouse or to his children. This is what is known as "an owner's' society."

But the capitalization of the saving for pensions also bears important advantages for the set of the society: major all that is the volume of investment and of risk taken, major capital will be the productivity of the economic factors, this is, greater will be its aptitude to generate revenue and to save, entering this way a virtuous circle of prosperity (more investment goes to more rent, more disposable rent to more saving, and more people save to more investment, through a capitalization pensions system).

The public pensions system at present current in almost the whole planet keeps, yet, scarce relation with the one that we have just described. Far from promoting the capitalization of the saving of every individual, the actual States proceed to carry out a necessary redistribution of this saving, due to changes in population levels: this is what is known as systems of share-out or pay-as-you-go systems.

In particular, the State pays the pensions of the current pensioners not by means of the revenue that acquires from the patrimony that these pensioners have accumulated during their productive years, but from the taxes crashing to the current working people. Said otherwise, it is the present generation of working people the one that pays the pensions to the present generation of pensioners. In exchange for it, obviously, when the present generation of working people turns into the future generation of pensioners, the future generation of work people will cover their pensions. It is a question of keep on paying, then, and of charging on the march (pay-as-you-go): the today working strengths support the today clerks and the tomorrow working strengths will support the tomorrow clerks. So, if nowadays the productive potential is higher, and rents go up, pensioners will receive higher pensions, but otherwise if in the future, the labor efficiency decrease, those workers who had generated higher wealth in the past will now receive scarce pensions.

In Spain, for example, every worker pays to the Social security almost 30 percent of his salary to support the pensions of the pensioners and, in exchange for it, he is earning a future right of service that, to today, is programmed so that it ends up by being the following way: retirement at the age of sixty-seven with a pension equivalent to the average salary of last twenty-five years (this average salary is known as "a regulatory base") any time it has been quoted thirty-seven years, which are the number of years you have to work in average to pay for your future pension (if they have been quoted fewer years, the pension is a progressively less percentage of the regulatory base). It happens, nevertheless, that these conditions of access to the pensions have been modified habitually by the State in the last thirty years: in 1984[145], for example, the working people had a right to retire at the age of sixty-five (not to the sixty-seven), their regulatory base was calculated from last two years of salary (not of the last twenty-five) and scarcely they were needed eight years (not thirty-seven) to gain access to the maximum pension; also, the same quotation to the Social security was serving to finance the public health (thing that does not happen already from 1994[146], moment in which it happened to be financed from the rest of taxes).

---

145 https://www.boe.es/diario_boe/txt.php?id=BOE-A-1984-1349
146 http://www.seg-social.es/Internet_1/Normativa/095093

This deterioration of the conditions of access to the pensions has not taken place for mere inept decisions of our politicians, but because the income of the system of share-out depends on two factors — the population in age of working and the productivity of the labor-capital— who have not been capable of compensating the evolution of other two factors that determine the expense — the number of pensioners and the engaged average pension, which is directly index linked to the Retail Price Index—. Said otherwise, since the current work people pay the services of the current pensioners, if the number of pensioners grows much more rapid than that of working people, there are only two ways of maintaining the system: or increasing what it produces and every worker pays even more or reducing what every pensioner receives, which is not even a solution.

The number of people between sixteen and sixty-four years was in almost eight times top Spain in 1961[147] to the number of people of more than sixty-five; in 2011, that ratio went down four points, so there were four workers per pensioner. Since the productivity between 1961 and the sufficient thing did not increase 2011 as to keep on financing the generous conditions of retirement promised to the Spanish, there did not stay another remedy to go worsening them. The problem is in that that one ratio will keep on diminishing to a worrying full rhythm, as just in 2015 we have two workers per pensioner[148]: in 2051, the demographic series of the National Institute of Statistics project that it is located in 1,4[149], in fact, the following graph speaks itself: in it there is gathered the evolution foreseen

[147] http://datos.bancomundial.org/indicador/SP.POP.65UP.TO.ZS?locations=ES
[148] http://www.eleconomista.es/economia/noticias/6662090/04/15/Solo-hay-dos-trabajadores-en-activo-por-cada-pensionista-en-Espana.html
[149] http://www.elespanol.com/economia/macroeconomia/20161023/165233925_0.html

by the INE of the number of sixty-seven-year-old elderly (that is to say, already considering the delay in the retirement age), which are pensioners and don't contribute to the Social Security, as well as a very optimistic projection of the number of occupied (assuming that 70 percent of the population between sixteen and sixty-seven years has a job, the maximum employment rates reached till now by Spain, in all the decade, taking into account the real-State boom).

Clearly, Spain will go through a demographic winter that will put seriously risk the system of share-out of pensions: unless the productivity of the working people is any more duplicated during the next four decades, the current average pensions will not even be able to be supported. For example, if in the year 2050, 70 percent of the Spanish in age of working enjoy an employment to a real average salary for 32.200 euros per year (what would be equivalent to a real growth of the salaries of 1 percent a year from 2014), the Social security will be scarcely able to pay an average pension for 10.500 euros for people older than 67 years[150], when today it is paying one nearby to the 12.000 for older than 65 years[151]: that is to say, under these not pessimistic at all supposed, the pension not only would deflate in relative terms opposite to the average but enclosed salary in absolute terms, as taxes on workers will be increased to maintain the pension system, which will have negative effects on the economic growth rate.

The problem, with everything, is not a specific of our country, but it is relative and applicable to any share-out system. After all, the share-out

[150] http://www.seg-social.es/Internet_1/Estadistica/FondodeReservadelaS48074/index.htm
[151] http://economia.elpais.com/economia/2016/03/22/actualidad/1458644632_840364.html

system was born in Germany with Bismarck in 1889[152], when the life expectancy of the Germans was nearly thirty-eight years, and originally the retirement age was established in seventy years. In the United States, Franklin Roosevelt implanted it in 1935[153] for the population older of sixty-five years, when the life expectancy in the country was sixty-one years. It is true that these numbers are inclined to the fall by the high infant mortality of the epoch, but nevertheless the life expectancy of a twenty-year-old American of age in 1935 only was climbing up to sixty-eight years, in a period of time of fewer than 50 years, since Bismarck took control over Germany in the 1890's

PENSIONERS IN SPAIN COMPARED TO LABOR FORCE:

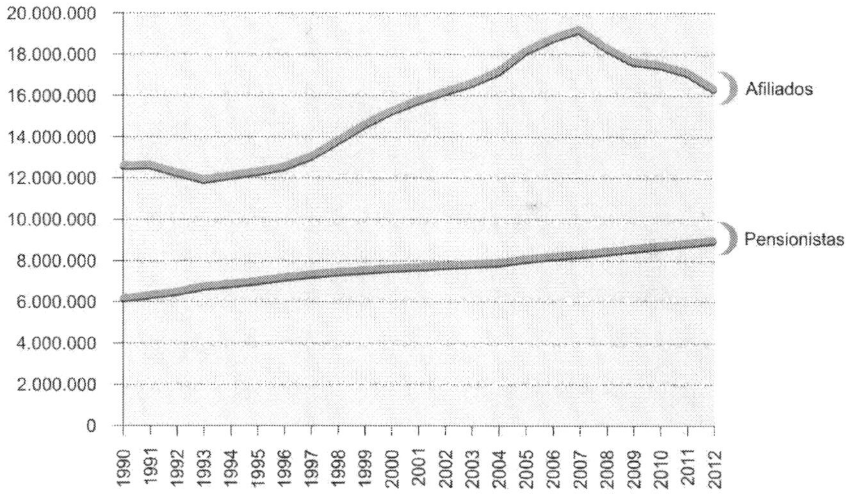

Finally, the creation of the systems of share-out was linked originally to the establishment of a network of State protection for those people

152 http://www.bde.es/f/webbde/SES/Secciones/Publicaciones/PublicacionesSeriadas/DocumentosTrabajo/14/Fich/dt1417e.pdf

153 http://famguardian.org/taxfreedom/History/President/1935-SSA.htm

who exceptionally were exceeding sixty-five years and were lacking patrimony, and not like the standard mechanism to finance the retirement of all the workers.

From here two types of solutions exist. The first one is to take the share-out system up to its last consequences: gross way, it would be a question of without promising any pension predetermined to the pensioners but simply of distributing every year between them the money that is collected by the affiliated to the Social security. Since in the future the number of working people will decrease, and that of pensioners will go up, this sustainable public system would be only capable of providing welfare, nearby pensions to guarantee the subsistence and little more, but in periods of downturn in the economy, the pensions will be harshly affected in this way.

The second one is to return to the system of the free market that would have developed in the absence of State interferences: the capitalization of the pensions.

Since we have already had occasion to comment, to capitalize the pensions it is the natural practice that the individuals would have continued to prepare for their retirement: basically, to save and to invest their revenue along all their labor life. Not in vain, even with the public retirement system in force, many individuals keep on saving and investing with the intention of complementing the lean pensions that the State promises them. Of what it would be a question, consequently, it is of adopting the same practice for that portion of our revenue that the State steals us on the pretext of supporting the Social security.

Right now, the quotations to the Social security directed to finance the pensions system promote 28,3%[154] of the salary of a worker for foreign account (also, the salary turns out to be decreased on account of the Social security for eight additional points directed to cover the unemployment, the professional training and the Fund of Wage Guarantee). That means that a worker who perceives a modal salary for 15.500 euros, is transferring to the public pensions system almost 4.400 euros per year. If the salary of this worker stays constant along its labor life and quotes for thirty-seven years, one will be able to retire the sixty-seven with an annual pension for 15.500 euros: he will have contributed 4.400 euros per year for thirty-seven years to perceive from sixty-seven years an annual revenue of 15.500 euros. If instead of working and quoting for thirty-seven years, he has done it during forty or forty-five, these additional contributions get lost: a person who has been paying to support the pensions system for forty-five years will have contributed to the system with 35.000 additional euros, according to the established normative[155] , which implies that a person who has quoted thirty-seven years and, nevertheless, both of them will perceive the same pension.

The question that we must formulate is what would happen if, instead of introducing these compelling contributions inside the pyramidal system of the State pensions, the worker had destined this capital to acquire real or financial assets. We can do an idea to ourselves looking at the historical evolution of the world stock exchanges: the average profitability of the world stock-exchange from 1900 even the actuality has

[154] http://www.seg-social.es/prdi00/groups/public/documents/binario/193632.pdf
[155] http://spainlawyer.com/guia-legal/pensiones-y-subsidios/las-prestaciones-contributivas

been located concerning 5,5 percent[156] per year, as soon as the inflation was deducted, with a level of actual 0.6%[157]. If we capitalize an annual saving for 4.400 euros to 5,5 percent for thirty-seven years, we obtain that the worker would retire at sixty-seven years with a financial patrimony of 525.000 euros. Just extracting annual profitability of 3 percent from this moment, its annual pension would promote to 15.750 euros, something higher than right now it promises the public system (if, on the other hand, the annual profitability should on being 5,5 percent, the annual pension would reach 29.000 euros, almost the double that the public system of share-out).

The result will be able to seem slightly overwhelming and incredible: if at the age of sixty-seven we reinvest to more conservative assets that provide profitability lower than 3 percent per year, the pension finally perceived under a system of capitalization will be practically the same one than under a share-out system. In what sense, can one affirm that the private system should be superior to the State one? (Perceive the irony here).

First, the worker reaches the retirement with an abundant financial patrimony of more than 500.000 euros. This patrimony is of his property and, therefore, he will be able to donate it to his spouse or to his sons at the moment of his death. With the State pensions system, the right to perceive a heritage becomes extinct with the contributing one, with the lone exception of the pensions of the widow and of the orphanage (that in any case become extinct with the death of the widow or with the adulthood of the orphans). The State snatches to them from the working

---

[156] http://data.worldbank.org/indicator/CM.MKT.TRAD.GD.ZS

[157] http://data.worldbank.org/indicator/NY.GDP.DEFL.KD.ZG?locations=ES

people the possibility of collecting an abundant patrimony that provides with financial stability both the taxpayer and his family. Secondly, as we have already summed up, those working people who quote more than thirty-seven years to the Social security does not get any type of compensation for it. In the case of a system privileged with capitalization, on the contrary, the saving of these working people is invested, and it is promoted, contributing to a larger future pension. And the difference is not by any means trivial: a worker who invests 4.400 euros per year from the twenty-two years, at the age of sixty-seven would end up by accumulating a patrimony for 850.000 euros and perceiving an annual pension for 25.500 euros (instead of 15.500 euros inside the State system). Or, for seeing it from another perspective, a worker who had begun to save and invest at the age of twenty-two, one might retire fifty-nine years after age (instead of to the sixty-seven inside the State system) perceiving an annual revenue of 15.750 euros per year).

Third, although the State quotations to the Social security on account of the retirement should be equivalent to 28,3 percent of the gross salary, already we have told that, by virtue of other concepts, the entire quotation reaches 36,25percent[158] for the worker for foreign account. These other concepts are basically the unemployment and the professional training: that is to say, a species of obligatory insurance to keep on perceiving a revenue in case of unemployment. Of course, and just as we will repeat soon, the worker can choose to destine this sum of money that monthly gets carried away forcing him to hire a voluntary insurance against the unemployment; but also their fits the possibility that

---

[158] http://www.seg-social.es/Internet_1/Trabajadores/CotizacionRecaudaci10777/Basesytiposdecotiza36537/index.htm

simply it uses this capital to increase even more its financial patrimony and to be protected this way opposite to the risk of loss of employment, diversifying his patrimony. After all, a worker who receives 15.500 euros is paying to the Spanish Social security approximately 1.100 euros per year as a way of unemployment insurance: capitalizing these numbers to 5,5 percent, would give a hereditary fund of more than 40.000 euros after twenty years, from which there might be supported its own investment (40.000 euros there is almost the double of the maximum welfare that can be perceived at present) and even his own formation. Consequently, if a worker with a salary of 15.500 euros saves and invests for thirty-seven years 36,25 percent of its revenue and does not go so far as to remain an unemployed man, he will end up by retiring with a financial patrimony for 675.000 euros and an annual pension of 20.200 euros.

In fourth place, at present, the pensioners are asphyxiated by all kinds of confiscatory taxes that reduce very substantially the pension that they perceive. A pensioner who receives a pension for 15.500 euros per year will pay concerning 1.500 euros in IRPF[159] and approximately 2.500 VAT[160]euros (if it consumes all its revenue), what leaves a real level revenue for 11.500 euros to him. On the contrary, with the privatization of the pensions and of almost all the other State services, already we saw that a tax would be enough on revenues or on the consumption of 6 percent, what would leave the pension resultant from the system of capitalization in 14.800 euros.

[159]http://www.agenciatributaria.es/AEAT.internet/Inicio/_componentes_/_Le_interesa_conocer/Retenciones_IRPF_2015_y_2016.shtml

[160] http://www.datosmacro.com/impuestos/iva

And I want to add, and probably more important: despite the last reforms of the pensions, the Social security system continues without being sustainable for a simple demographic question. Inevitably, the conditions of access to the retirement are going to keep on deteriorating, as it has come happening in the last decades. The following step will end up by being of lengthening the retirement age at your seventies, calculating the pension to be received dividing equally the whole labor life and demanding a minimum of forty years to perceive hundred percent of the pension. This way, a worker with a salary of 15.500 euros that he has quoted for forty years might have needed in a private system a patrimony for 634.000 euros and an annual pension of 19.000 euros (and not of 15.500, as in the pure share-out system).

Joining these five effects, the results of the system deprived of capitalization of pensions are much more visible. A worker who has begun to quote at the age of twenty-five, and who is retired at 70 and will capitalize 36,25 percent of his salary, which might end with a financial patrimony for 1,5 million euros and a pension after taxes for 41.800 euros, opposite to the lean pension for 11.500 euros after taxes, which would end inside the system of share-out and of the current over-dimensional State. Obviously, the number of 41.800 euros per year only would happen under all the handled assumptions, and also taking into account economic growth and a variable profitability of nearly 5,5% but in any case it is used to illustrate the enormous potential that possesses a system deprived of share-out pensions, differentiate from the one which is based on capitalization of the pension system, to obtain higher profitability and be able to maintain the public pensions, even though the taxes will be decreased enormously, allowing for higher levels of consumption, due to an increase in disposable income.

The pioneering country at the time of leaving the absurd and antisocial public pensions of the share-out system was Chile. Thanks to the work of Secretary of Labor José Piñera, the country initiated a transition from the public share-out system to the system deprived of capitalization. The Chileans whom this way were choosing it could migrate of one to another country under the following conditions: a government bond was recognized after them for the years that they had quoted till then to the public system of share-out (the called "bond of recognition"), and one was forcing them since then to invest 10 percent[161] of their salary in some of the Pension funds (private financial institutions entrusted to manage the saving and the pensions of the Chileans), and even though they were living in an exterior State, they would still receive their pensions when they went over 65 or 67 years old[162].

Despite the superiority of the systems of capitalization, it is quite frequent to expose them three types of more or less reasonable criticism that, ultimately, help to perpetuate the authority of the scheme of State share-out. As I say, it is not a question of random criticism, but of objections that are quite in defense of the private pensions and it must be taken very seriously although it is to understand better its real functioning: the problem of the transition, the problem of the high risks and the problem of the growth in a world without regular population growth rates.

---

[161] https://home.kpmg.com/xx/en/home/insights/2015/11/chile-other-taxes-and-levies.html
[162] http://www.oecd.org/els/public-pensions/2429310.pdf

The first one of this criticism is that, even if the private pensions could be preferable to the State ones, once the State has taken possession of the sector and has restored a share-out system, it is practically impossible to give step backwards: if the generation of current working people stops paying coactively the quotations to the Social security with the intention of beginning to save facing their own retirement, then the current pensioners will remain without pension; and if on the other hand, the work people keep on quoting, they will not have saved sufficient as their own private pension is constituted. Undoubtedly, the difficulties linked to the transition from a State system to one private one of capitalized pensions sounds very considerable, but in no case irrevocable. We have treated the matter with greater detail and explanation in the chapter dedicated to exhibiting how to change from a society linked to the State to a much freer one: at the moment, at least, let's bear in mind that in Chile the working people only needed to save 10 percent of their salary to reach reasonable pensions, as the taxes related to the pension system are only 10% of income[163], with difference to Spain, where workers pay nearly 25% [164]of their income to the pension system. This means in Spain still there would stay almost 20 points of quotation available for supporting the pensions of the current year to the Social security.

The second one of the criticism is that the private pensions are much riskier and uncertain than the public pensions, since they force citizens to depend on the volatile nature of the variable financial markets as essential as the moment, the quantity and the conditions of the retirement; on the other hand, the public share-out systems allows to

---

[163] http://www.oecd.org/finance/private-pensions/49497472.pdf

[164] http://www.bolsamania.com/declaracion-impuestos-renta/fiscalidad-del-ahorro-y-de-los-planes-de-pensiones-en-la-declaracion-de-la-renta/

guarantee how much we will receive and in what date we will be able to leave the labor market. And, certainly, most of the people feel a natural distaste for having its savings invested in stock-exchange actions or other financial assets, so that the protective cloak of the State seems to offer them a major safety. But this safety is more of posture than real.

In the first place, it is false that the State provides safety guaranteeing the pensions: the public share-out systems have been submitted to false statistics and interventionist incentives throughout last forty years because the promises that the governments were carrying out were turning out to be impossible to perform. That the State pleases to promise very much in all the ambiances does not mean that it is going to accomplish these objectives: in fact, the history shows to us that it tends to break them rather before the incredulity of a few citizens who could not foresee its corrupt and irresponsible behavior.

Second, a good part of the insecurity that the people feel at the time of managing their patrimony implies they have never had to do it: the excessive State tax system has disabled that big layers of the society privet financial participations, and that, consequently, were not feeling the need of improving their financial knowledge. But let's bear in mind that pacts and contracts involving financial operation involving an individual need a patrimony — and to obtain it is the natural result of the creation and wealth accumulation — necessary will turn out to be impelled to materialize this patrimony in assets that are risky; frequently more than the own deposit. Not in vain, two assets preferred by the Spanish to canalize its savings — the real State and the bank deposits — have been confirmed in the recent crisis like instruments of a potential risk superior to the stock-exchange actions: when you have wealth, to exhibit you to risks is inevitable, the question is to have enough financial culture as to minimize them, mainly by diversifying your financial portfolio into different markets or sectors.

Finally, the stock-exchange is not mainly composed of assets which are especially volatile and insecure for the long-term investor. It is normal that, before the absence of financial culture, a person feels unable to select actions of specific companies, but precisely for his investment funds which just are managed by a third or investment funds that limit themselves to answering the evolution of the stock exchange indexes: it would be enough that this person immobilizes his savings in funds diversified between all the world financial markets to obtain average profitabilities near to this 5,5 percent obtained throughout last ten years, taking into account also the economic recession years. Also, let's bear in mind that the normal thing is that, in the same way as a person is reaching the age in which he wants to retire, replace his most volatile short-term assets with other less volatile assets (for example, actions of big consolidated companies or fixed revenue), so that there does not even exist a high risk of suffering an important capital loss a few years before the retirement: for example, the more conservative type of investment funds inside the Chilean system (that one in which the working people most need to capitalize their revenues, are the ones next to their retirement age) scarcely suffered a few losses of 0,9 percent in the critical year 2008, with the explosion of the real-State bubble, and generating the greatest economic global depression in the last 25 years.

Certainly, the objection is reasonable: at last, the GDP of a country grows or because there are more people producing goods and services or because every person produces a major quantity of goods and services; unless the productivity of the employed people increases every year the sufficient thing as to compensate the number of people whom every year retire and stop producing, the GDP will fall down and if the GDP falls down, with direct consequences on the national income, the revenues of the pensioners will not be able to grow very much (since there will not be any more goods and services available for being acquired, due to a large contraction of supply in the market). In the limit, if Spain had only ten million workers and twenty million pensioners, it seems slightly probable that the pensioners wouldn't enjoy a very large purchasing power, as each worker will have to pay for two different pensioners, which has been previewed to happen in the years 2030-2040 according to statistics of the IMF[165].

---

165 http://economia.elpais.com/economia/2012/04/11/actualidad/1334133453_457282.html

PUBLIC EXPENDITURE IN PENSIONS IN THE WORLD:

Figure 2.1. **Public expenditure on old-age and survivors pensions, 2011**

Percentage of total government expenditure

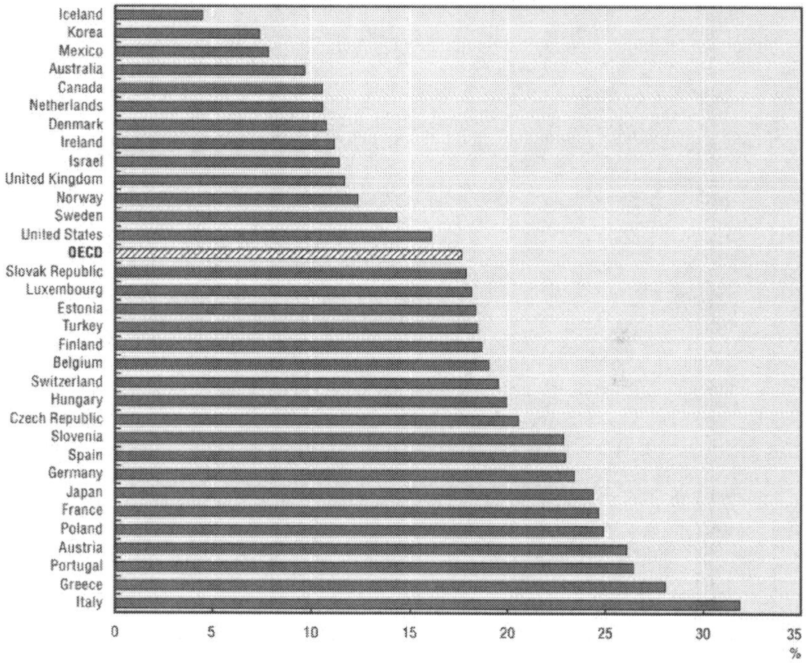

Source: OECD Social Expenditures Database (SOCX).

Finally, the habitual objections against the system of capitalization of the pensions are not solid, although they deserve to be taken into consideration. The natural mechanism to prepare the retirement on a free market and not taken control by the State is that it turns out to be preferable both for the proper individual and for the set of the society. In fact, those that wanted to join an intergenerational share-out system only would have to constitute it through a contract: with complete certainty by my side, that it would be exposed to failure, but it would be exactly due to a lack of legal backup to force the new working people to add it in an integrated way. So finally, with a pensions capitalization system, we will be able to pay a lower amount of taxes during the working period of our life, enjoying more disposable income, and later on, after our retirement we will receive higher returns, as all the money invested in the financial markets would have given a mean and constant profitability over capital.

The Spanish government should incentivize a reform of the pension system to save our people. This system is unsustainable and can't be handled anymore. There's just one solution and a very good one... a capitalization system, following the Chilean example. Through a capitalization system, citizens would destine 15 percentual points less from their income tax to pension funds, and they will see their capital conserved and revalued through time. But overall and the most important, pensions won't depend on workers at the time, but on your effort and dedication during your lifetime. It is more than a solution. It is a life project.

12- WE NEED TO PROVIDE EVERYONE WITH HEALTHCARE... BUT A PRIVATE ONE

Few sectors turn out to be so sensitive to the public like healthcare. Not even the education or pensions wake up so many cautions and stimulation of self-defense as the sanitary system. After all, on the health system our health and even our lives depend crucially. It does not seem, consequently, that the area is the most adaptable to do liberalizing experiments. Especially when, in accordance with the opinion of the experts, the Spanish public health is one of the best of the world while the American health — supposedly private — is quite dysfunctional. What sense must propose a privatization and liberalization of the health when the evidence seems to aim at that would end up in a worsening of the service and to an increase in the prices, especially in this so delicate sector for the citizen? (Please, notice the irony).

As in all the previous cases, it is complicated to anticipate what would have happened in a sanitary system that had never been centrally controlled and planned by the State, but, with enough safety, it would have exhibited certain characteristics.

The health is a physical condition that deteriorates for sustainable or unpredictable motives (paradigmatically, the age) and for relatively unforeseeable motives (illnesses and accidents). As well as soon as the human beings worry for their health — and it is a question of a quite sensible preoccupation — they will try to acquire the goods and necessary services to avoid or to minimize the deterioration of their health, preparing the risks that threaten it or having to enter into opportunity cost to be able to pay for the health system.

Now then, to be able to acquire these goods and services, every individual will have to be provided with sufficient capital, or in interventionist economies with enough disposable income. In the absence of the State and into the free market regulation, this capital can only come from three sources: the proper saving, the insurances and the donations of third people, as for example a heritage.

The proper saving is the source of logical financing for most of the expenses linked to the deterioration of the health for the age, affecting 20% of the population older than 65 years old[166]. If we are conscious of that in the future we will need of sanitary care and of medicines, we will have to save in the present to face this future expense. Overall let's preview that it will be this expense, the more we will have to save in the present.

For his part, the insurance companies are a financing source adapted to face most of the expenses of unpredictable nature, particularly, the risk that the sanitary condition of the subject deteriorates for developing chronic illnesses. An insurance is only a tool to cover risks inside a human group: if like average, 10 of every 100 people develops cancer, a group of hundred people can collaborate to eliminate the financial risk that some of them suffer from cancer, which will balance the costs incurred by the insurance company; it will be enough that all of

[166] http://www.apa.org/pi/aging/resources/guides/older.aspx

them promise to cover the cost of treating a cancer (let's put 100.000 euros) when one of them develops it (that is to say, each of 100 people would contribute 10.000 euros to the insurance to pay the treatment of the 10 who will endure cancer). Obviously, the person who must pay every insured debt will be related to its relative risk: for example, if the previous group fuses with another group of another 100 people who, on the other hand, supports the double of risk of suffering cancer (instead of 10 percent), the individual contribution of each of the members of this second group must be 20 percent the double that that of the first ones. In the opposite case, the people with a low risk of suffering cancer will have strong incentives to leave of the insurance and to collaborate with them, in an entirely private way.

Finally, the donations of third people imply that an individual covers the sanitary expenses of another individual, even if it is just for benevolence or for self-interest (for example, to avoid the epidemic risk).

Reached this point, the question is: when would each of the different methods tend to be used for financing? In general, most of the population would try to choose or for the proper saving or for the insurances, since the donations of third make your health rely on the wealth and on the complete will of another person. But, between both: which would they choose and when? We can answer this question analyzing a little more closely the functioning of the insurances.

For their configuration, it has not got a great sense that the insurances cover three types of sanitary expenses: those that affect to the totality of the group, those that take place to independent nature of one of the presented parts, and finally, those which price is relatively low. It does not make sense that it covers expenses that affect to the totality of the group because in such a case they do not serve as anything: if all the people inside a society are going to suffer cancer, and the cost of treating it is 100.000 euros, they will have to face all an expense for 100.000 euros, by which the type of insurance that they establish, shouldn't be contributive, as nowadays the mean costs for a cancer treatment oscillate around $141,000 for the first twelve weeks[167]. Also, it does not make sense either that the insurances cover expenses that depend on the discretional variable nature of the parts (for example, the aesthetic lifting for motives merely precarious): in such a case, every member of an insurer would have a "free" perspective to multiply his expenses at the cost of the others (and the others at the cost of him), being able to choose what to pay for if it is not a basic service. Finally, it does not make sense either having covered the expenses of low amount, where the mere costs of producing and managing the insurance are already superior to the proper amount to cover (for example, if a medicine to be taken only one time costs three euros, it is not logical to establish an insurance bigger than this price to reduce its risk), as what occurred with the proposition of medicines co-payment from the Spanish Health Minister, for jubilees with rents higher than 100,000 euros per year[168].

In this case the common sense seems to indicate that the smaller amount of the medical expenses of a person there would be covered with its personal savings, except those overloaded or crucial expenses (this is, those that do not depend on the individual, or very serious illnesses than won't be able to be paid off by the mean average wage) of high amount

---

167 https://www.drugwatch.com/2015/10/07/cost-of-cancer/

168 http://politica.elpais.com/politica/2017/01/09/actualidad/1483967577_767121.html

and that they do not affect to the set of the society, which would be supported by a few insurances where every individual would pay a quote linked at its level of risk: this person would cover, also, not only the current risk of developing chronical illnesses of high cost but also the risk that our future population increases the rate of developing these viruses. Finally, the medical needs of people with insufficient savings would be covered in an indeterminate amount by the donations of third people through a capitalized fund, or by the State in a unique type of fund for health care, independently on rent levels.

So far, I have exposed how the sanitary demand would be organized most likely in the absence of State influences. The offer, obviously, would tend to fit the needs of the population's demand: those illnesses endured by a major number of people would receive a major expense quantity and, consequently, they would monopolize a major capitalized fund for its prevention and treatment. The investment in capital assets and in investigation would tend to improve the capacity of diagnosis and of treatment of the different medical situations, reducing their average cost and extending their availability for the public sector, as this will be done through economies of scale, that will be obtained due to competition in the health care market, providing a more efficient service, and at a lower price (in a way similar to how it has happened historically with tuberculosis, cholera, malaria or the polio), what in turn would allow to be directing the resources for the resolution of other illnesses and, in general, to increase the life expectancy of the citizens, in consequence of higher living standards, as for example in the US, having no public healthcare but a life expectancy of 78.8 years[169], in contrast to China, having a State-financed health system, but a life expectancy of 76.1 years[170].

Nevertheless, and against what would turn out to be foreseeable, the average sanitary expense per person has not stopped increasing throughout the last fifty years, in Spain, and nobody has been worried about reducing it; even in the General State Budgets. Partly, clearly, because the societies have become richer and have chosen to destine a major percentage of their revenue to the health. But, even considering this factor, the cost of the health system has increased substantially in all the developed countries and the future previews, how as countries start to develop, increase taxes and fees to be able to raise public expenditure to provide many services, that could be managed in a much more efficient way, reducing costs and consequently fiscal charge on their citizens. This won't allow only for an increase in aggregate demand levels in the economy, generating a higher economic growth, but it will also permit citizens to improve those services offered by the State, using their own personal income, and as a private and not imposed choice.

---

[169] http://www.worldlifeexpectancy.com/usa/life-expectancy

[170]https://en.wikipedia.org/wiki/List_of_countries_by_life_expectancy#List_by_the_World_Health_Organization_.282015.29

COMPARISON OF PUBLIC EXPENDITURE IN HEALTHCARE OF DIFFERENT COUNTRIES:

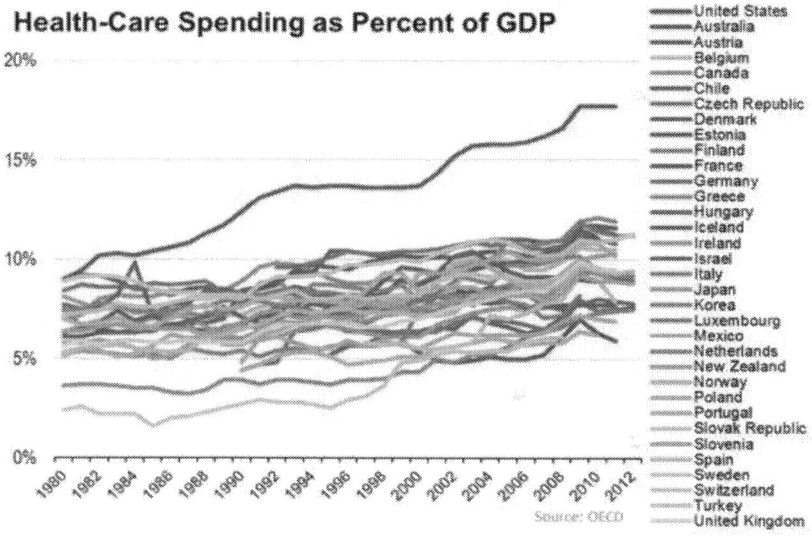

Although, as it was already happening with the education or the R+D, the expense of health looks like slightly upper in rising over the years, but seen as positive by the different States, which think that is convenient to increase it without limit, already we exhibited in its moment that the expansion of a sector takes place at the cost of others and, therefore, to increase healthcare without a formal reason and without a limit, shows that we are supposed to remain without any national income for the rest of services. Although the health is a good or service that the human beings employ in large numbers, it is not the only good that they want to enjoy or take advantage of: they also expect to receive free food in some cases, to be educated, to dress themselves, to buy a house, to travel, to enjoy themselves, to communicate, etc. This is known as the basic economic problem and theorem, as the population's needs and wants are unlimited but the resources (even private or public) are finite, which in many occasions produces scarcity. There must be, then, a balance between the different economic sectors that the State answers to the relative needs of the citizens. It is precisely for the previous thing, therefore, the boom of sanitary expense in the United States turns out to be so worrying: because if it continues in this way, in the end the society scarcely will be able to consume little more than sanitary services, as it is a society based historically on liberal and capitalist basis, and not used to high public expenditure, as we have been able to see with Spanish expenditure in public health care, which rose from 2.01% of the total GDP in 1970 to nearly 6.3% of GDP in the year 2015[171], taking into account the GDP increases and the variations in population.

Being necessary that the sanitary expense (like any other expense) rations and does not tend to increase without limits, the question happens to be: who must ration it? In the case of not having taken control of the State in the economy, already we have seen that the manager of rationing would be the proper patient or client in case of the private sector: he would choose what sanitary services he wants to consume and in what quantity. In Europe, since we will see next, in general, the State rations it across different mechanisms. But: what about the United States? The problem of the United States is that the sanitary expense is not rationed

[171] http://www.datosmacro.com/estado/gasto/salud/espana

by anybody so that the expected happens: that the expense goes off, and people have health scarcity in some cases. We can generate an idea of ourselves: according to the OECD, only 10 percent of all the sanitary expenses of the country are supported straight by the client (other 90 percent are paid by the State or the insurance companies)[172]; a percentage even lower than that of other countries with a predominant public sanitary system as Spain, where this number (of private expense in the health system) promotes 20 percent of the whole expense in healthcare[173], being in the mean of the OECD. In other words, an American can gain access to sanitary services valued at 100 dollars paying only 10 dollars by his pocket, something that obviously over dimensions the sanitary demand, due to greater competition in this sector.

As we were saying, other third payers pay 90 dollars: 45 the government and 45 the insurance companies. The government might ration its expense by means of the budgetary control, but in practice it does not do it: the Medicare (public sanitary insurance for elders) and the Medicaid (public sanitary insurance for people with low revenues), in the USA, it is more than twice its weight on the GDP, happening from 2 percent at the beginning of 1980 to 7 percent at present[174].

In turn, the insurance companies might ration their expense, by having to increase dramatically the consumer's quotes, that there pay the clients and not the State in any occasion (if an insurance covers too many services and its demand rises in excess, they will put up prices, its clients would begin to leave it and to look for other more accessible insurances).

[172] https://www.oecd.org/els/soc/OECD2014-Social-Expenditure-Update-Nov2014-8pages.pdf
[173] https://www.fundacionidis.com/wp-content/ponencia_manuel_vilches_director_general_de_idis.pdf
[174] https://www.oecd.org/health/health-systems/Focus-Health-Spending-2015.pdf

The obstacle so that the insurers ration their expense in the United States is that in 85 percent of the cases they are not the proper beneficiaries of the insurance who hire it, but their employees; that is to say, only 15 percent of the Americans with private insurance have hired it themselves and not across their company[175].

This enormous slant in favor of the sanitary insurances supported by the company does not seem to have internal logic too much since it does not happen with any other insurance. Except for causalities, it is not common that the companies take charge of the life insurance, of the insurance of the heart or of the insurance of motorcar or house. It has much more been common that the companies pay the salary entirely in cash to its working people (and that then these decide if they want to hire an insurance and what insurance to hire) instead of that a part of this salary should recover in part (in the form of public attached sanitary insurance). If in the United States it does not happen this way it is because, from 1943, the expense in sanitary insurances paid across the enterprise is free of tax. Bearing in mind that the marginal tax type of most of the American working people (counting IRPF and Social security) ranges concerning 35-40 percent[176], it is obvious that it is interesting for the working people to canalize "all" its sanitary expenses across an insurance supported for its businessman: if they incur straight a sanitary payment or hire a sanitary insurance themselves, the cost after taxes doubles. For example, if an American receives 5.000 monthly gross dollars and wants to make himself an operation that costs 10.000 dollars, he will need four months of clear salary (2.500 dollars) to finance it, but he will

[175] https://www.ssa.gov/policy/docs/ssb/v28n12/v28n12p3.pdf
[176] https://www.irs.com/articles/projected-us-tax-rates-2016

only need two months of gross salary (canalized across the insurances acquired by the company) to face it.

The American fiscal norms, consequently, have encouraged a distribution of the sanitary expense much differentiated to the one that would have prevailed on a free market and have sowed (together with the expansion without limit of the Medicaid) the seeds for the explosion of the sanitary expense in the country: the Americans can consume sanitary services which costs outsource to third people, inflating the global price, and generating inflation in the private sanitary system. It is as if a very wide group of friends was deciding to go to have dinner and distribute proportionally the cost of the meal with independence of how much each one consumes: the foreseeable result is that individually they would demand all more meal that if each of them had to finance the one that it consumes, and finally the ones consuming more will benefit, but the conservative ones will lose money through this operation, just as it happens with the unnecessary expenses in some facets of public health.

The previous reasoning might turn submitted to a quite common objection: for many perverse incentives on the demand that generates the insurances system, the sanitary expense of the population would not have to go off incredibly; after all, the medical needs of the Americans depend on the deterioration of health that they experience and it does not seem that the citizens are going to fall sick, and by the way to be able to make a more intensive use of the sanitary services.

The criticism would have a certain sense if, in fact, the demand for sanitary services only was dependent on the quantity of sanitary services of not crucial character that the patient receives. But there exist another three characteristics understood in the demand for sanitary services and that have been the determinants of its strong increase: the quantity of "preventive" sanitary services, the quality of the sanitary services and the facility with which these sanitary services are provided. The facility and the quality of the sanitary services do not need of many explanations: by quality of the sanitary service there is understood the treatment and diversity of medical specialists as well as the early adoption of the last technologies; in the offered facility rubric it is necessary to include all the not essential elements for the service of medical care but that turn it is more acceptable for the patient (number and closeness of ambulatory and hospitals, size of the rooms, equipment of the rooms, etc.). Obviously, when the citizen does not support straight the cost of these two dimensions of the sanitary demand, his preferences pass by increasing the quality and the service "with the independence of its cost." And, in effect, the United States is one of the countries with less number of medical general doctors as regards the most expensive medical specialists (only 12 percent of its medical population are a general practitioner[177], opposite to 50 percent of France or 30 percent of the United Kingdom[178]) and the country of the world where more quickly the last technologies are adopted.

A deeper explanation will be useful to present the variable of the quantity of preventive services. To understand why this part of the sanitary services turns out to be quite volatile at the price, it is enough to wonder the following thing: what is the previewing frequency, is it a scanner which is realized computerized, a mammography, a colonoscopy

[177] https://www.statista.com/topics/1244/physicians/

[178] http://www.gmc-uk.org/doctors/register/search_stats.asp

or a magnetic resonance with the intention of locating preventively any illness or structural defect? Every five years? Every year? Every half a year? It's impossible to determine it in an universal way. Of course, there exist guidelines recommended by the sanitary personnel for the average patient, since the preventive medicine also transports risks that must be considered (fundamentally, the false alarms: that is to say, the erroneous illnesses detection). But the question is that it should be every person who, after receiving the corresponding specialized counsels, was confronting the risks and the benefits of the preventive examinations and was proceeding to choose the intensity of treatment that he considers being ideal for his particular case. Now then, precisely for the previous thing, also it should be every patient who chooses to pass through a preventive examination, the one who supports the cost of these tests. If the patient is capable of stand for this cost on third — across the insurance — the global increment of the private expense into the sanitary market can be very considerable.

In sum, the socialization of the sanitary costs across the public and private insurances has incremented a type of sanitary demand especially expensive: the demand for services which are not crucial or preventive. A demand that, in more deepness, is quite insensitive to rise in prices, as the goods and services offered are demand and income inelastic: although the providers increase their tariff (with the intention not only of increasing their benefits but also of paying increasing wages to the sanitary personnel and of being capable of providing the last sanitary technologies at any cost), the demand does not shrink substantially. It is difficult in this context to understand what the competition in the private healthcare market produces: although the prices increase it gives place to an increase of the supply of sanitary services, the demand for the same ones grows even more rapid with independence what its price is, which makes revenues and income of firms in this sector increment rapidly over time.

It is necessary to bear in mind that, also, this potentially unlimited demand collides with a sanitary offer that, despite it is more liberalized than in most of Europe, remains submitted to very important restrictions that limit the competition between suppliers: in reference, very especially, to the State obligation of which the providers of sanitary services are provided with a medical license— granted by the proper professional schools of doctors, which are mainly located in universities— even to be able to give not medical services as it happens with the matrons, the nurses or the surgery. There are, therefore, the proper medical associations those who, as it would make any lobby worried for protecting the interests of its members, just as trade unions do, decide who and in what conditions can exercise the profession, independently of their knowledge or their skills, being constituted in fact as an oligopoly, which reduces competition in the market and brings productivity and efficiency down.

The consequence of this artificial regulative restriction of the offer before an explosive variation in demand is translated in that the wages and the benefits of the American sanitary sector are substantially superior to those who coexist in the rest of the world: in particular, and according to the report of the consultant McKinsey, the average wages of the general medical doctors in the USA are 46 percent[179] superior to those of the average of the OCDE (correcting the revenue differences per capita

[179] http://money.cnn.com/2016/01/27/pf/jobs/doctors-pay/

between countries) and those of the specialists 66 percent; in turn, the gross profit margins before interests go so far as to reach 35 percent in case of the ambulatory ones.

This sanitary over cost derived from the socialization; by the public sector, of the demand and of the restrictions of the offer is the one that generates, also, other well-known failures of the American sanitary system, very especially its economic inaccessibility for those individuals of low revenue. Although it is true that big part of the people without insurance are living under this situation for voluntary decision (young people with good health or people of high revenue who auto-insure themselves with their saving), there exists another important portion that lacks insurance for not being provided with a job, and most importantly if that insurance is public, and does not allow you to decide on the services coverage or the participation quote; there even exist people who see their sanitary coverage being in danger after losing their employs. Obviously, nothing of that would happen if the insurance policies were of an amount much more reduced, so prices of sanitary services fell, making the public-sector health unnecessary, and generating a healthcare allocative efficiency for the mean of the population (this can also be taken into account by private insurance) , which shows that a country can have the most accessible health, providing just the most essential sanitary services publicly; and only if the private market price of them exceeds enormously the mean wage rate or if the situation is of vital importance.

In sum, the sanitary system of the United States combines a limited freedom in the offer of sanitary services with a socialized and practically unlimited demand for the same ones (as much for the deprived insurance as well for the sanitary public expenditure).

The technical opposition of both factors has provoked what it would be necessary to preview taking account on the most basic economic theory: an explosion of the demand and of the prices. This implies that, even if the American sanitary system is partly deprived into establishment (let's not forget that 45 percent of the sanitary expenses in the USA are public, compared to 80% in most European countries), and what really differs its system of the one that would have declined in absence of the intervention of the State. Consequently, and not close from refuting a model of the effects of the private health, it will be necessary to consider the USA to be an example of the variable factors and its consequences of a certain type of State interventionism on the market like the sanitary one.

In Europe, the governments have made teal interest and intervention into quotes and restricted and controlled much of the sanitary expense of the society. Whenever during this crisis the sanitary cuts have been criticized, but it would be convenient to remember that the philosophy of the restriction of the sanitary expense is the basic characteristic of the different models of European healthcare: no European government has ever granted a blank check to its citizens so that they demand any quantity of sanitary services. Therefore, the predominant note of the European health is the repression and the bureaucratic expenditure of the civil diversification in health.

The essential difference between the American model of the European sanitary model is not the nationality, but in the European model, the governments have managed to establish the totally of the submission of the autonomy of its citizens to demand sanitary services. These have ended up by submitting to the closed menu of services that offer them, directly or by implication, the politicians. It is true that in Europe a universal and free access exists, but the consumption options are limited. Said in other words: in the United States, the citizen with insurance can choose to what hospital to go and what treatment to consume with the independence of its price; in Europe, the citizen can only go to that remedial center and take that service that the government indicates him.

Two mechanisms that the European governments have used to eliminate and to control the demand for sanitary services of its population have been the model of public health and the model of obligatory insurances taken control by the State, even though the major part of this insurances are private. The public health model is originally English; the much more modern one is Spanish: the State collects taxes, finances with them a sanitary system managed by the State where the providers are linked to the State, and recognizes a universal access to its citizens in the terms ruled by the State. The model of obligatory mutuality is German, the Dutch and, with certain peculiarities, but is also used by many French autonomies: the citizen is forced to spend a fixed part of its salary on hiring a mutuality to its election, which reaches up to cover the derivative payments of coming to the diverse medical general practitioners and private specialists that he needs, which even though still reflects State interventionism is better than the Spanish public health system.

Deeply, two European models have ended up looking sufficiently good enough: in exchange for the only obligatory tariff (taxes or insurance policy) the citizen enjoys free access (except certain copayments, as the dentist) to a letter of sanitary services regulated and enclose by the State. The differences between both systems are merely procedural and structural, not of the economical fund. It is a common target to reduce the autonomous demand of sanitary services of the citizen and to force him, so he submits to the conditions of sanitary provision of the State, given that it is assumed that the citizen is not financially prepared and cannot manage by himself his own health.

The deprivation of the European States at the time of suppressing the sanitary demand is so high that they even have chosen to censure the freedom of expression on the subject of medicines advertisement : the publicity of medicines subject to medical recipe is prohibited inside the European Union so that the citizens are not conscious of the different medical alternatives at their disposal, managing so the Ministry of Health could determine at his pleasure the medicines really provided by the public system of health. In other words, instead of allowing the patient to carry his own calculation cost - benefit out (is it convenient for me to pay more for a medicine just something better than a different one but cheaper?), the State says to carry it out in our place and imposes it on us with the intention of losing the price of its own costs, but forcing us to buy the chosen medicine and at a price set completely by them, not allowing for the opportunity cost.

In this sense, it is not necessary to doubt that the governmental restriction of the sanitary expense can be an effective mechanism to control its total expense, but on the other hand, reaching it at the cost of very excellent negative externalities for the population. The first one of them is the incorrect satisfaction of the demand, known mainly as market failure.

NUMBER OF AFFILIATES TO THE SOCIAL SECURITY IN SPAIN:

When it is not the consumer the one that reveals his preferences choosing on the market and when, consequently, the remuneration of the provider does not depend on the likes and tastes of goods that the consumer has chosen as his priorities, the services that offer him to this one do not have to meet by no means with his needs: not in terms of quantity of services, not neither of their quality, nor of their linked provision.

Probably, the most exuberant sign of that supposedly universal and free European sanitary systems do not provide a concrete with the totality of the needs of their citizens which is the important weight that in all the European countries keep on having the expense deprived in health: close to the fourth one part of its entire sanitary expense. Let's remember that in the United States this percentage was promoting 54 percent in the year 2010[180], which produced it to be slightly more of the double that the European average but, in any case, not a difference up to a greater point as to consider its completely private health and completely public financing paid off by taxpayers, or in greater motives by private banks.

The significant presence of the private sanitary expense reveals that a considerable part of the population does not see its specific sanitary needs covered inside the public system, and asks for an expansion of supply in the market. And it does not seem to be covering in three fronts that previously we have mentioned: quantity, quality, and service.

As for the quantity, the European public systems have turned out to be forced to limit the number of sanitary services of that their citizens can make use. At last, the health to cost zero (or) for the user generates at a low cost a level capable of supplying this demand to cost zero (if they were doing it, their sanitary expenses would go off). As a result of an offer lower than the demand, it becomes necessary to arbitrate mechanisms of rationing of the offer, taking it from different points that are not the price: a few mechanisms of rationing that can be beforehand or at a later stage employed by the government in the supplying of other public services.

Inside the first group — the rationing beforehand — there are those treatments that the public health does not cover or that covers only in a very restricted way: for example, in Spain the public health does not cover

[180] https://www.cdc.gov/mmwr/preview/mmwrhtml/su6103a2.htm

the attention of dental services and only in a way subject to quotes way through the preventive detection of three types of cancer (the breast cancer sifted one only once every two years and for women of between fifty and sixty-nine years; that of cancer of colon, once every two years for people between fifty and sixty-nine years; and of cervix, only every three years, per 100 people into the modal class), let's remember that one of the factors that were contributing to a greater extent to the superior hyper-regulation of the sanitary expenses in the United States was the very intensive use of the preventive medicine, so limited in case of Spain and other sanitary systems rationed by the State. Also, it is necessary to include inside this group of rationing mechanisms from the sanitary expense to the copayments. The copayment supposes doing the patient a tool of coverage for the cost of its treatment, along with the State, with the target to reduce its demand for sanitary services to cost zero; although it is not very much extended in Spain (only fond of the medicines), and only proposed by Ciudadanos, while in the European sanitary systems it has a much wider presence in all the senses: for example, in Germany, the hospitalization transports have copayment for 10 more daily euros[181], and 10 percent of the entire cost of tests and treatments; in Belgium and France, the copayment in primary health care, specialists and urgencies ranges, for most of the population, between 30 percent and 40[182] percent of the entire cost for most of the population; in Norway, the patient must cover 20 percent of the cost of the hospitalization[183], the totality of the price of the essential medicines (up to a maximum for 200 euros per year) and 38 percent of not essential medicines (up to a maximum for 270 euros

---

[181] http://ftp.iza.org/dp2290.pdf
[182] http://www.lse.ac.uk/LSEHealthAndSocialCare/pdf/eurohealth/VOL14No1/Durand-Zaleski.pdf
[183] http://international.commonwealthfund.org/countries/norway/

per year); and in Sweden the primary health care, the specialists and the first aid services have a cost of between 10 and 40 euros as visit[184], which overall allows the government to reduce taxes for higher citizens freedom and a more diversified sanitary system.

Inside the second group — the rationing at a later stage — the waiting lists are overcrowded in the public sector, that is to say, the rationing across derivates: as the demand overcomes the offer, part of the demand remains temporarily without coverage. According to the Spanish Ministry of Health, the waiting lists for specialties in Spain were in mean in 2012 a hundred days, this is, almost three months and a half. In some cases, like the neurosurgery or the digestive surgery, the waiting overcomes 150 days; but even in the vital cardiac surgery, the waiting lists exceed two months. The same rule recurs in other European systems, with the exception of German or the Belgium (whose waiting time they are similar to those of the United States, thanks to their biggest flexibility and decentralization of the offer of sanitary providers). In fact, the Euro Health Consumer Index[185] disapproves Spain, Italy, the United Kingdom, Sweden or Norway when it comes to times of waiting and accessibility to the medicine. Let's remember that the evidence points that the duration and expense of the waiting lists increases significantly the risk of mortality of the patients, so that this rationing of the expense is not a simple temporary inconvenience, but a critical element at the time of guaranteeing the effective access to the health of the population, which much better diversified and solved in the private sector.

---

[184] https://www.ncbi.nlm.nih.gov/pubmed/27477892
[185] http://www.healthpowerhouse.com/files/EHCI_2016/EHCI_2016_report.pdf

Nevertheless, the big problem of the public health is not its inadequate satisfaction of the demand of the patients, but its incapability to impel the technological innovation and of institutional models in relation to the priorities of the patients. Let's not forget that the public health not only restricts the present health demand, but also it plans its present offer and, what is worse, future offer, without having knowledge of any budget, income, private capabilities and facilities or even expenditure plans. It is the State who in a centralized way determines what illnesses will be attended and of what way they will be: it is more, it is the State who determines what lines of sanitary investigation it turns out to be priority to develop at present to attend to the sanitary needs for tomorrow, as it decides on the laboratories what investigations to carry on in relation to healthcare, and in many occasions without the crucial opinion of an expert in the theme.

On a free sanitary market, it would be ultimately the patients who, demanding and promoting the different treatments and different organization models, would determine where the investment flows and what is the most efficient way of providing the medical services. The entrepreneurs of the sector would present themselves to the government with different prices, although as the combinations of quantity / quality / facility and velocity of service of the healthcare, and the patients would choose (straight or with external consultancy), or even the government if it is the one who provides the services, even if managed by the private sector, in a way which they consider more efficient. In a totally public system, where the State determines in a mandatory way how the sanitary service is provided, similar schedules and decentralized experimentation are simply impossible, so much on the subject of innovation as institutional models. And the fact is that the State massive bureaucracy lack the information and the necessary incentives to alter significantly the way in which they have been giving the sanitary services: it is of general interest, for not being submitted to the pressure of the competition and to the mandate over the decision of the user, which is of minimizing his workload and of maximizing his remuneration at the cost of the taxpayer, not of improving the quality of the service to the benefit of the patient.

Just like we saw already, a sanitary system that had developed without the interference of the State is very improbable that had continued the course of the United States: the private and established insurance of the medical expenses has not too much sense from an economic and actual point of view. After all, both the American system and the European systems of health have ended up by being sanitary share-out systems (pay-as-you-go): most of sanitary expenses are materializing the same way as the person ages (with the important exception of the chronic patients), so that it is the healthy young people those who, across the payment of taxes or the insurance policies of the population (model of the United States), cover the expenses of the current users in exchange for the fact that the future young generations do the proper thing. The problems of the system of share-out of health are the same than in the case of the pensions: we need capitalization for social expenditure to cover the future payments. Hence it turned out to be necessary to go on to a system of capitalization of health, where it is the individual saving the one that covers most of the sanitary expenses, while the capitalized reserves of the insurance companies cover the cost of the catastrophic and chronic illnesses of a few insured people who have been paying along their lives a few higher quotes that reflect its real risk, as the higher frequency of illness the greater the price of the insurance, to be able to cover the expenses.

At present, we are not provided with examples of developed countries where the State has not ended up by controlling whole or partially the health, so it is complicated to offer evidence of the better functioning of the capitalization system. Nevertheless, there exist two countries where the health comes closer to a system of the free market (this are, countries where a good part of the sanitary expense not only is essential, but it is controlled by the patient and not by the insurer): as for example, Switzerland and, especially, Singapore.

In Switzerland, almost 40 percent of the whole sanitary expenses are for essential services through taxes[186] (the rest of the expense is directed to cover the basic and obligatory private insurance policy that the government imposes) and, in contrast to the United States, the three-quarters of parts of this expense are purely private and come from the money saving and investment of every patient and not of companies of insurance. The Swiss health system is very similar to German but with a smaller grade of State interventionism and major grade of administrative competition: the Swiss have an obligation to hire a basic sanitary, private insurance of between the different mutuality, which enjoy freedom to fix the insurance policy as the risks linked to the patient; on this obligatory sanitary insurance, there can be hired voluntary insurances that increase the sanitary coverage, just as simple as the car insurance works. The State intervenes in the market fixing through the minimal coverage of the obligatory insurance, financing and managing most of the hospitals,

[186] http://www.swedishhealthcare.com/about-sweden-and-swedish-healthcare/swedens-healthcare-system/

subsidizing the insurances and redistributing the benefits of the insurers according to the biggest cost of its consumers. The essential difference with the German model is that this redistribution of the benefits of the insurers is much more independent from the State and, therefore, the insurance companies can operate in many major ways like insurers of risks and not like provider of public services, paid off the contributions of the citizens, as their real benefit comes from extra coverage services hired by the citizens.

The expense of health of Switzerland represents entirely 10 percent of the GDP[187], in line with other European nations with the same revenue per capita that, nevertheless, have had to reduce their authority and independent mandate over the health care, and attend to a greater extend the demand of its citizens. Particularly the Swiss model — more similar to the one that would prevail in a free market that none of those that we have analyzed previously — joins the advantages of the American model and of the European States models: flexibility and adaptability of the offer depending on the demand of the citizens (waiting-lists prevail in absence and incorporation of the last and best technologies) and moderation of the costs. Nevertheless, even in Switzerland the State has been intervening increasingly in the health, bringing closer its system over to the German one.

Despite the merits of the sanitary free market, immense most of the population and good part of great economists keep on pushing it back for diverse motives. Perhaps the most popular are also the least relevancy: that the healthcare cannot be a business with which profit as an incentive.

---

[187] http://data.worldbank.org/indicator/SH.XPD.PUBL.ZS?locations=SE

In this sense, it is common to think that the health care cannot be controlled by an entrepreneur, and that by rule a businessman is only worried by the money that will provide and will tend to be much more deficient and expensive than the one that provides a tight fiscal pressure and managed by a responsible public sector: after all, the margin of benefits that the businessman adds to the costs has, out of necessity, to increase the final price of the product and, also, it will turn out to be seen very discouraged from him to reduce the offer of service to maximize his profit.

The reality, yet, is quite different. An entrepreneur obtains extraordinary benefits on the laid-down capital when the service that it provides is cheaper or of major quality than that of the competition, which is called differentiation factor: in the opposite case, the only yield that obtains is the linked one to the opportunity cost of the capital employed (that, although it is not taken into account, is also present in the State health); if a firm was lowering the quality of its service without reductions in its price, the citizens simply would change provider. The sanitary competition in the frame of a free market, consequently, tends to achieve a better service at a lower price and it is not a contradiction. Probably, most of people who affirm this opinion based on its erroneous perception on the false privatization of the health that takes place when it is overloaded the management of the State health to a private company: as they are the politicians who transfer to a few entrepreneurs; chosen by them, the money previously obtained from its citizens — and those who should be able decide what hospitals they will like to go — the risk that the company disturbs the quality to maximize profit is existent; but it is less probable, given that the revenue of the citizen keeps on being administered by the politicians and not to the proper individual, this is, because it is not a question of a free and competitive market but of the State of Well-being taken to a larger extent to companies.

Finally, referring as an example an average sanitary expense for Spanish of between 1.500 and 2.000 euros per year, a person would be completely insured if it was destining a third of this amount (between 500 and 667 euros) to cover the sanitary expenses of its current year through an insurance company, and not managed by the State in a share-out system, another third to be saved to face the future increase of its sanitary expenses and another third to insure itself against the risk of the deterioration of its health not linked at the age. In fact, it is probable that it was with much less, attending on the important reductions of sanitary costs at which we would be present in the absence of State regulations on offer. Also, those few citizens who could not face to these amounts after having eliminated almost all the taxes might receive the support of the private or State social work, providing everyone with a cheap, fast, efficient, high quality and private healthcare.

Reasons of weight do not exist, therefore, to assume that a planned and centralized sanitary system in a centralized way guarantees a wider access and of major quality to the sanitary services than one private and liberalized. Moreover, there exist deeply studied motives for thinking that it will be just the other way around: that a sanitary free market system will overcome in all the basic and technic aspects than one handled by the State in a totalitarian way.

The unique possible solution for a private healthcare system, where everyone is equally covered and where scarcity would not be present is through private insurances. The State should finance the private medical insurances of those sectors of the population at risk of poverty, while the rest of coverages should be privately financed. In addition, all public hospitals would be privatized, increasing the efficiency of its management, and reducing costs of production and consequently the prices of treatments due to larger competition in the sector. Everyone covered. Equally and freer. And with a reduced presence of the State.

13- YES! SOCIAL ASSISTANCE IS POSSIBLE IN A PURE MARKET ECONOMY

The future is uncertain in any society. But in those more dynamic and free societies, as they are capable of experiencing more fast and continuous changes, it is still more. The human being thinks about how to be protected in contrast to the uncertain and, for it, the same free societies offer it the whole series of economic policy instruments and social institutions. Between the first one's society emphasizes the saving and the insurances: to have a wide patrimony allows to accelerate and facilitate the revenue fluctuations and hire an insurance, allowing for socializing voluntarily the risks that affect a nation, as health, education or social welfare, representing in Spain a 24.6% of expenditure over GDP[188]. Between the second ones, it points out, especially, the familiar institution: the family is a small effective and juridical association where the revenue is consumed and redistributed in a communal way. A good part of the situations which can make a society fill impotent and without a defense that can emerge in a free society they are, therefore, changeable across the saving, the insurances, and the family investment. Nevertheless, there

[188] https://stats.oecd.org/Index.aspx?DataSetCode=SOCX_AGG

are good motives for thinking that the people we look for a level of top protection that comes out of the three previous mechanisms.

For fortune, the human being is an extremely social particular; he needs to live in society and enjoys being related to other human beings: the society brings him, on the one hand, safety opposite to a dangerous and harsh environment (" Stronger together") and, for other, affectivity. The union and preservation of the society, consequently, is essential for the human being, hence through evolution he has developed emotions that lead him to not worrying only for his particular well-being, but also for that of his environment: every human being has one, even if it is greater or less, an inclination to protect his society and to hope that his partners should protect him in difficult social.

In this sense, it is logical that the individuals are interested in that the society as a whole in which we live, to be provided with the institutions adapted to help those people in a transition project or structurally to fall down in a need situation: in the same way in that it is logical to worry why the provision of food, of electricity or of health is scarce sometimes. Also it is to worry for the social work provision. Deeply, it calms us down and encourages us to know that the other citizens ae not going to suffer or are not going to endure a life filled up with circumstances exempt to its control but partially inside ours; it is more, it makes us tranquil to know that the rest of people will not allow either to happen to us, which is called social welfare, which is merely based on the principle of solidarity. And, for it, the social work is a service more normal for which any society protects and promotes.

Different question, clearly, is the fact that the social work should be managed by the State by means of the compelling redistribution of the revenue, but which is a clear topic lie, as the Gini Index showed a reduced from 36.22 in 2005 to 32.57 points in the UK[189]in 2013, in one of the most free-market ruled societies of Europe. In effect, to today it is very habitual to affirm that on a free market there would not be a redistribution of the revenue, being such a competition instead of a proper monopoly of the State authority. The correct thing, nevertheless, is to affirm that on a completely free market there would not be "ambiguous" redistribution of the revenue since the voluntary redistributions (the mutual help, the charity or the voluntary action) would be completely legal and frequent. The definite question, consequently, is what role the State must play in this sector... if it is that it must play any.

The social work demand on the part of an individual answers to two different targets that, in turn, will give place to two different social work forms: on the one hand, an individual demands social work to be protected himself from the future unknown events(it encourages him to know that there is a safety network behind him that will help him in case of need); on the other hand, an individual demands social work to protect his environment of the future suspense (it encourages him to know that the others will not suffer). Obviously, not all the individuals worry the same way about their own safety or for that of their partners, but in a general norm, and excepting the extraordinarily delinquent people, we all possess both emotions in a greater or less grade. Now then, since the social work demand presents diversified purposes — to guarantee your own safety and to guarantee the foreign safety — the necessary

[189] http://data.worldbank.org/indicator/SI.POV.GINI?end=2014&locations=GB&start=1981&view=chart

organization to satisfy both social acre forms also will adopt two different forms.

When the individual tries to safeguard his safety, he will want the help that possibly could need does not depend on the will of anybody: his intention is of keeping on being autonomous in spite of the adverse circumstances that could have affected him. Little would satisfy us a social work that simply was moving us from a situation of being with no defense to be induced by unforeseeable adverse circumstances to another situation of impotence induced by the dependence on the unforeseeable optional will of the third. And so, this type of social work — the one that answers to our demand for personal protection — needs of horizontal structures based on the reciprocity (give and receive) and in the irrefutable action of the help. Its paradigm there would be the societies of mutual help, in contrast to tax-supported societies, as for example in Finland, where public expenditure overcomes 58% of the GDP[190].

When, on the other hand, the individual thinks about how to safeguard the safety of his partners, he will want to maintain a certain control on the help that he wants to deliver him. Precisely because we want to keep on being autonomous, we prefer to be able to modulate great or small help that, in the shape of time and resources, we grant the others (in the end, a person who had an obligation to live exclusively for the others help would be a slave, or at least very obnoxious). And so, this type of social work — the one that answers to our demand of protecting the nearby citizens will need of vertical structures based on the independent and on the voluntary fact of the help. This demonstrates that

[190] https://data.oecd.org/gga/general-government-spending.htm

societies are based on reciprocal help to each other, without the need of the State intervention and just because of their nature.

As I have said before, every person prefers to receive a social work based on the mutual help rather than on the charity. Therefore, in the absence of the State, immense most of the social work would tend to be provided by means of societies of mutual help, based on the existence of rights and obligations which will be given and received by their members, just as some ONG's help undeveloped countries and later receive money from contributors. Between their members: that person that a society of mutual help was integrating would have a right to receive the help from the rest of members in case he had to face some adversity that was happening and would have an obligation to have help and assistance provided to that member who was suffering the various difficulties. It is slightly probable that this help right was unlimited, but rather it would be estimated, conditional and supervised by the articles of association of the proper society with the intention of avoiding the abuses, from people benefiting from the system or even the State. The diverse societies of mutual help might give — and, in fact, they were big enough historically (as some ONGs as UNICEF nowadays), how then we will see — help in case of illness, retirement without savings, 'widowhood, orphanage or incapability: according to the target of every society, the rights (and the consistent obligations) acquired might be more or less extensive, depending on the situation, and solidarity will always be reciprocal and never imposed by the State. UNICEF is a good example, receiving only from the US and as an example of a free society, $7,361 thousand millions in the last year[191].

Nevertheless, these estimated causes would not have to be necessarily rigid and closed: precisely because the base of any society of mutual help is the confidence and empathy among its members, the causes that would justify the assuring of solidarity among its members should be flexible and adaptatively to initially unforeseen new adversities. This flexibility or discretional nature might be appreciated by the governmental bodies of these societies that, considering its contributive nature, probably they were democratic and changeable (like the neighbors' communities, or even nations as a whole): since they all are capable of showing in some moment the responsibility of governing the society of mutual help, they all would have incentives to treat the problematic problems and discussions related to empathy and generosityy (tomorrow the governor's roles and governed might change over time). In fact, one of the advantages of the societies of mutual help opposite to the insurances would be this one: while the second ones only provide a monetary indemnification in absolutely estimated cases (since it is a question of a capitalist company which intention is to preserve the benefits for its shareholders), the societies of mutual help not only would contemplate more forms of help (not only economic, but also human, psychological or even in labor matters), but they would be more flexible with the expenses and costs of this provided solidarity. In a certain way, to belong to a society of mutual help would be a clear objective for everyone: to make sure opposite to the adversities that I could not even have foreseen.

---

[191] http://www.opensecrets.org/orgs/totals.php?id=D000058062&cycle=A

The voluntary association looks like, consequently, the ideal form so that the different individuals guarantee a network of last and supplementary safety to which they already suppose other social and economic mechanisms of facing problems or even illnesses (like, for example, the familiar institution, the accumulation of a wide personal patrimony or the already mentioned hiring of insurances). Nevertheless, it is fully unclear that was happening herself and nor combining with economic models, which tend to normally be of the same type. First because, as we have already said, many people do not only want to be protected themselves, but they want to help others too. Second, because it is necessary to imagine diverse circumstances in which the societies of mutual help are not enough to solve the fragile elements of a society from the unknown: fundamentally, there can be people that, for any motive, societies of mutual help have decided not to integrate and there can be societies of mutual help who, for any motive, are not provided with enough resources to face certain adversities. It is here where it brings in the assignment of the economic-based societies.

The charity is not the ideal form of settling the personal opposition situations since it generates the people to turn in a position of inferiority and dependence. Therefore, far from constituting the general norm inside a free society, there would be rather the exception to a serious problem that cannot be settled by any other voluntary mechanism, or even the government. On the subject of charity, it is every person the one that chooses what part of his wealth and his time he wishes to destine to help the needed that lack other assistance networks. Although a portion of this time and of these resources might be managed straight by the proper donor (informal and spontaneous helps), most likely good part of the same ones would be canalized across companies, foundations and ONG specializing in redistributing it between the neediest, mainly in government, as it forces the citizen to destine a certain amount of their taxes even to church or to social work, having more than 500 ONGs nowadays only in Spain[192].

In contrast to the societies of mutual help, the charitable societies are managed, nor financed by the proper people who donate or receive the help, so that these would lack rights on the potential donors. The base of their relations would not be a mutual confidence and the reciprocal interest, but the generosity of some and the situation of need for others. This way, once the potential donor realizes that people needed help exist and once there is offered him an effective way of channeling his generosity towards these people, it will be able to take the decision with how helping every whom: every donor will choose those agents of his life, like any economic system, who more were lining up with his values and who are more efficient, responsible and productive at the time of settling the situations of social division and differentiation, just as when you vote for a certain party for its values.

Despite the differences between the societies of mutual help and the capitalist societies, both are forms of social work that, hence, share a common target: to help the one who needs help. This shows that both institutions also share two characteristics that it is worth highlighting: on the one hand, the help would tend to go exclusively to those people who need it and who deserve it, and not to be wasted, for other, the help of

[192] http://ong.consumer.es/alfabeticamente/?PARAM[searchFromResult]=0

everyone would be faced preferably to his most nearby social environment.

As for the first one of these characteristics, it seems obvious that, almost for definition, the social work only matters to those people who need it. Also, it is clear that, in the societies of mutual help, only there receive help those members who fulfill the requisites to receive it (if the society only was constituted to cover illness risks, probably I did not accept to cover the risk of hereditary recapitalization (economic problem due to heritage task, at advanced ages). Less clear turns out to be, nevertheless, the condition of "merit" in the charitable societies.

To outline its meaning, it is necessary to highlight the distinction that many States were carrying out between needed deserving of help (deserving poor) and needed not deserving of help (odd number of population- deserving poor): only those poor that could not work for personal incapability or for adverse economic conditions were having a right to take refuge in the State aid (it was not the case of those that, being able to work, were deciding not to do it on purpose and persistently). It seems credible that similar distinction was also prevailing between the donors of their time and their resources to the charity. After all, a person who is poor because deliberately he refuses to work — even if he has opportunities and capacities for it — probably does not deserve to receive any foreign assistance. There are rather people like the incapacitated or decapacitated permanent ones, the orphans or the elders without enough capital for some uncontrollable catastrophe who would be the main recipients of the private social help in the capital based society. The motive is slightly questionable: if the help is granted indiscriminately to those who do not deserve it, not only there diminishes the quantity of assistance available for those who really and purely deserve it, but also their multiplies the temptation of generating parasitic relations (to simulate need to live at the cost of the others), which really happens with the Universal Guaranteed Rent. The same happens, in fact, in the deep fund of this institution, called the State, which constitutes the most basic form of social work: the family. The parents are of course ready to maintain their son while this one is unable to find employment (deserving of help), but it is doubtful they would want to finance his expenses indefinitely even if this one pushes back from work alleging every time for vacancies (not deserving the help). It happens that the distinction between deserving and not deserving help people is replete with confusing areas and definitions. Are deserving of help a drug addict to whom his own addiction has led him to find himself without wanting to work, an elder who founds the savings of the whole life in the casino and then regrets of having done it, a young man who left early his education and does not find an employment or an adult who pushes back to hire a sanitary insurance, just to save ridiculously, and who suddenly suffers a serious and very expensive illness diagnose? Certainly, every reader will answer in a different way before each of these situations, but a common feature should be recognized: universalize the help without any type of control would encourage its abuse (for example, nobody would hire sanitary insurances) and refuse it in all the cases would give place to many situations of defenselessness that most of the citizens would reject.

The only possible solution is on an intermediate route, particularly, to allow every person who donates his money to the promotion of new business and independent institutions, to be able to choose whom to help and in what conditions to do it: it might to the drug addict demand to surrender to a detoxification program and to be precise actively I won't; or the ludopat might limit the elder the assistance to a minimum of subsistence, as the money is used to prevent him from playing in casinos; or to be used for the young man who left early the studies to be used for him and to promote that it completes his formation; and to the adult without sanitary insurance, which restores in the future a substantial part of the cost of his treatment, which will be paid by taxes in future quotes.

The second common characteristic to all form of social work — the help would be faced with the nearby environment of the one who gives it — it turns out to be quite understandable in case of the societies of mutual help: every member is only forced to give help to other members of the society, mainly through the form of tax, as in the Spanish rent, where we donate 1.4% of our taxes to social and charitable actions[193], therefore the time and the resources that he invests in society will result exclusively for the benefit of those who shape it (and let's remember that the affiliation to these societies of mutual help was not restrictive, but determined to fulfill the requisites that the proper group was imposing for the unique objective of maintaining the internal harmony). As for the charitable societies, it should not also be complicated to understand why the capitalization would be regulated to a great extent by this social principle: even if we could believe that we feel a deep love towards the humanity in its whole set, the people we want to benefit especially from the suffering that we contemplate around us, so that we are reduced and forced to solve these problems preferably. It is true that, in a regulated

193 http://www.agenciatributaria.es/static_files/AEAT/Contenidos_Comunes/La_Agencia_Tributaria/Modelos_y_formularios/Declaraciones/Modelos_100_al_199/151/M_151_Instrucciones.pdf

and authoritarian world, more and more people feel citizens of the world and it worry about the tragedies that could happen to thousands of kilometers of distance, but nevertheless it seems probable that, inside the universe of deserving individuals of help, those that are closer to the donor are who receive a preferential dealing to circumstances without taking into account equality. In fact, the State needs to supervise the acceptability and the merit of the dedicated help together perfectly with the preference for helping the people of the most extreme environment and poorest life conditions, by reducing all tax rates and reducing barriers to entering the labor market: it is much easier to know the needs and to monitor the merits of those nearby and well-known individuals than of the remote and unknown ones.

Consequently, in a free society, most of the social work would be canalized across the societies of mutual help, which mostly have a liberalized economy, and another portion would go to the donations by taxes. Inside this one, most of the charity would think about how to assist the community needs and, another part, there would be faced the people needed out of the proper community, due to strict labor conditions which exclude them from the labor market (a so much major portion the more the informative distances become closer, and investment in education and specialization increments); almost with entire safety, the latter portion of the donations would be canalized across foundations and reliable ONG that, being provided with ramifications and head offices in other territories, might provide personalized attention in a much more closer way to the poor people, as well as announce these situations to distant donors.

In spite of everything, until now we have described a stage purely speculative; credible, but speculative chance after all. Truly are there established motives for thinking that, in the absence of the State, the social work would develop for the routes that we have outlined previously? For fortune, the State of Well-being is a relatively recent social welfare tool in the Occident history, so that, simply, we can observe the history and study how the social work was pending before the State of Well-being and overall after the first world war through the League of Nations without the need of intervention by the State of Well-being.

It is a phenomenon sadly habitually thinking that, before the creation of the State of Well-being, in Spain in the 70's decade[194], immense most of the society was completely abandoned into facing adversities as frequent as the illness, the funeral expenses, not insured illnesses, the retirement or the labor incapability. And, certainly, the magnitude of the social work hundred fifty years before was much less that with the current Welfare States, but not because there were no social institutions that were allowing to resist the previous adversities but, simply, because Occident since a hundred fifty years, and mostly before the Industrial Revolution, was much poorer than now. Or said otherwise, even if it does a hundred fifty years they had installed the Welfare State just for themselves, these would have provided a social work much more scarce than the current one nowadays. Now then, at the level of available wealth in that time and into that situation, the extension and variety of the network of voluntary social work that emerged spontaneously for the Occident society turns out to be amazing and does not deserve the biggest of the praises, which mostly are enjoyed by their promoters.

[194] http://www.expansion.com/diccionario-economico/estado-de-bienestar.html

The services that these societies of mutual help were offering were very varied: the most common assistance was the compensation for the salaries lost in case of illness and the payment of the expenses by funeral, but throughout the XIXth century the trip expenses were made more and more frequent that also they were covering the sanitary payments, life insurances, retirement pensions, widowhood and orphanage or even by change of work, which nowadays is referred as frictional unemployment. The means with which they were provided for such ends were not simply nominal since they were capable of creating even schools where orphans could study and develop their lives until adulthood (71 only in the United States[195], for example), public residences for the elderly or top hospitals for the epoch.

To give this services variety, there existed diverse types of societies of mutual help; which in neither case the State was even thinking of financing, and still had the revenues to carry on the projects: the divisional societies (every member realized an annual monetary contribution to cover the expenses of the community and the surplus at the end of year it was distributed proportionally between all of them, so taxes were normally regulated in contrast to the expense in social works of each citizen); societies of unitary accumulation (societies where the surplus of the annual contributions of the members was not distributed among them, but it was accumulated to face the future adversities, which is very similar to nowadays States); societies of deposit (to the joint fund of the divisional or unitary societies there were added accounts of personal saving with which partly the retirement of every member was financed, just as the capitalization systems nowadays, as the funds were particular

[195] http://pages.jh.edu/jhumag/496web/orphange.html

and merely invested); burial societies (been in charge specially to provide different insurance, and where participation was forced); or industrial societies (created in the bosom of the company to instances of the proper interested capitalise in which its working people were provided with insurances against the unemployment, accidents or illness, just as labor insurances nowadays which were created and developed by trade unions during the Industrial Revolution).

In the beginning, the services provided by the societies of mutual help their members were independent of their contributions level, but with the time, and the same way as its members were thinking about how to insure themselves predetermined indemnifications quantities in case of adversity, a certain investment/coverage rate was restored between contribution and compensation (especially, in case of the retirement pensions). Also, to have the risks diversified, the societies tended to collaborate through a federation, so that if for example, most of the working people of a society were having to attend down all patients simultaneously, their indemnification was covered with the funds of the societies situated in other localities, which is nowadays done through institutions like the EU and is known as "regional assistance", used to increase investment in areas where unemployment is higher, and poverty is greater than in the rest of Europe, as whereas the last year the EU destined 49.1% of its funds to "inclusive growth" projects[196].

As we have indicated already, the members of the societies of mutual help had a right to receive the help from the society when there was happening some of the estimated adversities. Consequently, the

[196] http://ec.europa.eu/budget/figures/interactive/index_en.cfm

social work inside the friendly societies were collaboration was measured at a particular level and was set up as optional, was not deriving from the charity, but from the contractual labor incident's coverage. Now then, that the members were having a right to receive a service of the society does not mean that this one was not conditional: the supervision and the control between the members was permanent so that the production levels and potential was kept up and not unincentivized by insurances or forced rises of pay, and labor conditions between them were supported. For example, it was frequent that the ill people were visited with certain frequency by members of their society, and especially their employers and bosses, so much to be interested in its situation as to minimize the temptation to the fraud; and, obviously, while a person was in such a situation it could have certain unhealthy habits prohibited and restricted.

In any case, it seems reasonable to assume that the private monetary aid specially directed to the help of poor, and mainly disadvantaged people (and not to the exaltation or the maintenance of the trade union's orders) was ranging 0,3 percent and 0,4 percent of the GDP, in a moment in which the State aid was united to a coverage between 0,5 percent and 0,6 percent of the GDP. For scarce that could these numbers look, let's keep in mind that this monetary index allowed the government to finance an impressive range of varied services. According to the Real Commission, in England, during the Industrial Revolution epoch, there were 17 types different from capital based and social work organizations[197] that were giving services of care to children, young people, elders, homeless or incapacitated. Between them probably there stands out the impressive offer of voluntary hospitals that were free

[197] http://www.history.com/topics/industrial-revolution

for the poor with illnesses, and impressively were not public, showing that the private sector also has a solidarity factor to take into account (as we have remarked in previous chapters): so that we should generate ourselves an idea of its importance and extension, it is enough to say that in 1891 these hospitals were provided with 10 beds for every 10.000 English inhabitants, mostly in Manchester[198], and in 1931 with approximately 22 beds for every 10.000 inhabitants; this is, between a third and two-thirds of 33 beds for every 10.000 inhabitants with whom the whole English public health is provided nowadays, which is 80% less in comparison with which the private sector health provided at the time.

In any case, as we have exposed, the charitable organizations were playing a role merely secondary opposite to the societies of mutual help, who were the authentic nucleus of a system that, in England, was allowed to limit the number of people needed for State aid to 2,6 percent of the population at the end of the XIXth century. In fact, the interpretation most extended on the progressive development of solidarity based institutions and organizations, with the subsequent abolition of certain laws called "Poor Law"[199] in England is that they became irrelevant before the development of the friendly societies and the grown up of more sophisticated financial instruments (like the insurances with solid actuarial basis). Nevertheless, it tells nothing of this why the State of Well-being ended up by making off and dissolving the private social work that was lending in the shape of societies of mutual help and of charitable organizations.

[198] https://www.bl.uk/romantics-and-victorians/articles/manchester-in-the-19th-century
[199] http://www.nationalarchives.gov.uk/education/resources/1834-poor-law/

WELFARE STATE IN SPAIN:

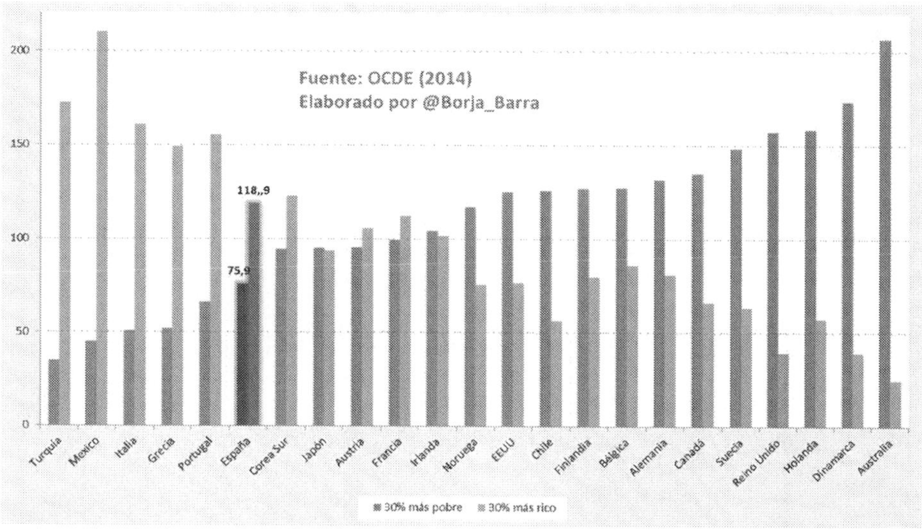

Bearing in mind the previous thing, the State participation on the subject of social work might seem unnecessary and even undesirable. And, certainly, this is a conclusion, with a completely reasonable point. Now then, as well as soon as the minimal State keeps on existing, it does not seem absolutely unacceptable either that this one acquires a subsidiary function and under a mandate to that of the voluntary private sector at the time of providing certain social work. It would be a question of constituting a network of last safety for the individuals, mainly at risk of exclusion, who have had the double misfortune of being in a situation of extreme poverty and of which they have not found answer in the private sector either, which would be already tried through societies of mutual help or of charitable organizations.

This network of State safety should be, nevertheless, much smaller than how it is nowadays. Most of the people tend to suppose that the help requires providing the unprotected ones of a massive redistribution of the revenue (taken from the labor capital in society) and, consequently, of the monstrous State. The error consists in thinking that the main social mechanism to protect us against the uncertainty — accidents, illnesses, catastrophes, loss of the job, etc. — it is to resort to the money of the others. But, to minimize these risks, we have diverse mechanisms, so much even of economic character: the constitution of a patrimony by means of the saving or the insurances; as institutionally: especially, the family, or even the government. Even if it is a question of a transitory problem, the individual can choose to get into debt: if a person remains without employment, he lacks savings and insurances against unemployment, but it is believed that it will turn out to be very simple to find employment in a few months' time, so anyone can choose to request a personal credit with which to cover his expenses meanwhile.

Mostly, all this happens already at present: the State does not protect us (or it does it slightly and with very high incurring costs) against the risk that our house catches fire, from earthquakes, of which they steal us, of that we remain unemployed for more than two years, etc. In all these cases, there are the insurances, and the personal or familiar saving is what liberates us from the absolute impotence, and allows us to be independent of the State. What it is a question, consequently, it is of that all the individuals take responsibility for other risks that today supposedly the State covers by means of the fiscal collection, used for social coverage, and that might be assumed in a better way across the capitalization, through investment, of our saving and of the hiring of insurances (life insurances, sanitary, private insurances against the unemployment, insurances against accidents, etc.). That the human being suffers reverses in life it does not mean automatically that he needs social work: once liberated from the fiscal oppression (and, therefore, allowing him to capitalize its saving and hire insurances), in immense most of cases he will not need any kind of help from the State, which has previously been paid extensively by taxation.

Nevertheless, there will keep on being people who will need help beyond the savings, the insurances, and the family. Let's imagine a baby who is born with a rare illness not covered by the insurances and with the highest cost of treatment, or an adolescent who, before beginning to work, suffers a tragic accident that impossibilities him to fulfill any task, or a woman who lacks personal patrimony and who, after the death of her husband, discovers that this one has wasted all the patrimony or a few parents who want to educate its son but who lack resources and, for the motive that is, they do not achieve a scholarship either. There will always be cases in which the social work will turn out to be necessary: but nothing of this implies that the State is essential to organize and distribute the resources: as we have seen, the private social work might take their charge perfectly as it did it up to the imposition of the State of Well-being.

In fact, before defending for principles or just for being "politically correct" the implantation of an enormous State bureaucracy entitled to monopolize and to manage in a centralized way the social work, we should think about how great in quantity there can be the cases that regularly inside a society will be able to need a help that they could not obtain across their savings, their insurances or their families. After all, if these assumptions were very scarce, we might be able to face them without informing the State or taking part minimally. The calculation is not easy to realize, but we will be able to bring it near with enough safety margin.

First, although most of the population tends to think that the Spanish wages are very low and that they would not allow supporting an education, a health or a few worthy pensions, let's bear in mind that only a 1,4 percent of the working people[200] on full time perceives the minimum wage: 9.034 euros per year that, in taxes absence, would be equivalent to more than 13.600 current euros. 64 percent of the Spanish receive wages, before taking into account taxes, of between 21.000 and 36.500 euros, and 33 remaining percent, superior to 36.500.[201]

Consequently, the revenue that the Spanish can obtain for working on 8 hours a day basis is not so low as it is usually thought: at present it is, and not because of a liberalized labor market system, but because the Government oppresses us to taxes.

Seen from here: what types of people can be considered to be really vulnerable and needed from any type of help?

First, incapacitated to work and that could not have needed a patrimony during its labor life. Second, the orphans whose parents could not have accumulated a patrimony (or they have not hired a life insurance) that provides assistance and maintenance to them. Third, the people of advanced age who for circumstances foreign to its responsibility could not have accumulated a sufficient patrimony as to obtain a revenue for a minimal retirement. In fourth place, the people who are unemployed, without patrimony and without insurance of unemployment

[200] http://ec.europa.eu/eurostat/statistics-explained/index.php/Minimum_wage_statistics
[201] http://ec.europa.eu/eurostat/statistics-explained/index.php/Income_distribution_statistics

for causes foreign to its will or that could not reinsert in the society. And finally to conscript, a variety of different expenses directed to cover social help in all these possible cases, and not to ensure extraordinary medical expenses and fees.

As for the first group of needed, in Spain there was in 2013, according to information on the Social security and approaching it upwards, approximately 930.000 people[202] who were receiving the contributory pension for permanent incapability and 200.000 people who were perceiving not contributory pension (paid entirely by the State) for invalidity. Nevertheless, we cannot take exactly these numbers as an estimation of incapacitated people needed from social work since, precisely, the benefactors of a contributory pension for permanent incapability have been quoting to the Social security and, consequently, some of them might have needed a patrimony of which to live and contribute publicly even without working. This way: what percentage of the permanent incapacitated 930.000 would really need of social assistance? In the last decade, only 38 percent of the high ones for incapability were corresponding to citizens younger than 50 years (in a capitalization system, the average pension of the people older than fifty years might overcome without too many difficulties the current amount of not contributory pensions): if we move this percentage, on the whole, we would have 350.000 incapacitated people[203], still in the contributory diet that might not have constituted a sufficient patrimony as to live from their previous revenues. In whole, then, we might include 550.000 people as incapacitated needed from social work, although the final number would

---

[202] http://www1.seg-social.es/ActivaInternet/groups/public/documents/rev_imagen/rev_031429.pdf
[203] http://www.ine.es/revistas/cifraine/1009.pdf

be slightly less since several of these people might have accidents insurances signed.

As for the second group, in Spain, there were in 2012 about 180.000 orphans younger than twenty-five years. Again, not all these orphans would need necessary of assistance, since some of them might be working and others might receive in heritage revenues of their deceased parents.

Thirdly, people who, for circumstances foreign to their will, could not have accumulated a sufficient patrimony to live from their revenues. In this sector, we would include the pensioners who could not have worked for variable circumstances, those that were not sufficiently trained to accomplish the labor market requirements, and other dependent relatives that had lost all their patrimony or which did not have any family left. Right now, in Spain, there are 250.000[204] not contributory retirement pensions. It would be necessary to add to this number a portion of the pensions of widowhood and in favor of relatives, as people rejected from the market (the whole amounts to 2,4 million): the portion, with everything, cannot be very high, since most of people at advanced ages (the average age of the pension's benefactors is seventy-six years), with what they might possess their own patrimony or the usufruct of that of his spouse to live from their revenues; in turn, the people who are incapacitated at the moment, but through formation and training can rejoin to the labor market and constitute their own patrimony. Although it is merely rough, we can assume for the high that the other quarter of the independent rejected people (or dependent relatives) would not have proper patrimony, they might not gain access to the rejoin of their income

---

[204] http://nadaesgratis.es/rubio-ramirez/diamond-y-las-pensiones-en-espana

or of the deceased, it would not rely on with relatives who could maintain it and might not return to the labor market: that is to say, 600.000 people. In whole (adding the contributory and not contributory pensions and social help), we would have 850.000 people needed from pension by the route of the social work.

Finally, we meet the unemployed people without sources of revenue or that are unemployable for some circumstance (drug addicts, mental patients, etc.). In normal circumstances and with a free labor market, Spain should not register a valuation of unemployment superior to 5 percent. Assuming that 20 percent of these people lack patrimony and insurance against the unemployment, we would have that 1 percent of the working population would need State assistance, this is, about 250.000 people.

Until now, then, we have reached the number of 1,83 million[205] people needed from social work; as presented in the BOE in 2013, otherwise, if we use the standards imposed by the interventionists, a quantity that to cover even more the basic needs we might increase up to two million. To cover the cost in social work terms, we need to determine the average payable pension for this group. This pension should be enough to survive but to be sufficiently low as to disincentive the moral risk of not saving or of not hiring insurances to be useful, AMD just uses up and take advantage of the safety network provided by the State. An acceptable quantity would be 6.000 euros per year since is over the current not contributory pension (5.000 euros), but it does not seem to be too high as to encourage irresponsible behaviors. In such a case, the entire

---

[205] https://www.boe.es/boe/dias/2013/12/31/pdfs/BOE-A-2013-13811.pdf

cost of the social work needed by unprotected people would amount to 12.000 million euros per year, about 1,2% of the Spanish GDP[206].

In spite of everything, the final number would be substantially smaller. First, because the quantity of people needed help was to be seen as overall merely inflated. Secondly, because the assistance should only cover the difference between other revenues that they were possessing, and the needed amount from help, and 6.000 euros (for example, if a worker remains incapacitated at the age of forty and it is already provided with a patrimony that offers him a revenue of 3.500 euros per year, it should only get 2.500 for social work). And third, because, in those cases in which it was possible (fundamentally, unemployed men), the revenue should be returnable: for example, the working people leisure without insurance might perceive it in exchange for the fact that, when they recover the employment, they return it (although it is without interests) the received total. Consequently, we can assume that the final cost would be rather about 1 percent of the GDP, and the State will be able to reduce the fiscal charge, incentivizing consumption and economic growth.

But the social work does not end with the pension that the unprotected people should perceive. Another part should go directed to cover the needs for health and education of those who, for not receiving sufficient revenue, could not gain access to them. Again, it is difficult to think what amounts would be necessary for it, since there are scarce references to which to consult: in Singapore, for example, the annual expense of the fund that finances the health of the poorest people (as there's no public health or minimum wage established) does not even

[206] https://www.statista.com/statistics/271079/distribution-of-gross-domestic-product-gdp-across-economic-sectors-in-spain/

represent 0,03 percent of its GDP and the level of sanitary coverage of the country is similar to the Spanish, it is still a question of a quantity probably insufficient for Spain. For our prediction in this chapter, we are going to raise the number up to 25.000 million euros for the social work in both atmospheres. This number is equivalent to something about 17 percent of the current public expenditure on health and education[207], what means that it would allow financing without cost the access to both services to 15 percent of its users. In fact, since in the majority of the cases, the State would not deal as with equal help hundred percent of the cost of the service, but only it would cover a part according to the revenue of the assisted person, as using this system the number of helped users will be major. This help, also, might be complementary to 6.000 euros per year in the form of social work by way of pension.

In whole, consequently, the social work that might need Spain would be about 30.000 million euros (3 percent of the GDP); probably, much less if we were adopting more realistic assumptions in our previous calculations. This total amount which we are speaking should be perfectly reachable across the private social work — societies of mutual help and private capital investment — in a country where the State scarcely will spend on social work 5 percent or 6 percent of the GDP, taking into account that all the public services expenditure will be diminished: since we have already seen, in the United States the private social investment societies merely charitable already rejoin 2 percent of the GDP although the fiscal pressure of the country overcomes 30 percent in this cases. Nevertheless, so that it does not keep you with a doubt that the basic needs of the population would be covered perfectly, we have reserved in

[207] http://www.datosmacro.com/estado/gasto/espana

our budget of the minimal State an expense equivalent to 2 percent of the GDP for social work, what added to 4 percent of the GDP of private investment societies, which manage their funds for social causes, that we might reach without difficulties (in collaboration with the United States), we come to 4 percent of public expenditure and forced to be in social work.

At the time of the truth, yet, the State would not even be needed to reach such a target. The private social work especially achieved by means of the auto-organization of the individuals in the shape of societies of mutual help would be most likely sufficient to cover all the welfare needs that come up in a nation. It is true that the private social work leaves seemingly the subsistence of most reach to reject many of the less favored people in society, but the same happens deeply in the State of Well-being: if in a democracy most of the voters were detecting the redistribution of the revenue, they might always vote for those parties that were proposing to repair it and, in such a case, needed from help also they would turn out to be rejected by their voters.

As soon as the State keeps on existing, which should of course persist, but in a minimized manner, there might still accept the existence of a protection network of the last instance that in a very restricted and subsidiary way it was guaranteeing that nobody will remain without resources, similar to the State of Well-being. Obviously, the cost of this network cannot be calculated beforehand, so it will depend on the particular circumstances of every society: I have estimated them at 2 percent of the GDP, although for the already exposed motives it is previewed that it would be quite low. If, in effect, the cost of the network of subsidies for people at risk of social exclusion was less than 2 percent before the crisis, and turning up to 29% afterwards[208], with the global size of the State — and the corresponding fiscal pressure — might diminish below 5 percent, increasing, even more, the well-being of the population (and, similarly, if for some years of hard depression, it was necessary to increase it at some points, it also might be done).

As Ronald Regan once said: *"Government exists to protect us from each other. Where government has gone beyond its limits is in deciding to protect us from ourselves."* The deeper meaning of this quote shows the overall intentions every government should have. I am not advocating for the total elimination of public expenditure in essential and basic services, but otherwise for an extreme reduction of its budgets. Citizens should be able to control the government and make sure that its expenditures are only used to prevent scarcity and poverty in the most basic ways, because over that all public services will be used as a political tool to buy our votes and make us slaves from our society. And remember, that we are always paying for the government, while the government is never paying for us. It is not a zero-sum game. We always lose, and market freedom is our last refuge against authoritarianism.

[208] http://economia.elpais.com/economia/2015/05/26/actualidad/1432626857_809310.html

14- SPAIN HAS STILL GOT TIME TO CHANGE... AND BECOME A FREE-MARKET ECONOMY!

Probably, the historical experience with most similar characteristics to the transition that we are proposing from the current social-democratic State (public expenditure near to 50 percent of the GDP)[209] up to the minimal State (public expenditure of 5-15 percent of the GDP)[210] is the transition that took place in East Europe from the socialist economies inside the Soviet orbit until the 1980 (public expenditure of 90 percent of the GDP)[211] up to their current social-democratic economies. Attending on the results of these processes of development of the State that began at the beginning of the decade of 1990, we were able to realize that the most important problems that can characterize this type of transitions are two.

The first one is of economical nature: as the State represents a gigantic portion of our economies, in the short term its decreasing size will carry along with it contractive effects. The productive potential of our societies will have to suffer a deep readjustment and transformation that

---

209 https://data.oecd.org/gga/general-government-spending.htm
210 http://people.tamu.edu/~sdaniel/Notes/politic4.html
211 https://www.quora.com/What-was-the-percentage-of-government-spending-in-the-Soviet-Unions-GDP

will extend during a certain period of time. At the end, not any company or public administration will be necessary and being managed actively, so that once they finally get adapted to the discipline and effective demand of the consumers, many of them will end up by disappearing so that they emerge alternative productive agents, which will be mainly private firms producing the same food at a higher quality. But all this takes time and, meanwhile, the production levels decrease, making necessary expansive economic policies to reactivate the economy. For example, the GDP of Hungary fell down 18 percent between 1989 and 1993[212], and it was not capable of reaching again the level of 1989 until the year 2000; Poland by its part, saw how its GDP was decreasing by 12 percent between 1989 and 1992[213], delaying until 1995 when the progress reached its activity level.

Even if the behavior of the post-socialist economies probably was not so bad as the registered one by the statistics — the increasing and fast developing private economy began in an expansive submerged economy not taken into account entirely in the official information — the descent of its GDP illustrates that any transition will transport in the short term a fall of the activity that had developed this economy; fall of the activity that, in case of being very hard, might stimulate the social deception and anger towards the reforms, which in many cases have happened and will continue to frustrate the liberalizing process. This implies that, before initiating good part of the round of decentralization, and start working on liberalizing reforms, it is essential to overcome the current economic crisis that nowadays prevails in Occident and, much in particular, in Spain; even though we are clearly solving the economic recession, mainly through a

[212] http://www.tradingeconomics.com/hungary/gdp
[213] https://data.oecd.org/gdp/gross-domestic-product-gdp.htm

labor market reform which has liberalized minimally the system and improved hiring conditions; reducing unemployment from 27.5% in the year 2012, down to 18.2% in 2016[214]: to overcome the problem relating to the moment of economic adjustment linked to the depression due mainly to the structural adjustment associated with the rate of model of the State which if it is excessively liberal from the beginning might become too painful in the short term, that's why a long transition period is required. Also, the first liberalizations that would be necessary to impose and start working on should be those that had a more immediate and favorable influence on the economic growth, for example, the commercial opening, the elimination of the subsidies or the liberalization of the labor market. But, in any case, a society which wants to reach greater freedom levels in economic matters will have to realize that in the short term its economic activity level very probably will suffer: the key is that the restructuring is completed as soon as possible, for which the economy will need a lot of flexibility, which will be developed over an extended period of time.

The second one of the problems is of juridical - institutional appearance, and it is much more serious than the previous one: the risk that the privatization of wide sectors of the State ends up by being captured by lobbies and institutions, just as it happens in the countries that apply Keynesian economics. As well as soon as the disappearance of the State bears the massive reassignment of rights of property inside a society, it exists more than the clear risk of which this readjustment is carried out in a deployable possible way for the joy of the lobbies, which receive nearly 30% of the total subsidies in the US[215]. To minimize this risk,

---

[214] http://elpais.com/elpais/2015/11/18/media/1447871942_778264.html
[215] http://www.ieb.ub.edu/files/PapersWSFF2015/WSPEPF2015Groll.pdf

the transition should be carried out lower above and not above, particularly, of what it is a question it is of that the State moves back from those areas that it should never have occupied and not of that which we have planned a new liberal order from zero, in other words, the State doesn't have to change of areas, it just has to be reduced.

Finally, the essential fact to reach the minimal State is that the society wants to reach this minimal State, the desire of the people is the most important: it is not a function of the politicians to impose its reform programs to the convictions of the population, but they must be the citizens the ones that demand and claim the retreat of the State. In turn, there where it should be possible, the State should limit to recognize the actual or informal property rights instead of creating them from zero: to know, there where there existed in advance private ownership (State nationalizations) or there where it keeps on existing although the State does not recognize it formally, will have to limit to returning or respect these property rights, which will be done through privatizations. But with this, we will continue without answering to the question of how we will develop and establish property rights on State domains like the schools, the hospitals, the public enterprises or the highways, which will have to be partially privatized to reach the minimum State.

THE THEOREM OF THE PRIVATIZATIONS

Those State properties that could not be returned to their original owners or investors would have to surrender to a privatization process. To determine the possibilities of privatizable properties, it turns out to be reviewable to allow all the citizens to realize their own proposals on what specific properties to privatize instead of that they are the State bureaucrats who decide on the process: this way the State manages to make use of the dispersed present private knowledge in a society. As soon as the properties diversification was determined to privatize, it stays to proceed to do it. Three routes exist essentially for it: their auction to the best buyer, so who offers the most for the property, their transference to its working people and agents, and their transference to the set of the citizens, which would have the option to be a shareholder of the institution. The three have its advantages and disadvantages so that the formula finally adopted should consist probably of a combination of the three according to the circumstances and the characteristics of the good that it wants to privatize. The sale of properties in public auction allows to the State to collect substantial sums of money with which to amortize and balance part of its public debt or face the transition costs of the system of pensions. The weak point of this option is that, on the one hand, the massive and simultaneous sale of State properties is closely linked to decreasing their price massively, since enough capital cannot exist to attend to all the supply; on the other hand, as to the beginning a very precarious knowledge exists on the real value of a lot of the privatized properties, the politicians possess an excessive influence at the time of determining who acquire what properties (what accentuates the risk of corruption during the process, which has already happened in the actual situation with some privatizations). In sum, the price of privatization of the State properties will depend on the sale conditions, and they are the bureaucrats of the State, or the citizens, which determine these conditions. As an example we found how after Margaret Thatcher's privatization program, the British economy reached an economic growth of nearly 5.2%, having risen up from an economic deflation of -2.5%[216].

The second possibility is to deliver the public ownership to the people who work or are related to it. The apparent advantage of this method is that the property remains in the hands of those that had managed it, so that they do not have why to give him significant changes in its functioning; also, the resistances to the privatization on the part of the officials and other lobbies tend to decrease when this one redounds to its own benefit. Nevertheless, the disadvantages of this privatization system are also notable: on the one hand, the State working people obtain very significant resources transference at the cost of the rest of the society; for other, the incentives of the new working people - owners usually consist of expanding or exploiting everything possible new capital that they have received (for example, giving himself the same very high salaries or reducing its working days), what ends up by displacing them out of the market, and making them inefficient into the economic system.

And, finally, there fits the possibility of transferring this public shares to the set of the citizens by means of the share-out of participations or shares on the same ones. This way, the State goods would remain automatically privatized and reinvest it in the hands of the citizens that they financed the State partly. The disadvantage is that the shares and participations or derivates share-out develop and secures enormously the control on a property, turning it in many cases hardly questionable, as which occurred with Bankia's launch into the Spanish

[216] http://www.tradingeconomics.com/united-kingdom/gdp-growth

stock exchange market in 2011 and having devalued its active by more than 83%[217] since its first day. The socialist country in which this method was used more extensively was Czechoslovakia: the citizens support the entire cost of the State at very low price through participations and with those you pay and support, as they could bid for the shares of the big companies that were privatized or transfer them to investment funds, where large numbers of those were in charge of grouping the costs to buy valuable portions of the privatized properties.

As it has been indicated, there do not exist methods objectively better than others to privatize and, consequently, it will be necessary to attend on the circumstances and concrete characteristics of every State property. As general rule, we can indicate that the big companies and the properties that, like the hospitals, imply an enormous investment in fixed capital should be privatized by means of systems of share-out between the citizens; the properties which value derives essentially from the task that they fulfill through its labor (as it happens with the schools) might be distributed among them; and the grounds, buildings and infrastructures in hands of the State — whose evaluation is simpler than that of a company and in many cases they must be sold off only one piece — might will be sold through means of public auction.

THE FLOW OF MONEY IN A LIBERAL MARKET

Just like we have already seen, at present the money is a State monopoly based on the role and the inconvertible currency. The decentralization of the money constitutes a priority to minimize the magnitude of the economic depressions that consequently endure the

[217] http://www.expansion.com/2012/07/15/empresas/banca/1342378286.html

capitalism as a result of the State interventionism in monetary subjects, as what's happening right now with Bitcoin, which in the last year incremented its value up to $2000 from $435 just two years ago[218].The strategy to allow the election and the production of the money to return to hands of the society can constitute two ways: one, in which simply one stops imposing a legal currency money and it is allowed that other capitals of private origin compete with him; which will be a great utopia and merely impossible to develop, and other, wherein parallel with this abandonment of the money of legal currency there tries to become stable the value of the State currency by means of its convertibility in gold.

The second of these ways is the simplest. At present, the citizens of a country keep on using the paper money (euros, dollars, yens or you free) for three motives: because the State imposes its use in the private deals (laws of legal currency), because the profit in national currency derived from the possession of foreign currency is directly related to the appreciations and derived tax and because the State has to pay the taxes in paper money. The minimal State that we are describing would allow getting over these three obstacles: first, the State would eliminate the legal currency laws, allowing the citizens to compromise with absolute freedom what currency to use in their deals, independently to what central bank it belongs, second, the heritage profit derived from the transference of different currency from a different nation would not be subject to any taxation; third, the fiscal pressure would be so low (5 percent of the GDP), as for example Guatemala, charging an income tax of 7%[219] or just all the Arab Countries which don't charge income tax at all,

---

[218] http://www.economicswire.net/bitcoin-capitalization-rose-to-record-value.html
[219] http://www.tradingeconomics.com/country-list/personal-income-tax-rate

having a rate of 0%. That the State scarcely would influence in what currency the citizens need to employ in their financial transactions. With these three reforms, consequently, the State money would happen to compete in an equal way with other forms deprived of money that could emerge (or with currencies of foreign central banks) particularly: the citizens might choose what money they employ in their financial transactions and operations. And as soon as the euro underwent to the competitive pressure of alternative coins, simply it would be necessary to privatize the European Central Bank for some of three routes presented beforehand in this book, which will increase the efficiency of their function, making the euro currency more competitive internationally, consequently raising its value.

Now then, it seems reasonable that, while the State buries its monopoly on the currency, tries to improve simultaneously the quality of its inconvertible paper money, so that it is not necessary to exchange it for other currencies, due to the high taxes imposed on it, which shows that it is advocated to become extinct and to disappear along the competitive process with the rest of international currencies. The way of improving the quality of the euros or of the dollars is restoring their convertibility in gold, this is, using the golden reservations that the current central banks still possess to produce that the notes in circulation are payable in certain quantities of gold.

The second difficulty has relation to the exchange rate that would be established between the euro and the rest of currencies. The gold standard was a monetary system essentially internationalist, where the exchange rates between coins were fixed (what was the price of the gold of each of the currencies). To stabilize the value of the euro with the gold might be distortion and really volatile if the main commercial nations with which the Europeans exchange through exports and imports (the United States and China, especially) will not stabilize in turn their currencies with the gold standard.

Consequently, the return to the gold standard should be carried out in a gradual and with multiple factors involved way. On the one hand, the main central banks of the world should declare their intention of restoring the convertibility of its currencies with the gold standard (something to what they might be an incentive to do, pushed by the increasing competition that the international currencies market would suppose). For another side, before opening the options and expectations for the conversion in gold, it would be necessary that the private banks and the BCE were undoing the enormous take off period (expansionary monetary policy period) that they exhibit at present, that is to say, that will limit themselves to being big enough in the short term against its short-term debts and that to be big enough in the long term (mortgages, managerial loans, credits to the consumption...) meaning that they had to receive long-term capitals, even through loans, shares, derivate, State bonds... With these two conditions, the euros, dollars, pounds sterling or yuans currencies might return to the gold standard without big difficulties and without major needs for reservations of this metal, and just establishing a fixed value for the currencies, used to stabilize the economy, and prevent devaluations as last year's yuan one of more than 7% in a period of 6 months long into the second quarter of 2016[220].

---

[220] https://www.dailyfx.com/forex/market_alert/2017/01/03/Chinese-Yuan-Devaluation-Looks-Like-a-Long-Shot.html

ECONOMIC FREEDOM LEVELS AND INCOME PER CAPITA IN DIRECT RELATION:

Economic Freedom and Per Capita Income

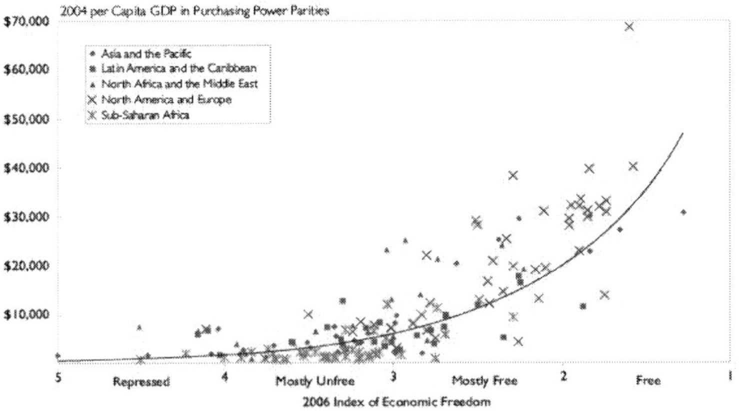

Sources: World Bank, *World Development Indicators Online*, available by subscription at *www.worldbank.org/data*; Central Intelligence Agency, *The World Factbook 2005*, available at *www.cia.gov/cia/publications/factbook/index.html*, for the following countries: Bahamas, Bahrain, Barbados, Burma, Cuba, Equatorial Guinea, Iraq, Kuwait, North Korea, Libya, Qatar, Suriname, Taiwan, United Arab Emirates, Zimbabwe; Marc A. Miles, Kim R. Holmes, and Mary Anastasia O'Grady, *2006 Index of Economic Freedom* (Washington, D.C.: The Heritage Foundation and Dow Jones & Company, Inc., 2006), at *www.heritage.org/index*.

<u>AND WHAT WOULD HAPPEN WITH THE HEALTH SYSTEM?</u>

Although the privatization of the health system could seem quite different from the privatization of the system of pensions, up to certain grade they keep a few important parallelisms, even though the health system will keep on being public in more than 40%, but in contrast to the Spanish model right now with a health expenditure of 6.29%[221], having more than 80% of the market share dominated by the public sector. Since I explained already in its moment, part of the extraordinary expenditure of the health should be financed across the hiring of medical insurances by every citizen. The hiring at early ages of an insurance allows the insurer to capitalize during more time the quotes paid by the client, and, this way, to support future sanitary expenditure of adverse and mainly unexpected character to him: the way of covering in an accessible way the very high medical payments of the retired citizens is to hire a sanitary insurance from the first years of the youth ages, to be able to expand these capital funds and cover future risks and adversities that could be created, generating a positive or at least break even balance of account, which can only be reached through a private management of the healthcare system.

Now then, the negative implication of the previous thing is that, if the health is privatized without much cooperation from public institutions, which will produce that any State financing will be cut to the same one, the aged people or who were already suffering chronic illnesses might not gain access to a safe medical insurance at a disproportionate cost. It is for it that also it would turn out to be necessary that, during a time, the State was taking charge of the sanitary expenses of this part of the population, just to allow the privet sector to establish financially on some basis, to be able to offer lower prices for frequent users in the future, increasing their

[221] http://www.datosmacro.com/estado/gasto/salud/espana

aggregate demand. We can also observe a parallelism with the privatization of the pensions: the public sanitary system is nowadays similar, as if the State was hiring a public medical insurance to all the Spanish, which could be contrasted by the adult people who have earned a right to a sanitary service of which the State cannot make ignorance (as he could not reject either of the right already settled to earn a pension), but many young people could have their taxes decreased and be themselves the ones that choose what sanitary insurance to hire.

Consequently, the privatization of the health will also need a process of transition during which the State would cover whole or partially the sanitary payments of a part of the population, but not of the rest, which should already begin to hire their own insurances, increasing the portion of this part of the population through time, and completing the process of privatization. The part of the covered population should be that to the one that the established conditions have already localized him at the moment of the privatization or that it has already reached an age that prevents them from capitalizing enough patrimony as to have its sanitary expenses covered in the future. For it, it would be enough that the State was offering to the people older than thirty years and those minors of thirty who have diagnosed certain illnesses the following offer in exchange for promising to constitute a few accounts of sanitary saving, their expenses will be decreased, but they will have to hire an insurance just for complementary health services.

Obviously, the State should prevent the socialization of most of the sanitary expense from allowing to the private suppliers, as hospitals or medical centers to make a profit raising the prices and multiplying the services offer: as I have already exposed, the combination of a liberalized offer and of a socialized demand is the worst possible one, given that it leads to excessive and controlled character of the costs. In this sense, the State should devote to do the same as inside the public system, particularly, to ration the sanitary expenditure, with the only difference of being private. For it, it would be necessary to define the services and the providers whose cost covers the State; in fact, in its overall quality mainly monophonic (it would be the major buyer for many years, so finally the demander will dominate the market being able to have control over prices), the State should even come to the point of negotiating prices to the fall with these providers to whom a fixed demand assures them.

With these conditions, we can calculate the sanitary expenditure of the main citizen would keep on being a charge of the State during the transition. Attending to the information that the Spanish Ministry of Health offers, the age group between fifty-five and sixty-four years supposes an average sanitary expense for inhabitant for 1.950 euros[222]; between sixty-five and seventy-four, of 3.250 euros and over seventy-five it goes up to 4.125 euros. Since the State only would take charge of the part not covered by the capital of the accounts of sanitary saving, or the sanitary insurances, the necessary entire payments from 2015 would range between 20.000 and 30.000 million euros per year[223], to then start falling consequently from 2040. Namely, the sanitary socialization of the expense would disappear in fifty years.

[222] https://www.msssi.gob.es/estadEstudios/estadisticas/docs/EGSP2008/egspPrincipalesResultados.pdf

[223] http://www.msssi.gob.es/estadEstudios/estadisticas/inforRecopilaciones/gastoSanitario2005/home.htm

And so, the financing of the sanitary expense that the State would keep on covering would need a tax of 3 percent on the revenues of the work and of the capital, what joined the necessary tax to finance the pensions would take the abusive tax system to reduce the State of well-being between 11,5 percent and 13,5 percent[224].

IS THERE PUBLIC DEBT IN A CAPITAL-BASED STATE?

There is nothing necessarily wrong in that the State generates public debt to finance expenses which afterwards will come out and be paid out of several exercises: since it would do any family or private enterprise, the long-term investments of the State can be supported by its future fiscal income and, for it, it is possible to generate public debt.

In the budget that we have artificially created for the minimal State, nevertheless, there does not appear any portion directed to support the interests of the public debt. The motive is that any debt emission should have a long development character (a long-term specific investment) and, therefore, its annual amortization and the balance of its financial costs should be extracted from the annual budgetary planning expenses for every sector inside the budget. This way, for example, if the State announced debt to ten years to construct several military airports and the annual cost of the return of the main one and of the payment of interests of this debt is 500 million euros, this total should take off from the annual allocation of the budget of Defense, reducing it until all the expenditure or investment costs have been paid..

[224] http://documentos.fedea.net/pubs/dt/2016/dt2016-09.pdf

The problem is that, at present, the expense of interests, and just in interests, of the debt on the part of the Spanish State arises close to 4 percent of the GDP, this is, almost the double of the entire public expenditure with which there should be provided the minimal State that we have proposed. Assuming that the public debt at the end of 2016 has become stable concerning 1,2 trillion euros[225], in the actual State, the interests payment might go so far as to represent up to 5 percent of the GDP. How to manage to re-conduct the situation so that it does not suppose an excessive financial load for the taxpayer, and preventing a higher financial charge on income? Exactly, the last one of the State obligations that must be progressively amortized during the transition to the minimal State is the public debt.

The States have managed to end up traditionally with its public debt excesses without resorting to the non-payment by means of three mechanisms: first, the budgetary balance combined with the growth, and mainly powered by major exports; the second one, to destine a great portion from the fiscal collection to amortize public debt; third, to sell off State assets and to use you them prove to amortize the debt, mainly through privatization.

The effect of the budgetary balance combined with the growth can become quite notable. For example, if between 2016 and 2050 the public debt will freeze in 1,2 trillion euros and the real GDP would be growing at an average of 2 percent per year[226] (from 1 trillion euros up to 1,96 trillion), the weight of the public debt would fall down from 120 percent to 61 percent and the interests of 5 percent of 2,5 percent. We also have

[225] http://www.datosmacro.com/deuda/espana
[226] http://www.oecd.org/eco/outlook/spain-economic-forecast-summary.htm

to bear in mind that we are considering inflation in absence, or at a much reduced rate and being around 2% all the time. If on the other hand, we were assuming a growth of 4 percent of the mean wages per year, allowing for consumption levels to rise by the same percentage, the weight of the debt would come down to 31 percent and the interests of 1,2 percent.

Finally, if the previous economic growth politics without deficit and of liquidation of State assets, we were combining them with a clear and persistent debt amortization, the result would be even more profitable: destining every year 3 percent of the GDP to pay so much the interests as to amortize public debt, the State debts would have disappeared completely in the year 2050. In fact, if we were considering the very realistic idea or theorem of which all this expansive program of amortization of public debt should serve to reduce the average interests of the debt up to 2 percent (due to the high credibility and safety that the Spanish State debts would offer, increasing this way international investments), it would be enough for us to use 2 percent of the GDP every year to get rid entirely of the public debt in the year 2050, while there will not be a clear necessity of cutting off any type of service, as the planned economic growth would be 2 percent of the GDP per year.

COMPARATIVE OF MARKET FREEDOM G20-USA:

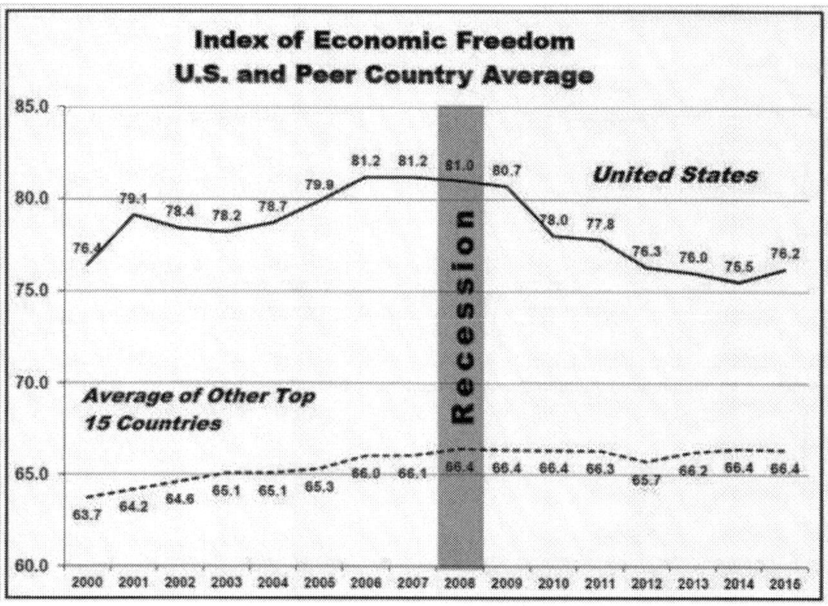

And so, the hyper-regulated State might be replaced by the minimal State of 5 percent of the GDP in the middle of the XXIst century. The transition is gradual but entirely achievable so that the only reasons not to develop it are not of technical character but only ideological and financial. In the end, the main opposition to a powerful reduction of the size of the State comes from these two fronts: those who feel an ideological and almost emotional fidelity towards the enormous State and its expenditure, even if it carries an outrage against their own interests or those of their communities (it would be the case of the antiliberal well-intentioned ones who believe honestly that the State promotes the social harmony, as for example pure Socialists or Communists); and others that have been capable of taking advantage of the bureaucracy and the branches of the power of the State and that, consequently, arrange it in their own benefit making them believe the rest of citizens who are trying to obtain the common good, as it would be the case of the politicians, of the lobbies and of the trade unions, who comfortably enjoy revenues guaranteed at the cost of the taxpayer without need to compete for their maintenance, which the State won't be generating value for them in the frame of a free market. Public workers are not the problem if there is not an excess, the problem are public parasites and spoilers of private money, whom each year steal us nearly 50% of our income recurring to the simplistic argument of: "how will we build up roads if not?" It is clear as noon: let's defend market freedom.

15- WHAT WOULD I DO IF... I WAS THE MINISTER OF ECONOMY[227]

Being Spain's minister of economy is not even one of my dreams or objectives in life, I am not saying that I would not accept the charge once reached the case in the future... but I know that I will not be chosen at any time or any moment. Why? Very simple. As you have been able to see, along this book I have been politically incorrect in many topics, which might have disguised a large part of my readers, but along with it goes my opinion and my true economic values, which in contrast of other economists are not utopias or closed proposals; as mines have been reinforced with arguments and common sense, offering diverse ways to reach the same objective: economic liberalism. And as the title says, we are *"In Defense Of Freedom,"* well, in that case... let me present you my troops, which will fight to convert Spain into a totally economically free nation:

DECREASE TAXES TO THE LIMIT- SPECIALLY DURING A RECESSION[228]:

The increase or descent of taxes during a crisis is usually one of the main topics of economic gathering. There are several opinions about this

[227] ALL DATA EXPOSED ON THIS CHAPTER HAS BEEN EXTRACTED AND PREVIOUSLY ANALYZED FROM MY PERSONAL ECONOMIC BLOG: *WWW.ELRINCONDELPARQUET.COM* -REFERENCES TO ARTRICLES WILL BE ATTACHED FOR EACH SECTION.

[228] http://www.elrincondelparquet.com/news/%C2%BFes-necesario-subir-los-impuestos-en-una-crisis/

matter since one of the main causes are slows down in the cycle of production and consumption during the recession period.

First of all, the economic crises are periods during which the private sector is hardly damaged since it is in an epoch in which it needs that the demand for its product increases. Looking at this point, we can take up account, that to raise the taxes in this case would generate that the consumption levels were diminishing, after which, the companies would reduce its production, after the demand turns out to be lowered, which they would try to apply a descent to the production costs, generally referring to the labor, what has a direct relation to the unemployment increases. After the unemployment rises, generates by an excess supply of labor in the market, the government would turn out to be forced to offer more helps to stop poverty levels from rising and to try to increment through this measures the commerce, which would raise the public expenditure brutally, generating consequently higher levels of debt.

Next, reached this situation, we identify as a fact that the companies would be completely shanked into debt, for which, it would suppose an entire drowning, which to the majority would make them end in payments suspension. All this, it would affect in the straight and direct way many families, which would see their income reduced or even eliminated, what again would reduce the aggregate demand levels, even more, breaking this way the production levels and reducing supply in the market.

In the third place, we can observe, that in crisis times, the main regenerating tool there exists are the foreign investments, for the ones which a taxes increase is very negative since it reduces straight the benefits of the long-term fixed revenue. In this situation, the investors would choose for countries with the major liquidity of assets and less governmental intervention, for investment options with long-term future. Without foreign investment, the country would turn out to be exposed to a very slow and less intense recovery, and in many times if the public debt keeps on increasing, even to depression.

Really, it is funny hearing by television and radio to certain political and economic personalities, when referring to foreign investment and jobs as favors granted to our country, simply because the image that is giving or tries to give. And all these people expect, that when Spain has reached a debt of 100% over GDP, with levels similar to Japan; people still have the desire to continue to invest, also knowing in consciousness that in recent years, in Spain a program of increased debt over GDP, deficit delays, and a tremendous fiscal drowning which has done more to curb growth, has been severely developed. But that is not the worst, and is that the people of "*the smile revolution*", or those politicians who try to pretend to be Leonardo Di Caprio, dare to say that the increase in debt is due to austerity programmes carried out during the last mandate, which have been based on the reduction of taxes as much as possible increasing 4% growth in comparison with previous years, as many companies have become to see incentive to lay their premises in Spain, being rewarding in most for their efforts.

In this country, it has been thought for a long time that the best solution for the creation of employment and reduction of debt is based on an increase in public expenditure, which has proven to be a very wrong attitude. If we look back we can see how meaningless public spending doubled in the time before the economic crisis, or as being already in times of recession not to paralyze useless public works projects, such as always empty, or AVE lines that connect two cities, whose trip is faster by car, and that makes half of the wagons to be empty, but yes, we continue showing off our great and unnecessary infrastructure. A particular case which we can take note as an example is the rescue of public savings banks, which boasted of being one of greater solvency of European banks while hiding red numbers after the back-filled leaves, that yes, even though rescued, just in case if perhaps there wasn't enough spending. My favorite case is that of the autonomic communities, which are intended for more than 40,000 million a year, by a pure motive of representation, and a nice excuse for false growth; which confirms the typical utopia that rising expenditure reduces the debt. We have heard for years that liberal policies in the economic term are extremely austere and may be harmful to the population, but they have not thought that if it were not for those economic policies would not lower the deficit 4 points, or are growing at 3% annually? Or but simply because we are leaders in job creation in Europe?

HERE YOU CAN SEE A GRAPH DEPICTING THE PROGRESS OF ECONOMIC GROWTH IN SPAIN IN RECENT YEARS:

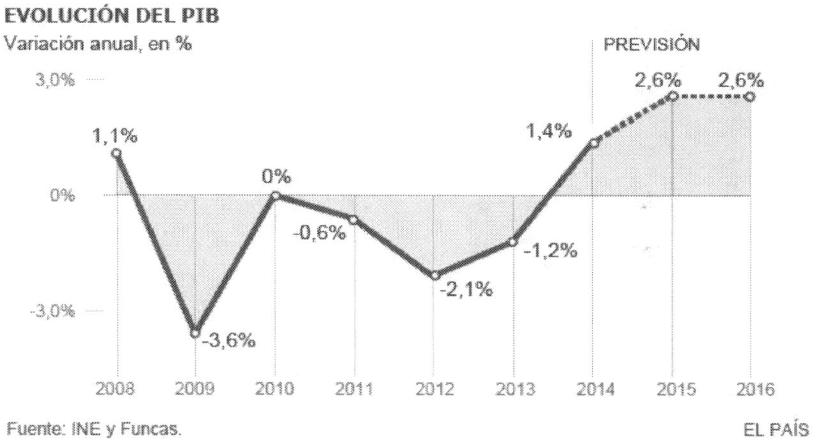

This past week we have seen one of the new proposals of Spanish interventionists, and this was to create another tax[229], this time earmarked for the Pension Fund, similar to the tax which was established in France in 1966, and which has made that pensions to be steadily cut since then. We have seen that higher taxes do not make more effective or sustainable the pension system, and the only necessary solution to make this Fund increase and our elders to be able to enjoy a better standard of living, is through the promotion of job creation in the private sector, which is produced directly by a higher rate of consumption, and leads to greater economic growth, due to increased productivity and efficiency in the market.

---

[229] http://www.elrincondelparquet.com/news/do-you-want-a-solution-lower-taxes/

In the end, the solution to everything is lowering taxes, as we have already seen in certain countries of the European Union in recent years, which have raised much more money and had a higher rate of growth. A great example can be the United Kingdom, that reduced the tax to all businesses, and raised a 2.4% to the previous year in terms of corporation tax, which shows that a greater liberalization of the economy and a policy of retrenchment have worked in this country. Spain, a country that was the bankruptcy of the EU, and suffered one of the biggest economic crises in its history, has managed to move to a 3% growth-based reduction of taxes and incentives to consumption, in a period of just four years. Greater job creation has also been achieved, due to an increase in exports and a major opening of the market to the outside.

THIS GRAPH REPRESENTS THE VARIATION OF INCOME TAX OVER THE PAST DECADE, AND ITS EVOLUTION IN COMPARISON TO GDP:

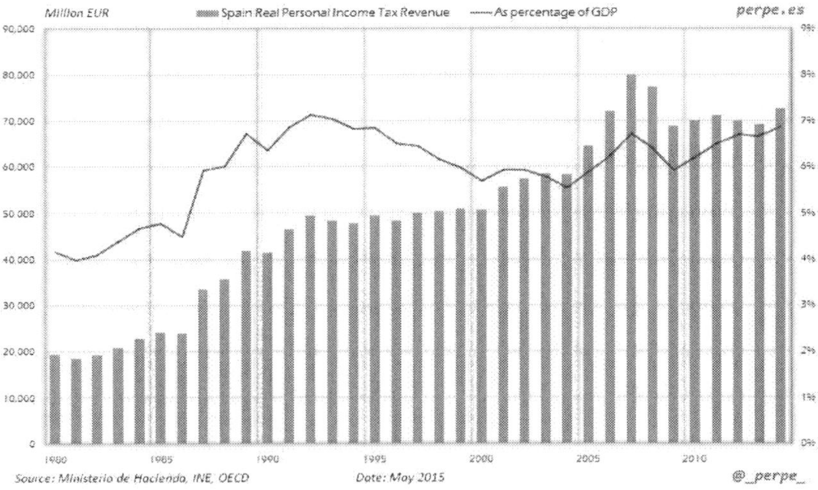

Interventionism has already shown its ineffectiveness and poor practices, producing tax hikes and increases in deficit due to higher public spending marked for thousands of secondary reasons, breach of all economic targets which were fixed by those of "the revolution of the smile." Now is liberalism's turn, since we are in a new time in which the Government has to defend a lower fiscal drowning for the support of entrepreneurship, thus producing higher employment, which has their wages linked to the productivity of the company, increasing efficiency in the market. And remember, as the great Milton Friedman said once: "A society that puts equality above freedom will end without equality nor freedom."

ELIMINATE AUTONOMIC COMMUNITIES IN SPAIN[230]:

And now it is me who wonders: Why? Why do we have to keep on wasting money in this bottomless system well-called autonomies?

We know in abundance, although some of them do not admit it, that one of the big holes of the Spanish economy is the autonomic model. The topic is not alone in 17 different legislations, which for their account produce not even a euro... But they spend the triple, but apart from all this, they make difficult the free creation of employment and the general economic recovery of Spain.

Every year, the government destines about 85.000 million euros to the autonomies, which go out of the pocket of all the Spanish. Apart, if there did not exist the autonomies, the education, health, the system of

[230] http://www.elrincondelparquet.com/news/es-el-momento-de-recortar-a-las-autonomias/

pensions... They would be centralized and managed by the Government, for what political parties as CIU might not remove the education in Castilian or Compromís which passed a law in 2015 related to education quality without permission of the Central government.

With the CCAA, and looking at the labor model, the only thing that is done, is to create more and more not productive public employment, and according to a study by the Complutense University of Madrid, for every not productive public job that is created, 3 private jobs are destroyed, since even more taxes are needed to maintain not necessary officials, or in other words... close friends of politicians who did not know how to do a single thing in life. According to the same study, in Spain, there remain 1.000.000 of positions of public work, and 900.000 of them come from the autonomic system, which, in conclusion, means that the Spanish citizen is paying nearly 80.000 million euros to an inefficient system which lacks productivity, which has a name and surname... Autonomic Communities.

DECREASE OR ELIMINATE THE MINIMUM WAGE IN SPAIN[231]:

Since the last general elections in Spain, we have seen several political leaders declare in favor of a higher minimum wage rate in this country in the next year. Their proposals about this theme are mainly centered on the government being the principal character, and forcing to introduce a higher minimum salary into the labor market, having no correlation with the local economic growth. But there is one thing that

[231] http://www.elrincondelparquet.com/news/did-you-know-that-increasing-the-minimum-wage-in-spain-doesnt-benefit-workers/

these left-wing new parties have not thought about, and that is productivity. Anyone who has received a pair of economics lessons should know that wages are directly related to the productivity of the human capital of a firm, so in general terms, if a company produces higher amounts of its product, they will be able to sell it at a low price in the market and be more competitive, raising its benefits and automatically (in theory), the wages of the workers of that firm. Actually, the minimum wage rate in Spain is fixed at 658,20 euros per month, having some new proposals of certain parties wanting to increase it until 950 euros in the period of a year, increasing it by a 22% in the first two years, and 45% by the end of their legislature. But, what will be the consequences of a rise in the minimum wage of these characteristics?

Firstly, salaries are directly correlated, as well as prices of any good or service, to the demand for each of them and the level of production of each company. Salaries can not be fixed by law in a general way, as this will create very high economic instability and will make the demand for labor in the market fall immediately, as the production costs of companies will increase in an enormous way, but the levels of output will remain the same, generating major loses. A very high minimum wage in contrast to a low level of productivity will end up generating higher unemployment levels; hiring new workers for companies will simply be not profitable. Forcing a very high minimum salary will be especially harmful for low qualified workers, as if their jobs are very simple, there will very high supply of labor, and with a high minimum wage, the demand for those workers will go down, as their jobs will be replaced by automation, which will be far more profitable for companies, and will create higher competition in the market, as we know that machines are much more productive than humans in almost all aspects of production.

There is an example that applies perfectly to this situation. It was the year 2009 when the federal government of the USA fixed a minimum wage rate of 7,25 dollars per hour, but one of its States, Seattle, decided that they were going to impose a different, and much higher minimum salary, of exactly 15 dollars per hour. At first, almost everybody in Seattle saw this as a very good decision that would increase the supply of labor, and it did, but what they did not realize was that the demand for labor would fall enormously. We could see how in the year 2013, all the employment that had been created in the last decade had been almost destructed completely by the incredibly big levels of unemployment, that had increased more than one point. The labor market just restructured when the economy stalled again, following the economic growth rate, which made the demand for labor increase freely, reducing unemployment. When the minimum wage rate rises, normally the GDP of a country does not seem to be greatly affected, but the labor productivity decreases enormously.

IN THIS GRAPH WE CAN OBSERVE HOW AS THE MINIMUM WAGE RATE RISES, THE LABOR PRODUCTIVITY DECREASES, WHICH MAKES UNEMPLOYMENT GO UP (APPLIED TO SPAIN):

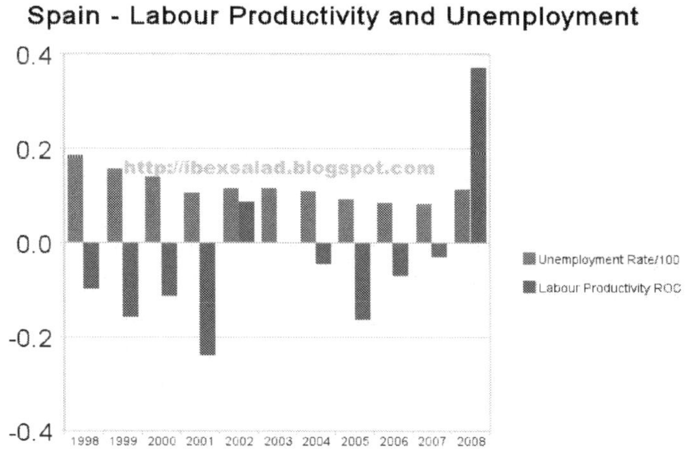

Sources: OECD, Eurostat and INE

Secondly, we can see that when the minimum wage rate rises significantly, the possibilities of losing their job increases between the low productive workers, affecting overall the young people, and adults over 45 years old. In this two years groups, as we have said before the most affected ones are the low qualified people, mostly in the secondary sector, as there is a very large amount of supply of labor. Many governments, countries and political leaders talk magnificently about the Nordic countries and their perfectly balanced labor market. But political parties that support a high minimum wage are ignoring, that these countries are the ones enjoying the lowest minimum salary, and the lowest unemployment rate, also complemented by the highest wages in the entire EU. This is caused because employers can reduce the costs when they set up their company, having a faster economic growth process, and be easier for them to develop the firm, and as the workers show high productivity levels, they will be rewarded with higher wages to balance the costs and benefits of the enterprise.

HERE WE CAN SEE HOW THE MINIMUM WAGE RATE HAS BEEN RISEN THROUGH THE LAST DECADE IN SPAIN, INCREASING THE UNEMPLOYMENT RATE:

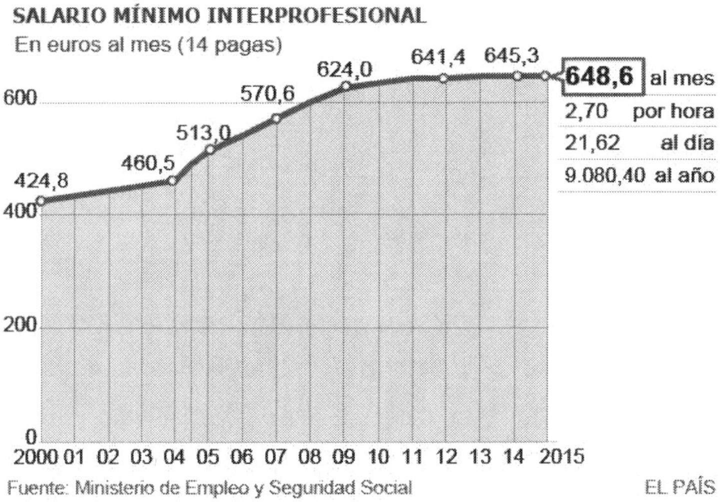

In conclusion, the economies with the most flexible labor markets, which don´t even have a minimum wage rate or any type of costs related to firing the worker, are the ones that enjoy the lowest unemployment rates and highest salaries for the standard worker. The most interventionist labor market models as Greece are the ones that have lowest salaries of the EU, as many companies just adjust their costs to the minimum wage rate. These countries are also the ones with highest unemployment levels, as we have seen recently, caused by the scarce demand for labor and the minimum new companies that are set up in those economies. So we could say that the countries with highest liberty and flexibility in labor matter are the most beneficial labor markets for the mean worker, as through competition in the market, the salaries will be naturally risen, with no need for intervention from the government. Because as Frederick Hayek said: "The ultimate ends of the activities of reasonable beings are never economic. Money is one of the greatest instruments of freedom ever invented by man."

In my opinion, minimum wage rates should be totally eliminated, but the governments should introduce an obligatory productivity bonus to the salaries of each worker. This will link productivity totally to the wages, motivating workers to produce much more, making them more efficient, and allowing wages to increase, according to the economic growth, which will help to balance the labor market model. On top of it, this will make the intern demand of the country rise in general terms, as consumers will have more disposable income to spend on goods and services.

REDUCE TRADE UNIONS' NUMBER AND INFLUENCE[232]:

From the very beginning of an established labor market, trade unions have been present and have interfered, whether positively or negatively into this market. The competition between companies in the labor market is one of the factors that are most affected by this type of associations. Many economists have fought against trade unions during their whole life, giving arguments against them, but we do not have to

[232] http://www.elrincondelparquet.com/news/why-are-trade-unions-harmful-for-the-economy/

think about their effect just on workers, but on the economic system and labor market.

We all know that through competition in the market, higher wages will be produced, as companies will grow in the mean term, and will want to increase their labor investment, to be able to supply more. Here is where labor unions intervene; as if a firm wants to increase their profits, they will try to balance their production costs, having to provide lower salaries to be able to hire more workers. Trade unions will try to force the government to raise the minimum wage rate, creating much more labor supply, but decreasing the demand for labor in an astonishing way, leading to unemployment.

Here we can see a linear graph representing how higher wages produce less labor demand and more unemployment applied to the market system:

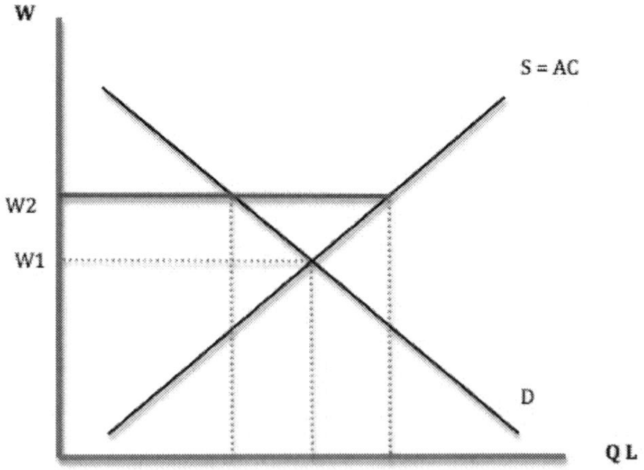

This occurs because trade unions are just worried about their own members, and their interests, without thinking about the direct and indirect effects this purposes and measures could have on the general labor market. We can find a very clear example of this, when in the year 2013, the principal Spanish trade union, UGT, proposed to the government to take a measure to close mean and big businesses on weekends and festivities, trying to ban the commercial liberty. So this shows, that they were just thinking about the income of their major members, without taking into account all the jobs that will be lost, if commences as *El Corte Ingles* will have to close on festivities and weekends.

Trade unions tend to promote general and partial strikes almost five times a year, which makes workers be really unproductive, making this lead to loss of sales and output, making the company lose money, and be unable to hire any workers at the end, and in case they are small firms, even go out of business. In a more moderate plan, trade unions support that workers work up to rule, so just in their established working time, independently of their productivity or efficiency, making the company in the enormous majority of cases being forced to fire the worker.

Inflation is one of the principal effects of trade unions, even though this only occurs in countries where trade unions have a very powerful representation. If unions bargain for higher wages and they lead to set them over the rate of inflation, this will lead to economic problems in the whole nation, leading to inflation of the country itself, as they will be unable to support all the present unemployment. If we look back at recent economic history, in the UK in 1979, a similar case occurred, where the minimum wage rate was increased by 27% in a one-year period, by the pressing of trade unions on the government, which generated enormous quantities of unemployment. It is true that if we find ourselves in a monopoly market system, trade unions will be able to balance wages without reducing unemployment, but this would be very strange cases, as in a normal system, higher wages lead to lower demand for labor.

If we look at this chart, we can see how production in manufacturing increased in a huge way when there are no unions intervening in the labor market:

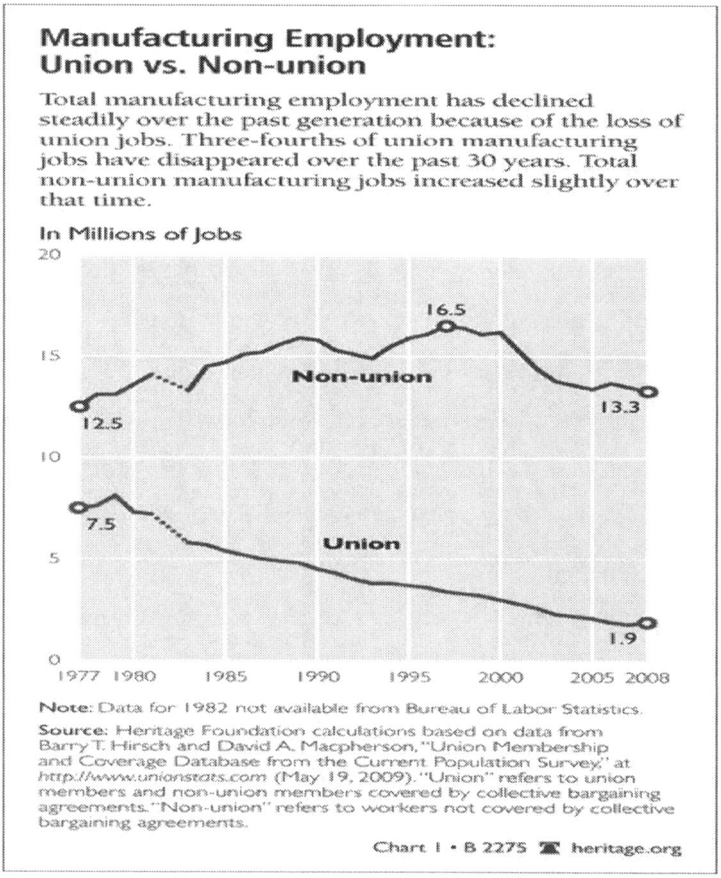

Many governments give subsidies to unions and it is more; many trade unions live from the subsidies governments give them. The solution for eliminating trade unions partially, or just reducing their power, is giving more protection to standard workers, but also taking care at the same time of employer firms production and revenues, as having a balanced labor market is essential for any type of country, but mostly on those where the tertiary sector is the principal one, where economic freedom is the base, and the only useful tool to fight against inflation and unemployment. Because if an economy works well, higher wages will come by their own feet, as forcing them is not the solution, because everything has its own time, and there is time for everything.

In conclusion, trade unions restrict employment by just increasing the wages of their own members, which produces a cut on supply and revenues of the employer companies. The conditions and effects of trade unions in the economy, lead companies to automation, to reduce costs, which will lead to a permanent loss in jobs availability. If we balance the labor market, we can see that trade union force increases in wages of approximately 10%, but this leads of rises in unemployment of 13% in the long term, which makes the market to be less competitive and efficient. As always, the solution: economic and commercial freedom, which provides major reinvesting in production, to increase the supply of their product by a bigger demand.

PROMOTE AND SIGN AS SOON AS POSSIBLE THE TTIP[233]:

In the last months, we have been able to see, how the main political leaders have stopped negotiating the main conditions, of which will be the biggest free trade agreement in Europe and the USA in all history, since between these two economic powers, they compose 50 % of the GDP on a global scale. We see many praises towards this new agreement, but also certain criticism, which comes from those who are afraid of looking on the

233 http://www.elrincondelparquet.com/news/%C2%A1saquemos-adelante-el-ttip%21/

outside and prefer to encourage only the internal consumption. But I can assure you, that the barrier elimination to the commerce, tariffs and legal obstacles, is always beneficial for the market freedom, which later is later on developed in the form of benefits and profit. The TTIP will mean the death of the barriers and regulative tariffs between the USA and the EU, creating a big competitiveness ambiance between companies, encouraging this way the international trade and competitiveness. Right now, the most important thing of eliminating barriers in relation to the exports and imports are the legal barriers between both commercial sectors, both the European and the American. All these proposals try to impel the commerce increasing this way the demand and the foreign investment, giving place to major growth and offering greater growth opportunities to the PYMES and small companies.

In two sectors the elimination of these tariffs will mean principally that firms which are not located in an inefficient sector will benefit from it since the barriers that exist between these blocks and are very difficult to exceed. If we center our opinion on the last study of the Centre for Economic Policy Research, we can observe that this new agreement will increase the GDP permanently in 3,9 % for the USA, and 4,8 % for the European Union. If we look at this increase in the GDP per family inside the EU, we can see that every family budget would have an average increase of 550 euros per year. As for companies, the TTIP, will influence especially the PYMES and small enterprises, since eliminating the commerce barriers would help to the internationalization of these companies, reducing its production costs and increasing its offer facing the exterior, what in the mean term gives place to a big reinvestment in the company directly and in many occasions, even in the short term.

There is a great book written by the economist Adam Smith, called "The Wealth of Nations," which I still have not had the opportunity to read, but that applied to the topic can turn out to be very positive. Inside many famous phrases of this book a very well-known one is:" What any good family does in particular form for prudence, hardly can be a senselessness in the government of a big nation", what means that if another country can give us a product cheaper than it takes place in ours, what favors us is to buy it, even trading with it to expand our markets and generate greater economic growth. The same reasoning expresses itself in many of the measures of the expansive economy of the TTIP. First of all, and as we have already said earlier, this new agreement would destroy 80 % of the tariffs that right now exist in the commerce between the EU and the USA, what would give place to a much more opened economy between both sides of the planet, giving many other opportunities to the PYMES and small enterprise, across contributing with more resources for the production and reducing the costs, but in turn, increasing the demand and the international investment. If the commerce increases, it is basic that the employment follows it in the same way, since it has been estimated that the GDP generated by the industrial sector of the EU will pass from 15 % to 20 % after the agreement, what shows that the revenue would give place to a few new 150.000 workplaces in the short term in the country, climbing this way, of average per capita 6 % in the long term. For the EU, it would suppose personally an increase of its Treasury arks in 120.000 million euros per year, according to information of the CEPR. Afterwards, we have to think that Spain is the ninth country with more investment in the USA, being also the American nation the second one that invests more in Spain, so this agreement would be positive for both, seen from the atmosphere of the national territory, since it would generate approximately 20.000 million euros per year in Spain, dedicated to the sector of the motorcar and the food or even agriculture industry, since there would obtain benefit of the lower cost of exportation and the consumption of goods imported for a minor price than the habitual one.

IN THIS CHART WE CAN SEE IN DETAIL THE CHANGES THAT THE ECONOMY WILL OBSERVE IN RELATION TO COMMERCE WITH THE TTIP:

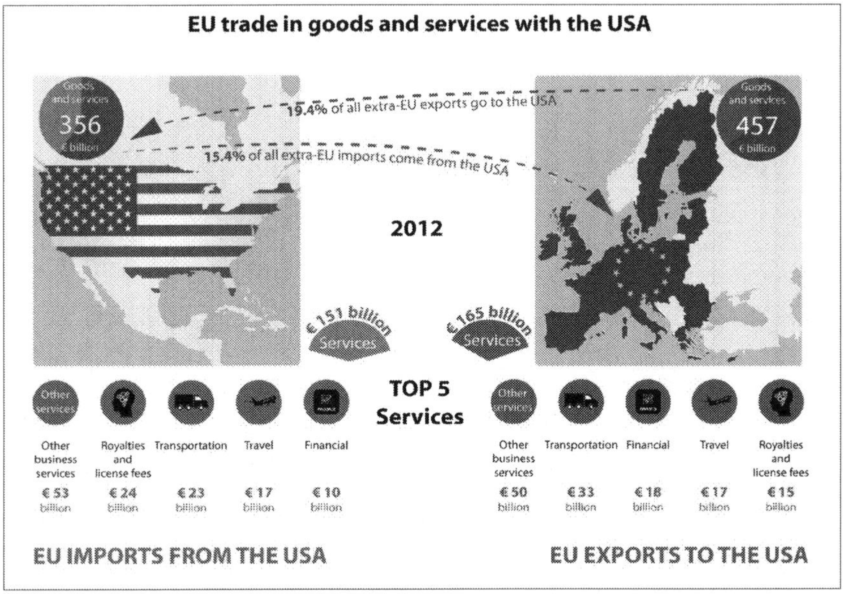

If we look towards the developed countries, the economies with a major index of economic freedom were those who grew more, in average an ascent of 2,35% of the GDP in the last ten years, while the economies which were mainly closed and protectionists, grew of average 0,7 %. The liberalization of the commerce of a country is very important since it achieves a major efficiency in its companies and the production index increases its growth, as it would have promoted the exterior demand, generating higher increments on exports.

Finally, the TTIP will give place to the elimination of many tariffs in the commerce, achieving this way a major fluency, which will give the consumer a major variation of products and services and also a greater range of sectors, while the companies will have the opportunity to reduce costs and to increase demand, without the need to do an adaptation of their goods and services, either prices or production factors.

PREVENT PUBLIC BANKING... THE FINANCIAL SYSTEM SHOULD BE 100% PRIVATE[234]:

There is a proposal which calls my attention greatly, that is in where they coincide Podemos and Izquierda Unida, which tries to bring back to life the public banking system, which devotes itself to give 'loans and deposits to citizens at cost zero, and to take different deposits without any type of commission, since according to the propulsors of this idea: "this banking would not look for any type of benefit". But everything that glitters is not gold, and after this utopian proposal, there is its way of being financed, that it is like many other times, across taxes. It seems that Spain does not learn of the disaster of the banking and the public banks, which created the biggest public debt, which was one of the biggest causes of the recession suffered in our country, but yes, apparently, some of them want to repeat...

A bank for definition does not matter of that type it is, must ask for money in loans to be able to be big enough, creating this way an indebtedness, which often in the long term generates a benefit, thanks to the interests. Well, since we imagine the same model in the public banking, which since it does not receive interests, has to auto finance itself, creating a big expenditure hole, on many occasions being converted

[234] http://www.elrincondelparquet.com/news/%C2%BFbanca-publica-%C2%A1otra-vez-no%21/

into a losses hole, that in the long term, means that the public sector of the banking falls into debt much more than the private one, since most of its services do not generate any type of benefits. After getting into debt, there will begin to come the difficult times, for which, in the model of private banking, they are the shareholders and the bondholders those who are in charge of keeping on the float the entity, doing an expansion in capital, but having simultaneously the option to rescue its investments. Meanwhile, in the public banking, for definition, the shareholders are all the Spanish citizens, that in this case, we should take charge of its rescues and its endless losses, generating in the medium term the highest taxes increase, since this type of banking carries out operations of minimal profitability.

In the case of having to produce a rescue operation to the public banking; as we have said earlier, this would run in charge of the citizen, being he the one that is forced to increase capitalization of the State, without having dialogue or not even option. We have seen multitude of examples like this one, so much in the case of Greece, the same year, or in Italy and its famous "control panel of capital", in the year 2012, and the coincidence shows that both events took place due to the decline of the public banking system, in relation to the financial crisis.

WE CAN OBSERVE A GRAPH THAT REFLECTS THE DEBT INCREASE BECAUSE OF THE PUBLIC BANKING IN GREECE FROM 2006:

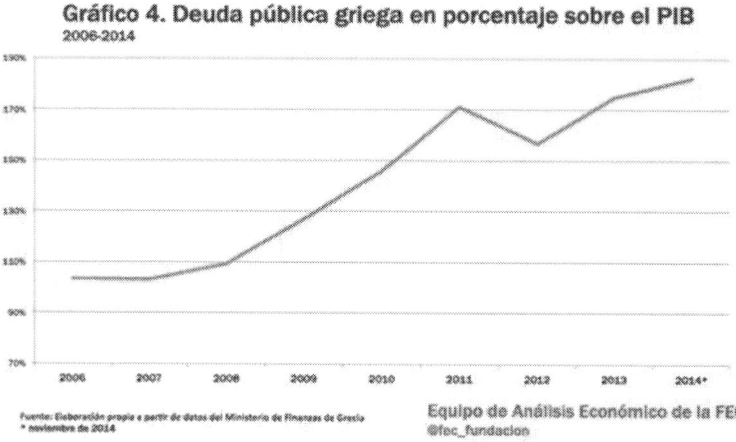

In the side of the credits, we know in abundance that the private banks have better information about reliable and profitable credits, managing better the field of the risks and the benefits. On having talked each other about public banking, this type of banking does not reach a profitability target, therefore assumes major risks at the time of giving credits, on not having had anybody who obtains benefits of this operation. All this leads to the final solution that in the majority of occasions, the credits donated by the public banking are lost almost to the full of their percentages.

A lot of the people who support a model of public bank system believe that this one provides a major safety opposite to the economic recessions, due to a major regulation. This information is not true, since first of all the regulation of the EU in regard to the banking system is equal both for the public sector and for the private one, removing any demand from public organisms about any type of benefit from the public sector. Therefore there are no penalizations for big losses. On the other hand in the private banking, we have seen a multitude of cases like those of the landesbanks in which the EU had them asphyxiated in their moment of greatest depression. Due to a large number of public banking located in the European countries in 2007-2012, the debt increased in a big way, taking Europe to one of the biggest economic depressions (not caused by the war) of our history.

The public banking possesses a very small capital handling since it is the proper taxpayer the one that assumes the financing of this sector, paying it through taxes, and rescuing it with even more taxes when it sinks. An enormous difference exists with the private banking in this sense, and the fact is that the private financial sector looks for a profitability increase on assets, trying to encourage the benefits increase, investing only in those projects that are considered to be strategic, and with better profitability margins. Meanwhile, the public banking, destines its investments to civil, social causes, what as it is logical, does not have any profitability, since the public banking is expert at subsidizing projects particularly in inefficient and unproductive sectors, making us call it "sustainable economy", as we saw with regard to China and its transition of assets from the private into the public sector into the business of the coal mines. In Spain also we had a slightly similar situation during the government of Zapatero, when, across financing which was not necessary, and in not profitable industrial sectors; we had losses of more than 200.000 million euros, with the excuse of which this type of projects would encourage the aggregate demand in the real State market of the country, which we still keep on waiting sat down.

ON THE OTHER HAND, HERE WE CAN OBSERVE A GRAPH OF THE ROA OF THE SPANISH PRIVATE BANKING IN THE LAST YEARS:

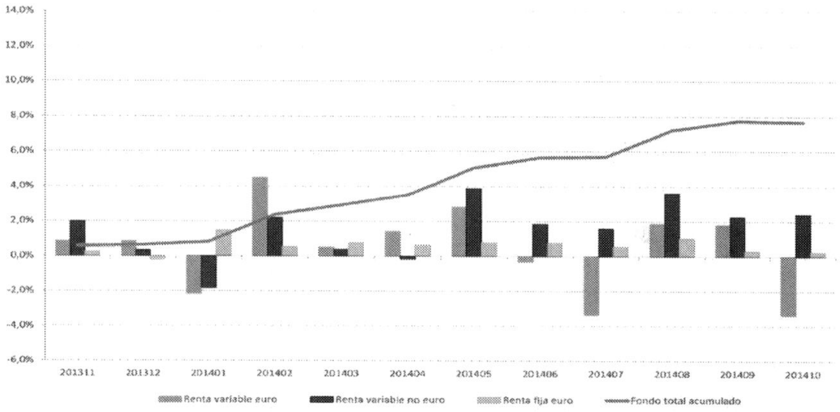

To end up with this topic, and after everything above mentioned, we can observe clearly that the best bank system for a country is one which is completely private, since as you could have observed, the cost for the investor is much lower in case of decline, since the private bank system is formed by shareholders, who can rely on an increase in capital to solve the financial problem. On the other hand this, in the public banking it runs in charge "of the people," since we have gone so far as to see rescues to the public banking; in some countries like Greece, of almost 70 % of its value, and completely financed by the citizens. The index of productivity and efficiency of the public banking is almost nonexistent since it is not provided with the factor of targets of benefit and profitability, increasing this way the public debt in a continuous way. Someday we will learn that in Spain the sole time the public sector works when it is a question of primary and essential services, as at any time they do not suppose any risk for the internal economy since it is necessary to remember, that the account... goes to the charge of citizens.

PROMOTE TEMPORARY CONTRACTS AND LABOR ROTATION[235]:

Lately, we have been speaking about the proposal of Ciudadanos to forbid definitely the temporary contracts in Spain; in all their facets, differentiating first of all the fixed contracts and those of certain duration, or seasonal contracts. We have to remember, that these contracts were legalized in Spain in the 80s, used this way to provide more freedom to the labor market. After this, there have always been several socio-economic discussions on the matter, but: why are the temporary contracts beneficial?

In the last years, and as regard to the economic crisis, we could have seen how it was lowering the index of temporary contracts in Spain, but not owed principally to the creation of new contracts of indeterminate duration, but to the increase of the general rate of unemployment. Nevertheless, from the year 2011, we have seen Spain overcame for the double the EU in percentage of temporary contracts on the employment rate, which has been produced by an attempt of fast economic growth, which the primes and the autonomous workers have charged on their backs, raising this way the number of contracts of certain duration.

IN THIS GRAPH WE CAN OBSERVE THE COMPARATIVE OF TEMPORARY CONTRACTS BETWEEN SEVERAL COUNTRIES AND THE EU:

---

[235] http://www.elrincondelparquet.com/news/%C2%BFpor-que-decir-si-a-los-contratos-temporales/

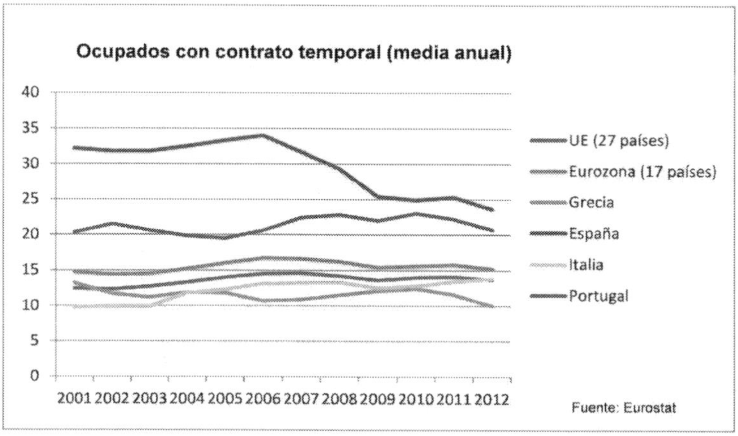

The temporary contracts prevail mostly inside the private sector, and the hired main ones on determined time are usually women younger than 25 years. As for the sectors, in which a major number of temporary contracts we will find they are those ones in relation to agriculture, construction, manufacture and occupations of primary education.

Surely we cannot deny the importance of the temporary contracts inside the economy and the labor market, but like everything, they have their advantages and their disadvantages. First of all, we can stand out, from the managerial side, that with a temporary contract, the entire adaptation of a worker is not achieved by the company, by what this type of contracts are usually used for is when the company is not ready to invest a lot of money in the formation of this concrete worker but it needs to hire someone at a lower average cost. Also, we are able to notice that in the last years a breach has been opened in the labor market between the fixed and temporary contracts. The contracts of certain duration suppose a major labor rotation, what at the expense of the government supposes an increase of the public expenditure in help to the unemployment or wage complements. If we were getting into the mind of a temporary worker, we might see that this one reduces its expenses in an enormous way, being known that this income is going to be short-term only, what releases on a lower internal consumption into the way - long term, in the national term.

Meanwhile, if we look at the positive side, we can see that a temporary contract serves for liberalizing and adding flexibility to the needs both of the company and of the worker, allowing both to get to an agreement. When a company is insecure on the hiring of an individual, a temporary contract can be the perfect tool for a process of a test of validity. In companies of variable production or regulated by the seasonal economic cycle, a contract of certain duration allows to adapt himself to the productive needs of every company. In favor of the companies, I have to say that the temporary contracts suppose a minimum or very limited dismissal cost compared to the contracts of indeterminate duration.

It has always been thought that the companies with major percentage of temporary contracts usually have less productivity, in fact that is completely false, because the most productive sectors in Spain, like construction or tourism (being those which contribute to more fiscal income to the State), they usually stand out for the large number of temporary contracts inside its companies, what in the short term supposes an increase of the internal consumption in the country generated by an ascent of general income.

As an alternative to the temporary contracts, we find the contracts of indefinite duration. This type of contracts emphasize for the stability that they promote, making feels more strengthened both the worker and the company, what frequently turns out be firstly more productive. Although frequently it is thought that they suppose for the most part disadvantages for the entrepreneurs, we can demonstrate that this is not completely true, since for example, the contracts of indefinite duration present a year of test for the worker, a time in which the businessman can value the productivity of the employee; and time after which the dismissal does not bear settlement, as after the labor reform, the costs of laying off a worker in their trial period will be barely minimum. Fiscally, this type of contracts also supposes an advantage for the company, since, for every new worker younger than 30 years, hired of fixed contract, the company achieves a deduction for 3000 euros maximum on the subject of taxes. If it is true, that this type of hiring also has its negative side, observing that the company has to deliver its working people for the dismissal, a settlement of 45 days of salary for every worked and earned wage year in the company. Moreover, an excess of contracts of indefinite duration reduces the general hiring, deflating the rotation and the competitiveness of the labor market.

HERE WE CAN OBSERVE A GRAPH REPRESENTING THE GROWTH OF THE CONTRACTS OF INDETERMINATE DURATION IN THE LAST YEARS IN SPAIN:

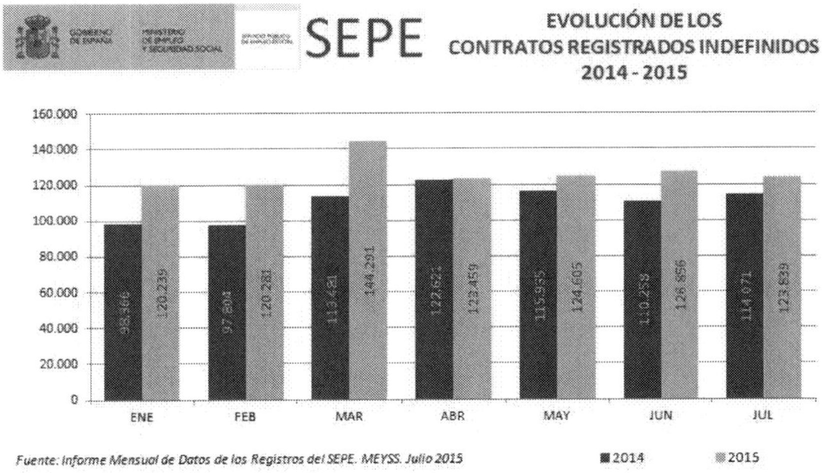

So, although the contracts of indeterminate duration are a big option that contributes and promotes safety, the employment of short-term should not be forbidden under any circumstance. The temporary contracts suppose a great liberalization of the labor market, leading this way to a rapid reduction of the unemployment, since it generates that part of the population which earlier was without work, happens to be part of a company quickly, reducing mainly frictional and cyclical unemployment. This way, seems to be the easiest to replace the working people with the temporary contracts, which apart from the previous mentioned characteristics, encourages the competition inside the labor market, what can be very beneficial for companies, since it can go so far as to reduce the wage targets and rates of the average worker, and at the same time it will be reducing unemployment.

DEREGULATE COMMERCIAL SCHEDULES![236]:

Practically official is the fact that the economic crisis that Spain has been dragging since 2008 has finished. And I do not say this in vain. I rest principally on information of the Spanish department of economy, to know that the sector sales grew in the latter year 6.1 %, increasing and reaching the number of 40,978 million, since the Spanish paid out 3.2 % more of their income in the recounted to this sector, which demonstrates that the demand for this type of products exists, and in many cases it would be necessary to extend the offer. But not only because of it, but because the average of commerce related to sales they received 1.907 million visits in the year 2015, which is an increase of 5.8 % as for the previous year, dismantling statistics of the epoch of crisis where one believed that it was necessary to create aggregated demand to revitalize this sector after two consecutive demand descents of close to 2 % in the years 2012 and 2013. But employment has also been created thanks to this sector, as unemployment in the sales market decreased by 0.8%, and the Spanish commerce integrates now nearly 3,400,000 million of workers in them.

The market share that shopping malls have in the market towards small shops is only 17.85%, and in 2008 this was nearly 14%, which shows that not regulating schedules will not be harmful to small commerce, as they have more that 83% of the market domination, which makes them

---

[236] http://www.elrincondelparquet.com/news/deregulate-commercial-schedules/

capable of competing against big companies, shopping malls or centers for a lower price or through product differentiation.

Consumer's demand has changed over time, and just as the suppliers have adapted their offer, governments should do the same, and reduce their protectionist measurements in order to allow for a better service to be given, increasing the elasticity of the supply of much commerce. Electronic shopping is now one of the big deals of our time, with nearly 13,100 million sales in 2015, which creates an enormous competition against small businesses, that can't have online platforms, but the intelligent ones use this situation to reduce prices by contacting with cheaper suppliers and innovating in their production, becoming much more efficient and productive, which will promote traditional shopping, in contrast to nowadays technology. In this part, not scheduling for small businesses will be much more beneficial, as they will be able to supply at different types of the day adapting themselves much more to the consumer and offering them a higher quality service with a lower price, which demonstrates that without market barriers, through efficiency in production, small firms can also compete against big platforms.

HERE WE CAN SEE A GRAPH SHOWING THE RESTRICTIVE LEVELS OF EACH COUNTRY IN COMMERCE SCHEDULING:

Figura 32
Límite a los horarios de apertura para la venta minorista

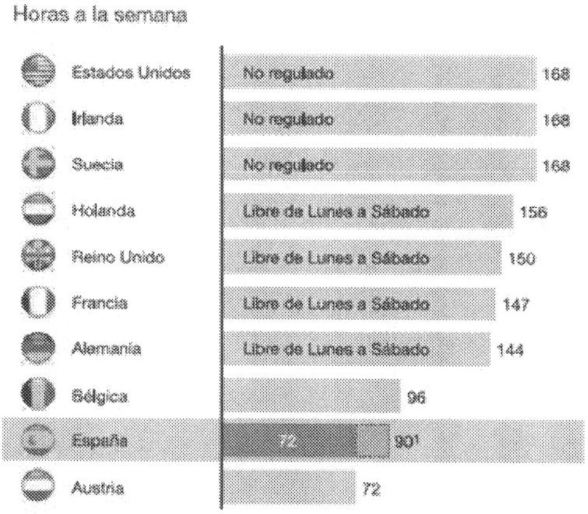

1 España tiene un límite mínimo de horas semanales de 72 horas. Existe, sin embargo, cierta flexibilidad en algunas regiones (en concreto, en 5 CC.AA.) donde han extendido dicho límite a 90 horas semanales

Fuente: Planet retail

In Spain, we should eliminate all of the 17 legislations that refer to small and medium commerce scheduling, as consumer's needs are of any governmental interests, and businesses should be able to modify their supply for the demander. And as always the government should be a help and not a barrier to economic growth in the market. All shops, malls, and centers should be allowed to open on Sundays and festivities, as it is very difficult to grow organically with 17 different legislations, each one providing different rules and reducing productive flexibility, as Sundays tend to be the second day of bigger consumer of all the week, according to data of the CNMC. Tourism is a really important sector in the Spanish economy, and it shouldn't be forgotten in these cases, as the type of consumer offered by this sector tends to be much different to the national one, and suppliers should be able to adapt their profile to them, and this can only be possible through bigger economic freedom and major flexibility. We are nearly world leaders in tourism in percentage of comparison to population, following not many countries, but our income levels in this sector, also in contrast to our national GDP it's very far away to countries as France, Holland or the United Kingdom, which implies that tourists consume less in our nation, or cheaper products, which rapports less benefit to our society. A direct effect that liberalizing schedules will have in relation to tourism will be the creation of 50,000 new jobs, as the vacant hours should be covered by new workers if there is enough demand for it. This has a direct relationship with the GDP and the economic growth of the country, making internal demand and consume rise in the mean term. But all of this should be done through reforms that impulse flexibility and liberalization and allow commerce, independently of their size; for internal growth into the market.

WE CAN OBSERVE A GRAPH REPRESENTING TOURISM IN SPAIN DURING THE LAST YEARS:

In conclusion, by liberalizing the commerce schedules and banning the actual legislation, which forbids most of the mean and big companies to open on Sundays; will improve Spain's touristic offer, which actually receives nearly 57 million visits. So if tourists are able of buying more and they increase their demand towards national products, this will generate much more jobs, reducing unemployment, and increasing international competitiveness towards other countries. There are people that think that there won't be enough labor supply to work on Sundays, but in my opinion with the unemployment levels, we actually have, nearly 50,000 new jobs will be covered completely in a few weeks. Tourism is a very important source of incomes that we cannot give up, and while there's no labor abuse, having labor rotation each 8 hours to expand the schedules will be positive for economic growth and will impulse reinvestment. Why can't we compete with the English, the French or the German, which are allowed to have all their commerce opened on Sundays and festivities? And overall, why don't we let business owners take their own decisions and invest their money the way they want, expanding or not their schedules, without the government having to intervene?

REDUCE SUBSIDIES FROM THE MARKET[237]:

In one of my cultural visits of this summer vacation, we went to a farm which was surrounded by gardens and all kind of agricultural land in Nice. I had the opportunity to talk to a man, who was never really interested in agriculture or the countryside, and who overall lived in Monaco and had many other businesses apart from supplying nearly all the markets from the region with fruit and vegetables. During our visit, I asked him why he started with the idea of the plantations and the agriculture business, and he answered me that they are provided with good working capital and conditions for it, even though that the benefit margin was not very big. Later on, one of his assistants explained us the costs and the machinery involved in the production, and with such a high input, I doubted about any benefit at all... and that was my next question. You would have made the same face I did, when they told me that right now they were at a breakeven point, but that they made benefits thanks to the subsidies from the government, which was one of the reasons why they did not want to expand anymore, as if not they will get into red numbers. Incredible. They were receiving much more public income than any hospital, police station or school from the area. And that is the problem. The main agent against free markets is always interventionism, and this time the virus had a new name... subsidies.

---

[237] http://www.elrincondelparquet.com/news/why-should-we-eliminate-subsidies-from-all-economic-activity/

All economic activities we can think about receive subsidies from the government, in a bigger or smaller way, but they actually do. These subsidies go against competition, the consumer and of course the liberalization of the economy, in two different ways: higher taxes and an increase in prices forced by an intervened economic cycle. We can observe that Spain is one of the most controlled economies of the Eurozone, and in most ways, because during the economic recessions period much more subsidies were given by the European Union, who was trying to increase supply, never thinking that the problem came from scarce demand and consumed. International investors are not stupid, and they know that an intervened economy will always have higher prices and less incentive to consumption, which will leave a lower productive margin, making them emigrate with their money to much more free economic systems as Hong Kong, Ireland, Switzerland or the USA. The main factor of this is because over controlled economies are always tied to any regulatory or political changes, which increases the uncertainty in the market, and money tends to fear.

HERE WE CAN SEE A GRAPH DEMONSTRATING THE GOVERNMENT EXPENDITURE IN SUBSIDIES ALONG THE YEARS IN SPAIN, COMPARED TO THE CAPITAL EXPENDITURE:

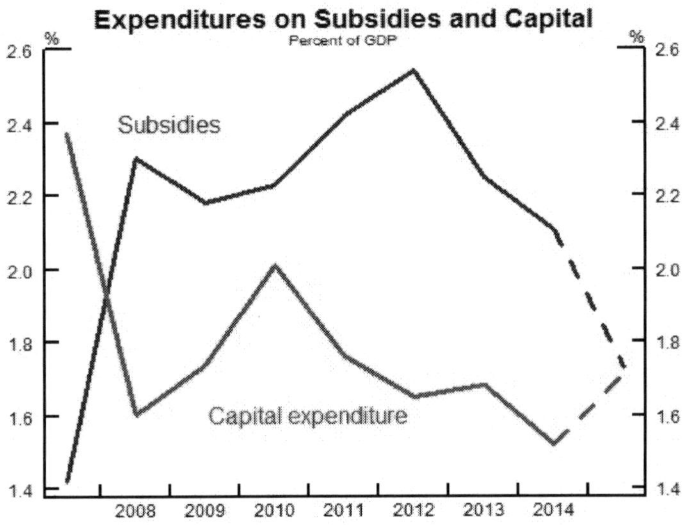

Reducing subsidies, we will be able to adequate the investment demand and the real profitability, evading economic bubbles and of course reducing turnover effects of the economic cycle. The effect of subsidies in the market is really harmful in the mean long term as it helps to generate a false effect of false demand to later on create an overcapacity leading to excess of supply, causing an increase in the cost of production and a consequent rise in prices which are harmful for the demand of consumers and reducing the demand for labor, as this two factors are generally derived, which will finally lead to higher unemployment rates, which will make many companies and industries break down in the long term, due to allocative inefficiency in the market.

Spain's general expenditure in subsidies and economic aids to different sectors is now nearly 5% of the country's GDP, but during the periods of economic crisis, these numbers have not been reduced, but they have actually increased trying to impulse the economy, which generated an economic bubble in some sectors of the market as the construction one. In Spain, economic subsidies are present in everyday life of many companies and big enterprise, which makes them much more heavy and dependent on new government decisions , as receiving income constantly from the public sector, makes many firms overload their debt capacity, and prevents them from diversifying their supply and expanding their production to try and be more efficient, as, with subsidies in fixed levels, this will lead them to higher costs and a loss of revenue, which makes reinvestment and internal growth much more difficult.

WE CAN OBSERVE A SIMPLE LINE GRAPH REPRESENTING THE EFFECT OF SUBSIDIES ON PRICE AND DEMAND FOR THE CONSUMER IN THE MARKET:

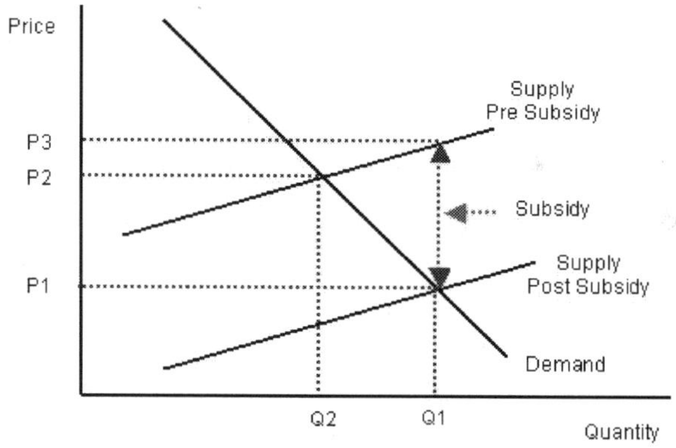

We can see that each day and more often companies are taking subsidies into account in their risk and debt analysis, giving them viability as a normal and fixed input element, which should not be like that. Many valuations of costs and revenues consider subsidies as a fixed element of income for production, but they do not take into account that governments change the regulatory systems very often, leading to an excess of supply in the long term, and overloading the production capacity of the just mentioned enterprise.

And that is why international investors fear towards hyper-regulated economic systems, as they understand that an atmosphere of business driven by government and public organizations will reduce enormously competition, efficiency, and innovation due to their dependence on political decisions and governmental actions.

It is essential to change subsidies policies nowadays, reducing direct expenditure to try and decrease debt levels of public organisms, and try to increase consumption and production through fiscal incentives, mainly lower taxes and fewer barriers to entry the market, preventing bubbles and overloads in the sector. In the USA a few years ago, with Reagan as president the government introduced a measure called the tax credits, which not only reduced the Government public expenditure, but also helped to increase the internal demand and the international investment, through lower prices and higher wages, which lead to a bigger efficiency and made production and productivity levels rise enormously in a very small period of time, which was very attractive for capital and new enterprising, as the model was based on extreme competition in the market generating more efficient business plans, which is exactly what we need right now for Spain.

In conclusion, subsidies nowadays just generate an increase in taxes and credit tariffs, which is automatically followed by an increase in prices, which will reduce the demand of consumers, overloading the market with excessive supply, and creating allocative inefficiency. This is similar to reducing the wages of efficient workers and increasing those of inefficient, doesn't it sound crazy? Well, think about it... because subsidies are not the solution for a slow economy or for uncompetitive markets, and the only one who benefits from this is the government, which makes the economy much more dependent on them for much more strict regulatory measures.

DEVELOP AUTOMATION AND ADAPT THE LABOR MARKET TO IT[238]:

In recent times, we have been observing how automation has been introduced into companies in the form of computers, machines, and even robots, that are replacing humans in many tasks, and in many cases doing it better and faster than it was done before. We thought that the introduction of new technology was just affecting the big manufacturers greatly, but following a study was done by the Oxford university two years ago, we can see that 47% of the companies in the tertiary sector around the world have introduced some elements of automation to their production process in the last five years (up to 2014). Technological development has brought many different advances to the business world, like big data, automate robots or even artificial intelligence, that is able to take managing decisions by itself. There have been many debates about the intervention of the various governments in this development process, but if we see the entire technological sector growing at this speed, it might be because of something, so how efficient is really automation for a standard firm?

The introduction of robots, software, and computers into companies in the last years is a fact that has had a tremendous

[238] http://www.elrincondelparquet.com/news/automation-the-key-of-efficiency/

repercussion in the economy, but overall in the labor market, as it has destroyed many employment sins the secondary sector to move them into the services, and make the workers have the need for a higher specialization and differentiation in the market. Computers used in production nowadays can manage data through patterns and generate codes to organize it in more efficient and faster ways. Artificial intelligence is mainly used in the human resources departments to explore the productivity of each worker and discuss its salary in balance to the benefits it generates for the firm; this allows firms to increase their human capital and workers to be highly motivated by the incentive of new working schemes. The productivity of machines in contrast to humans is greater in most of the cases, as we can imagine that for example machines don't need rest breaks or lunch pauses each day, producing higher levels of output. The production line also becomes much more flexible in terms of rotation, as workers can get ill and have to be replaced, and with technology, the entrepreneur assures that the production process is always covered fully. Machines also have great effects on social benefits, as there will be higher innovation in the market if the technological sector rises, followed by the creation of more developed goods and services, generating fierce competition and making firms reduce their prices and offer a wider range of products, which overall will increase the living standards of the population.

In the first place, automation will help firms to stay competitive in the new technological markets, as old companies that do not renovate their production methods will have higher costs and stay obsolete, so technology will help firms to leverage more margins in their production. In contrast to human workers, the introduction of new machinery will reduce the errors in the production line, as machines will be much more specialized and precise. This will make the production speed increase, as it will enable more units of output to be produced in a smaller period of time, which will increase supply in an enormous way, supposedly having positive effects on profit. The reinvestment of profits into new machinery products will make the output be multiplied generating higher income levels in the mean term, and help to build up the volume and size of the company, because, remember that the increase of automation will also be taken into account of a firm's total capital. By removing the human element from many manufacturing processes, we will be able to increase compliance through a reduction of waste and externalities, as for example pollution... Automation will bring the possibility to the major part of the companies to increase their capabilities, as it will optimize the working methods and increase capacity, resulting in increased revenue in the mean long term. Overall, technological equipment will bring a rise in productivity, as the more automation a firm employs, the more output per unit of input it will develop, and employing less time in the production, which will improve business operations.

IN THIS GRAPH WE CAN OBSERVE HOW AUTOMATION HAS BROUGHT HIGHER PRODUCTIVITY IN MANY COUNTRIES:

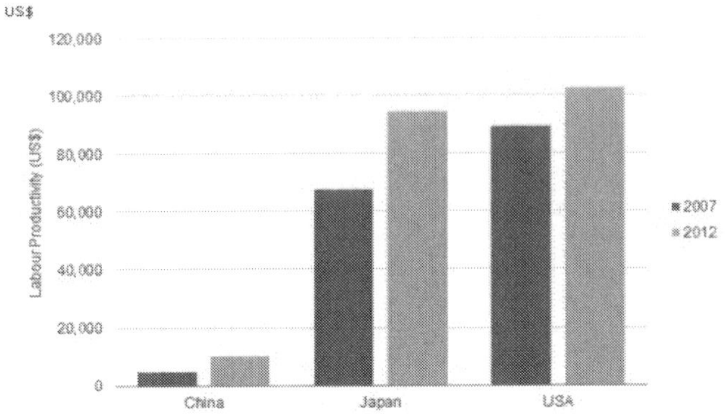

Many people who are against the use of automation in production argue that this will destroy many jobs and create unemployment, but this is not true at all. Workers will need to be upgraded and acquire new working skills to be able to stand still in front of the new automation stampede. New kind of jobs will be developed with the arrival of technology, and industries will be in need of another type of resources, for which employment will be created. Low skilled workers will be the most vulnerable ones to this renovation, but governments all around the world could help by increasing the expenditure in training and education for technology, which needs to be seen more as an investment, as it will produce large economic growth in the future, and it has shown to be a sustainable and renewable market. Many job opportunities will emerge from the development of technology, but the issue is that this time, humans are the ones in need of adaptation to automation. This adapting process has been shown in the last decades through de-industrialization, which has caused the fall of the secondary sector in many countries in contrast to the up rise of the tertiary, where the workers have been positioned after having acquired new skills.

WE CAN OBSERVE A GRAPH THAT REPRESENTS THE DE-INDUSTRIALIZATION PROCESS IN THE LAST DECADES:

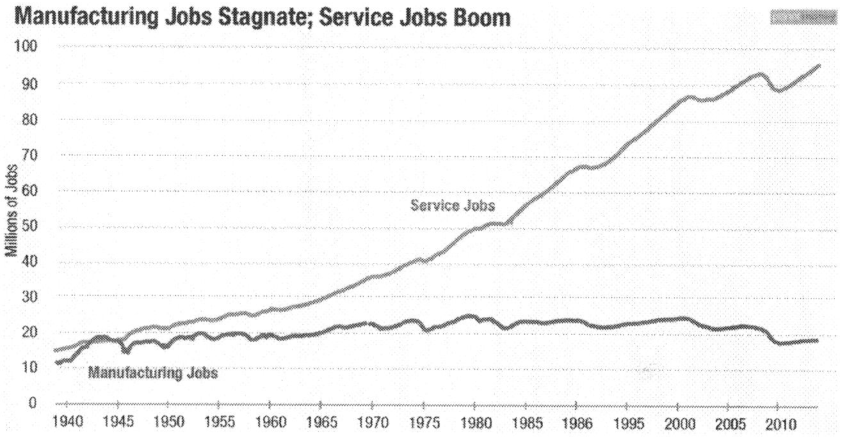

As we have seen, the rise in automation will automatically provoke deindustrialization. But we don't have to see deindustrialization from the bad side; totally at the contrary, as it is the sign of the development of a nation, and an increase of its economic growth caused by a greater efficiency. This process will bring higher salaries, as according to the mean data, the tertiary sector workers are normally better paid than in manufacturing. If the population has higher disposable income, this will allow them to increase they are consumer on local products, making internal demand rise. One of the principal signs of deindustrialization is the shift in the demand of standard consumers towards professional services, which implies that the people prefer to spend the major part of their wages on finance, lawyers, doctors, education... instead of necessities, which demonstrates economic sufficiency. All these factors will generate a higher GDP, which as a sign of higher efficiency and more productivity, which will allow governments to reduce taxes or otherwise offer better public services to their citizens. As John Maynard Keynes said: *"The difficulty lies not so much in developing new ideas as in escaping from the old ones."*

LET'S KILL INTERVENTIONIST UNICORNS![239]:

During last years, we have been able to hear and see several economic proposals from the different political parties in Spain, and what scares me principally is that were the promises the ones in the face of the newspapers, without doing a real economic analysis of their effects in the long term. The ECB re-edited the estimations of economic growth and debt for Spain in 2015, but not positively, at contrary, it decreased its objectives in the short mean time, estimating a new growth rate of just 2,4%, which reflects the enormous political uncertainty that we are leaving at the moment in the country, and what negative effects does it have on external direct investment.

Last year, we were able to observe an increase in monetary mass, followed by growth in the public expenditure rate, which made the State debt to increase by a 9% of the GDP, not generating the previous economic growth expectative or accomplishing the deficit reduction that people was waiting for. But what is most surprising at all, is the fact that it was not only the ECB the one who did wrong growth and debt reduction estimations for Spain, but the IMF committed the same error, and in the same way. The cause of this fault was nor previewing the negative impact that some intervention markets, as China could have in Spain, which have an excess of stimulus in the economy, and make international trade

---

[239] http://www.elrincondelparquet.com/news/no-gastemos-mas-de-lo-que-tenemos/

decrease, as their coin is usually evaluated, and inflation is caused in cases as China's. It has been deeply proved that the economies that set up policies of extreme public expenditure to reduce unemployment, and increase economic growth tend to fail in the mean term, as their interventionist plans only work in a really short term, as these policies tend to go against economic cycles, which make their estimations to be reduced, and which is a good reason to stop believing in unicorns.

In Spain, journalists and politicians do not really care or look at statistics, mathematics or just numbers, as political parties just promise, and promise and continue promising unicorns, unicorns that will be paid with or money, and that will be used to finance the excessive generosity of those who didn't realize that their promises were not reliable and that increasing taxes and public expenditure will not make the economic growth rate rise, which is one of the general motives for most of the financial recessions along history. One of the principal fake purposes I heard this week came from Unidos Podemos, which promised that they would increase taxes to cover the debt hole, but they will increase taxes just to the "rich ones." We have to take into account that in Spain, there are around 4,500 people that earn over 600,000 euros per year, which will just be an option to cover a minimum fraction of all the populist political expenditure. But in Spain, by many economic specialists, at the moment you can be considered as rich if you earn more than 60,000 euros per year, and taking into account that entire people, which will be an increment of or that 32% of IRPF, which will make local demand and imports decrease, generating market failure and higher private debts.

HERE WE CAN SEE A GRAPH SHOWING THE SPANISH PUBLIC EXPENDITURE AND INCOME OVER THE YEARS:

One of the most unfair taxes that we can be able to talk about is the successions tax, as it charges citizens for things that have been already paid for previously, and which is the nucleus of familiar richness, that normally tends to be located in properties like houses, cars or luxurious objects. From the economic program, we can see that what they call a progressive tax is really a rate that can get to 86% of the total wage in cases of the highest salaries, decreasing internal investment, and housing market demand. The fake promise of just increasing taxes on the rich, really means raising the general tax and becoming more interventionist, as they also exalt that Spain should do "expansive monetary policies", which can be reduced to increasing monetary mass, forcing a decrease of prices, and giving more public subsidies, which will end up just in a devaluation of the euro, higher debt rates and an enormous inflation, which will produce allocative inefficiency, as we have been able to see in Greece, with the government of Syriza.

One of the most ridicule economic unicorns, is the proposal of ALL parties to cover the enormous debt hole, and to reduce deficit, by just fighting against tax fraud, firstly because it is a concept that we should set up as secondary or tertiary, and not as our primary source of income, because it is unstable, and not very efficient, as in most of the cases to reach a certain objective in this policy, public expenditure should be increased, for example to hire more inspectors, which will reduce the productivity of this economic activity. Following official data from the ECB, and its estimations, just by fighting fiscal fraud, the incomes will just rise by 1.4%, which is a ridiculous amount compared to our debt of more than 100% of the GDP, so we can call this proposal a unicorn.

GRAPH SHOWING THE EVOLUTION OF SPAIN'S DEFICIT OVER TIME:

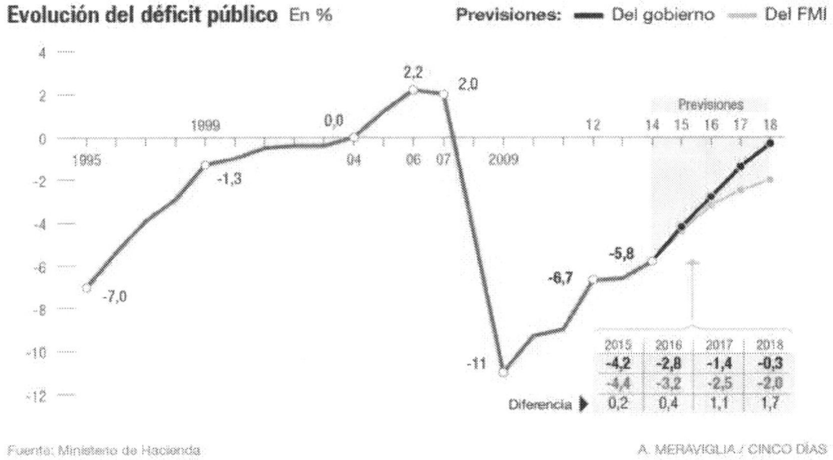

From this, we can now appreciate why Podemos presents its program as an Ikea catalog, as they try to sell you their ideas as free and beneficial, but at the end, you are paying more than expected, as they are only beneficial in the very short term. They also seem to be doing everything for you, and that you will not be in need of working anymore, but in the meantime you have to work harder to develop your life and family, and as in everything in life, low quality and cheap proposals, which have no aggregate value, end up costing higher than anybody expected, and who ends up paying it?... Yes, you and me, the normal citizens, and how?... Through higher taxes, which make local demand and imports decrease, generating a higher debt, and making inflation rise. Because now it's our time to choose, between false proposals, which are directed to an increase in debt rate, higher prices and a less efficient market and labor system, or real and stable ideas, which promise lower taxes, greater economic freedom, and growth of companies, which will increase international competitiveness. Now it's our time, the time to kill unicorns, and fight for economic liberalism!

If you haven't got enough with this book, and you want to continue battling from the trenches for economic liberalism visit my personal economic blog:

www.elrincondelparquet.com

9291429R00195

Printed in Germany
by Amazon Distribution
GmbH, Leipzig